Fine
SHOTGUNS

Fine SHOTGUNS

The History, Science, and Art of the Finest Shotguns
from Around the World

John M. Taylor

Skyhorse Publishing

Skyhorse Publishing books may be purchased in bulk at special discounts for sales promotion, corporate gifts, fund-raising, or educational purposes. Special editions can also be created to specifications. For details, contact the Special Sales Department, Skyhorse Publishing, 555 Eighth Avenue, Suite 903, New York, NY 10018 or info@skyhorsepublishing.com.

www.skyhorsepublishing.com

10 9 8 7 6 5 4 3 2 1

Library of Congress Cataloging-in-Publication Data is available on file.

Cover design by Richard Rossiter

Print ISBN: 978-1-63450-315-0
Ebook ISBN: 978-1-5107-0096-3

Printed in China

To Peggy, who enjoys fine shotguns and shoots them well. Few women have visited as many shotgun factories, gunsmiths, and gun shops as she, and fewer yet say, "The next new shotgun in the house is mine." She is the joy and light of my life, and without her sweet kindness, this book would never have been possible.

Contents

CONTENTS

Foreword

To build a fine rifle, a gunmaker must be a competent mechanic and have an artist's eye for line and proportion. But to build a fine shotgun, it takes all that and a little black magic as well.

Rifle shooting, which is at stationary targets, is static, but all shotgun shooting is dynamic because what you shoot at is always moving. For this sort of enterprise, you need a dynamic gun, and a shotgun that does not possess that intangible mixture of balance and weight and feel that makes it an extension of your will can never be a fine shotgun. British shooters, who have studied shotgunning as intensively as anyone, call such firearms "numb," as in no feeling, unable to respond.

They call them worse, too. Many years ago I had a coaching session with Holland & Holland's great shooting instructor Rex Gage. The only decent shotgun I owned at the time was an American-made over/under that had found great favor among trap and skeet shooters because it weighed a ton, and once you got it swinging you couldn't stop it.

When I pulled it out of the case, Gage's face fell.

"Oh my dear chap," he said, "you're not going to hit a thing with that dreadful club."

He was right, and out of sympathy he loaned me a Holland shotgun for the lesson.

A skilled rifle shot can pick up almost any good rifle and do about as well with it as he can with any other good rifle. But a skilled shotgun shooter will always shoot best with one particular gun. After long (and usually costly) experimentation, he will have found that shotgun which, by its unique combination of fit, balance, weight, and sight picture, and unknown voodoo, lets him shoot better than anything else.

As Gene Hill, a formidable shotgun shooter, once told me in his mushy mumble:

"David, my lad, if you ever find a shotgun that really fits, shoot the thing until it falls apart in your hands."

That one magic gun is more than likely to be a fine one.

And there are other benefits.

In the early 1970s, when I shot ATA trap seriously, I used a highly popular semi-auto gas gun. It threw lovely patterns, and was very unpunishing to shoot, but it broke so often that I eventually owned three. One I shot; one was kept in the trunk of my car to replace the one I was shooting when it broke, and one was always at the gunsmith being repaired.

In 1985 I got tired of this and bought a Perazzi MX-3, through which I have poured ammunition for 25 years. It has never broken or hollered for mercy in any form. Fine shotguns will do this. They go on and on unfailingly. It's one of the things that you spend all that money for.

A word or two about engraving and inlaying, since they are an intrinsic part of most fine shotguns. Much of what you see ranges from ghastly to unspeakable, and even expensive guns can be blighted by rotten work. Winchester Model 21s, in particular, are often afflicted with gold inlay work that looks like I did it. There are comparatively few artists who have really mastered this art, and their work is very expensive.

Two kinds of shooters can get away with engraved guns: very rich shooters (because the very rich can get away with nearly anything) and very competent shooters. Going back to my trapshooting days, there was a fellow on our circuit who owned a Ljutic (pronounced loo-tic) with a colossal gold inlay on the receiver flat. When the sun shone on it you could see the thing from the far end of the trap line. Normally, this massive mound of gold would have subjected him to mockery, scorn, and derision, except that he was a sensational shooter, and when he showed up everyone else suddenly remembered they had to mow their lawns. No one laughed at his gold blob, or at him.

My favorite inlay consists of neat gold lettering on the rear face of the barrels of a London Best live-pigeon gun that I examined 20 years ago. The letters said:

"Kill it, dumbass."

I don't think this gun was built for a British shooter.

Now, a word or two about this book. It is a damned good one, but it can't make you an expert on fine shotguns. That takes, quite literally, a good chunk of your life, tons of shooting, and a chance to learn from people who have all sorts of arcane knowledge. At a Safari Club International convention, at the Fabbri booth, I once listened in awe as the gentleman who ran it delivered a lecture on how to detect non-factory modifications on Fabbris. It revealed a depth of knowledge that I didn't dream of.

There is also opinion in these pages. For example, Mr. Taylor states that his Perazzi Sporting model is not a fine shotgun. I happen to own one, and think that not only is Mr. Taylor wrong, but that he actually deserves a beating for saying such a thing. Nor do I see a chapter devoted to the Italian firm of Fratelli Piotti, which makes guns of heart-wrenching loveliness and Herculean strength, but there is a chapter on Siace, of which I have barely heard.

But then John Taylor is the expert and I am not. If I were, I would have written it. In any event, it is a damned good book and a very useful one, and when you finish it you will know worlds more than you did when you started.

Also, you'll enjoy it. I know I did.

—David E. Petzal,
Field Editor, *Field & Stream*
June 12, 2010

Acknowledgments

A book such as this could not have been written without the help of many friends and professional acquaintances. My wife, Peggy, has been a constant source of inspiration, and the occasional gentle nudge when the pace of work slackened.

It would be impossible to categorize all the help and advice I've received during the production of this book, but certainly Catherine Williams, the former communications manager of Beretta USA, was instrumental in allowing me to tour the Beretta manufacturing facilities in Gardone Val Trompia, Italy. The tour not only provided insights into the modern manufacturing processes of high-grade shotguns, but afforded me the opportunity to take many of the photos you will see herein. In addition, Jarno Antonelli and Guisy Di Dio of Beretta Italia provided excellent translations of all my many questions, and also knew of every wonderful restaurant along the way. Dr. Ugo Gussalli Beretta was a wonderful, warm host,

both at the Beretta factory and at his family's historic home.

Elsewhere in Italy, Dott. Stefano Madau, director of Meccania del Sarca, Beretta's wood-processing facility at the tip of beautiful Lake Garda, gave me great access to how Beretta dries, selects, and processes their walnut. Dott. Ing. Antonio Girlando, director of the Banco Nazionale di Prova (the Italian National Proof House) also provided unlimited access to and an excellent description of the very exacting proofing process employed by the Italian proof authorities.

On these shores, David Cruz of Holland & Holland, New York, was most helpful in allowing me to photograph at their gun room, and has been generous in answering my many questions. I also thank Anthony Galazan, whose Connecticut Shotgun Manufacturing Company produces the only all-American-made high-grade shotguns, for his help with photos and the use of his extensive dating guide to many firearms. At one time, another shotgun, Ithaca Classic Doubles, was largely manufactured on these shores by Steve Lamboy, who unfortunately was forced into bankruptcy before his dreams could be fully realized, but hosted me for a visit to his factory. That visit provided me with further insights into the classic manufacture of fine side-by-side shotguns. Lamboy's top engraver, Jack Jones, greatly increased my knowledge of how fine engraving is accomplished. Too, Giulio Timpini, Beretta's master engraver, further expanded my knowledge during my visit to the Beretta Uno facility in Gardone Val Trompia.

The well-known British shooting instructor and shotgun expert Chris Batha, who now produces the Charles Boswell over-and-under that won the Medal de Concours at the 2004 Vintagers Cup, gave me considerable insight about how the London gun trade operates. Batha got his start by moving shotguns in various states of finish between outworkers in the London gun district. His knowledge of the whole gunmaking world is profound. His knowledge of gun fitting, which he generously shared with me, is equally vast.

Thanks to Daryl Greatrex, managing director of Holland & Holland who was a most gracious host during our visit to their London gun room, the factory, and finally the shooting grounds. He and his staff showed me their classic factory and the many facets of why a Holland & Holland rifle or shotgun is truly one of the world's best. Too, it was revealing to see their extensive computer lab and the

advanced computer-driven machinery that has taken them and others in the British gun trade into the 21st century. Thanks, too, to Nigel Beaumont and his staff at James Purdey for their cordial reception and wonderful tour of their gun room including the historic Long Room.

I cannot ever begin to thank Chuck Webb, former general manager of Briley Manufacturing in Houston, Texas, for decades of advice and top barrel and shotgun work. There doesn't seem to be anything the folks at Briley can't do with a shotgun. In that vein, Doug Turnbull does some of the most authentic firearms restoration anywhere. His secret case-hardening process produces some of the very best, and is complemented by his historically correct bluing. My most heartfelt thanks go to top-notch custom gunsmith Gregory Wolf of Easton, Maryland. For nearly 30 years, Greg has helped me with numerous stories, answered endless questions, and always been there when I needed his advice or stellar craftsmanship.

Olin/Winchester's Michael Jordan has been a source of information and friendship for several decades. He has always been a font of knowledge about Winchester ammunition and the historic development of the modern shotshell. Thanks also to Bryan Bilinski, proprietor of Fieldsport, for his insights into gun fitting. Giacomo Arighini, who owns Giacomo Sporting, was extremely helpful with Italian shotguns. Thanks also go to my friend Joe Prather, who is the former president of Griffin & Howe. Joe made available the Griffin

& Howe store for photos, and gave me much good advice for the book. Last but far from least are two of my colleagues, Michael McIntosh and Nick Sisley. Both have been helpful over the years through their articles and books, but of far more value have been their friendship, advice, and counsel. I've no doubt left someone out, and for that I apologize.

—**J. M. T., Summer 2010**

CHAPTER 1

What Is a High-Grade Shotgun?

"Beauty is in the eye of the beholder." However tired that old saying might be, it goes a long way toward defining a high-grade shotgun. How *do* we define a high-grade shotgun? Cost, engraving, wood, the maker's name, its age, who owned it? One person might think granddad's nearly worthless side-by-side is a high-grade gun, while another might feel only a gold-inlaid, jewel-encrusted shotgun owned by Czar Nicholas defines the term. The gulf between the two views is vast, as vast as it is between the guy whose Browning Auto-5 is his high-grade shotgun, and likely as high a grade shotgun as he will ever own, and collectors whose fancy is tickled only by the most elaborate and exclusive shotguns. As I said, beauty is in the eye of the beholder, and between these two extremes there are many shotguns, and defining them is the purpose of this book.

Among the many things I do in the milieu of gun writing is to answer letters from National Rifle Association members. Out of every batch I receive, perhaps 70 percent deal with a shotgun that is either a family heirloom or bought at a gun show or yard sale. In each case, one can sense that the writer is not only seeking the "who made it and when," but hoping that his shotgun is somewhat valuable. The truth is that most of these old shotguns have no paper trail, and the serial numbers were more assembly numbers and inventory-control numbers than traceable, factual numbers that can tell something of the history of the gun. And with the exception of the top American makers—Parker, Winchester, Ithaca, A. H. Fox, L. C. Smith, and shotguns from the major British makers—serial numbers are meaningless. In more than a decade of answering literally hundreds of these letters, I can recall only one instance where the individual's shotgun was really valuable: That was a Holland & Holland Paradox—a side-by-side shotgun whose barrels are rifled for about the last 6 or

A high-grade Beretta sidelock over-and-under. Stocked with exhibition-grade wood with intricate checkering, and the exquisite engraving inlaid with gold, it is the epitome of today's finest shotguns.

8 inches to provide better accuracy with round balls, yet be usable with shot. This guy wanted a load to shoot rabbits with this obviously aged, blackpowder-proofed but valuable relic. I directed him to Holland & Holland's New York gun room with the suggestion that his shotgun—of which Holland & Holland made about 1,500—even in the less than pristine condition he described, might be worth more to a collector than as a rabbit gun.

To American tastes, wood and engraving seem to be the primary defining assets of a high-grade shotgun, followed by the maker. To many people the grain is paramount, and the finish, often the shinier the better, defines perfection. Frequently overlooked is the way in which the wood joins the metal. Watch a high-grade shotgun aficionado or dealer check the wood. He runs his hands over it like a groom his bride on their first night. Most don't even look at the wood-to-metal fit, simply the grain and checkering.

Checkering on many shotguns is now done with a computer numeric control (CNC) checkering machine. When this technique came on the market, perhaps first with the Remington 3200 in 1973, mistakes were purposely programmed in, to make the checkering appear to be hand-cut. Although truly artistic checkering can be machine-cut, the hand of a master really makes a difference. The more elaborate the pattern and the finer the checkering, the more likely it is hand-cut, and that the work is truly high-grade.

Engraving fools many, as often rolled-on engraving that takes mere minutes to execute is lumped with hand-cut excellence that may take several hours or days to accomplish. Only when precious metals are inlaid does the average gun buyer take note. The advent of the laser clouds the waters even further. Perhaps the most unfortunate engraving is that on shotguns brought back from Asia by servicemen who served on Okinawa and in other areas where inexpensive engraving flourished. Even with inlays—that more often than not have popped out—I've yet to see an example of this GI, Southeast Asia–style engraving that added to the aesthetics of

any shotgun. Engraving that doesn't belong is indicative of something being amiss. Recently, on the used-gun rack at our shooting club, I spotted a nicely refinished side-by-side by one of the lesser-known British makers. It was a quality Birmingham, England–made shotgun, and the refinish wasn't bad either, but the engraving. Oh my God! I've never seen a jumping Nebraska pheasant—it had to be from the Midwest since the pheasant was jumping from among some cornstalks—on the bottom of the action of any original-maker-engraved shotgun. Something else adorned the side of the action—I can't remember, so traumatized was I at the pheasant. Poorly executed (this was apparent under close examination), it was as gauche as an exotic

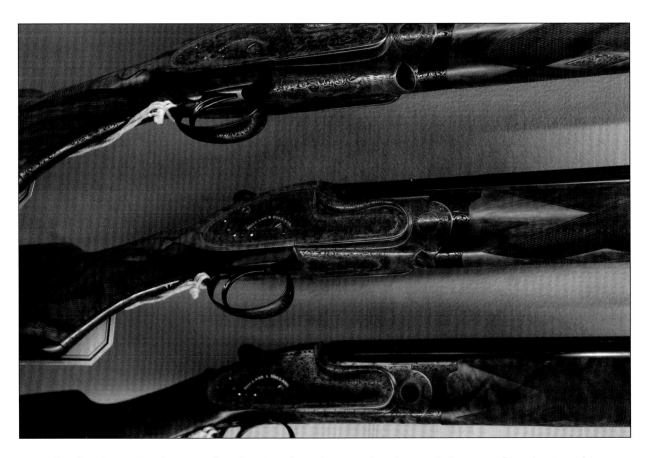

Several Holland & Holland over-and-unders that show the typical understated elegance of London Best shotguns.

dancer with a peg leg. I'm sure the guy who had the engraving done thought it would set off his pheasant gun, but when it came time to resell it, it sat unloved until finally and mercifully the owner took it back home.

Another measuring stick is price. Parker shotguns, regardless of grade and somewhat disregarding condition, carry hefty price tags. Winchester 21s likewise are drawing crowds and high sticker prices as well. Both are side-by-sides, and interest in this style of shotgun has grown by leaps and bounds in the past fifteen years. At one time side-by-sides were thought to be a dying breed, but no longer. Of course with the name

comes the price, and shotguns from the major American makers have shot up in value, whether warranted or not.

Price alone cannot define a high-grade shotgun. I have a Perazzi MX8 Sporting model that cost a lot, but I'd certainly not consider it for a minute a high-grade gun; high-priced, perhaps, but not high-grade. Yet, close by in the safe is my A. H. Fox HE-Grade Super Fox, which because of its rarity—Fox only made about 300 HEs—is a much more high-grade gun. Too, the fact that it undoubtedly passed through the hands of Nash Buckingham, the greatest proponent of the HE-Grade Fox and one of the great gun writers of the first half-plus of the 20th century, gives it special provenance. Provenance can have much to do with high-grade shotguns. One fellow sent me a letter regarding a Belgian-made side-by-side with Wells Fargo branded or cut into its buttstock. He stated that the person he purchased it from claimed Wells Fargo used it to guard its stage-coaches. The only *documented* Wells Fargo shotguns were made prior to 1915 by the Ithaca Gun Company. Other than these—and there were only about 50 made—the rest must be suspect as being frauds. The only exception could be written provenance from a known Wells Fargo guard stating he used it; something that verifies that the gun was owned by a certain person or company. In the case of my Fox, I know from the copies of the original shipping and manufacturing tags that accompanied the gun that my particular Fox HE was shipped to

« Showing two high-grade stock blanks that have been rubbed with oil to verify their grain.

Historic stocks, bullet-casting molds, and other tools displayed in Holland & Holland's New York gun room.

Buckingham, Ensley, and Carrigan in Memphis, Tennessee, in June of 1924, when Nash Buckingham was a partner in the sporting goods firm, and most assuredly handled this shotgun when it arrived. Merely saying that Uncle Fred got it from King Edward VII isn't good enough; *Antiques Roadshow* has made that plain.

Sometimes what provenance is available can come from production records. Virtually every gunmaking firm of any note in the British Isles kept scrupulous records of each shotgun, and many of these survived the various mergers of the gunmaking trade as it contracted following the Great Depression and World War II. Certainly, some of these makers' records did not survive. There is an entire book of some

412 pages (in small type) devoted to British gunmakers, *Boothroyd's Revised Directory of British Gunmakers* (Sand Lake Press, Amity, OR, 1997), and unless they amalgamated with one of the major and surviving gunmakers, the possibility is slight that the records from the majority of these various makers are available. However, those records that are available can provide a great deal of detail about how and when a particular shotgun was made, and often for whom it was made. In addition, *The Blue Book of Gun Values* (Blue Book Publications, Inc., Minneapolis, MN, 2004), and Tony Galazan's Connecticut Shotgun Manufacturing Company catalog both provide good lists of dates of about twenty-eight shotgun manufacturers by serial number (see

5

« Even though thought to be obsolete by some, there is great fun to be had shooting fine hammer guns. Here, J. D. Shank is shooting a Damascus-barreled American-made Parker. Note he wears a heavy leather glove in the event that one of the barrels might split.

Appendix B). So, it is possible to obtain information on select shotguns, but the number is small in relation to the many manufacturers and trade name shotguns made.

Trade name shotguns are another matter. From approximately 1880 through about 1910, huge numbers of inexpensively made side-by-sides were imported for resale, mainly from Belgium. Domestically, Crescent Arms company of Norwich, Connecticut, made great numbers of shotguns and imported even more, again from Belgium, that were sold to wholesalers, sporting goods stores, gun shops, and hardware stores under dozens of trade names from 1888 through about 1932. Although Crescent made shotguns for years, the company was sold and resold several times until its ultimate demise in 1932. In 1883, H&D Folsom, whose offices were in New York City, bought a controlling interest in Crescent, which continued to produce shotguns for Folsom, as well as the Crescent line of house

brand shotguns. In 1929, at the beginning of the Great Depression, the Crescent Fire Arms Company merged with the N. R. Davis Firearms Company, then owned by the Warner Arms Company, becoming the Davis-Crescent Arms Company. The newly merged company succumbed to the national economic crisis, and was bought by the Savage Arms Company in 1931. In 1932, the city of Norwich, Connecticut, foreclosed on the Crescent property for back taxes.

Below is a list of the known names of shotguns produced—all essentially the same gun with only cosmetic changes in engraving. Probably not complete, the following list includes brand and trade names of Crescent-made and Folsom-imported shotguns: American Gun Co., Bacon Arms, Baker Gun Co., T. Barker (for Sears), Carolina Arms Co., Central Arms Co., Cherokee Arms Co., Chesapeake Gun Co., Compeer, Cruso, Cumberland Arms Co., Elgin Arms Co., Elmira Arms Co., Empire

A historic Purdey shotgun. Although a valuable shotgun by nature of its maker, any time a historical figure, occasion, or place can be positively linked through provenance, the value can markedly increase. On the other hand, spoken legend and lore without provenance must be taken as only hearsay.

Arms Co., Enders Oak Leaf, Enders Royal Service, Essex, Faultless, The Field, F. F. Forbes, C. W. Franklin, Harrison Arms Co., Hartford Arms Co., Harvard, Henry Gun Co., Hermitage Arms Co., Hermitage Gun Co., Howard Arms Co., Hummer, Interstate Arms Co., Jackson Arms Co., Kingsland Special, Kingsland 10 Star, Knickerbocker, Knox-All, Lakeside, J. H. Lau & Co., Leader Gun Co., Lee Special, Lee's Munner Special, Leige Arms Co., J. Manton & Co., Marshwood, Massachusetts Arms Co., Metropolitan, Minnesota Arms Co., Mississippi Valley Arms Co., Mohawk, Monitor, Wm. Moore and Co., Mt. Vernon Arms Co., National Arms Co., New Rival, New York Arms Co., Nitro Bird, Nitro Hunter, Norwich Arms Co., Not-Nac Manufacturing Co., Oxford Arms Co., C. Parker & Co., Peerless, Perfection, Piedmont, Pioneer Arms Co., Quail, Queen City, Rev-O-Noc, W. Richards (not related to the British gunmaker Westley Richards), Richter, Rickard Arms Co., Royal Service, Rummel, Shue's Special, Sickel's Arms Co., Southern Arms Co., Special Service, Spencer Gun Co., Sportsmen, Springfield Arms Co., Square Deal, Stanley, State Arms, H. J. Sterling, St. Louis Arms Co., Sullivan Arms Co., Ten Star, Ten Star Heavy Duty, Tiger, Triumph, U.S. Arms Co., Victor, Victor Special, Virginia Arms Co., Volunteer, Vulcan Arms Co., Warren

Arms Co., Wilkinson Arms Co., Wilmont Arms Co., Wilshire Arms Co., Wiltshire Arms Co., Winfield Arms Co., Winoca Arms Co., Wolverine, and Worthington Arms Co.

To repeat, none of these are more than inexpensively made, solid shotguns. None, absolutely none, has any collector value or interest. If you've got one that belonged to Uncle Ned or your granddad, it's a wonderful keepsake, but not a high-grade gun worth five figures. My father owned two shotguns, a well-worn Winchester Model 1897 and a 1957-vintage Browning Auto-5 Light 12. Both are precious to me, but together have little monetary value.

Although side-by-sides and over-and-unders dominate the fine-gun market, we should not ignore repeaters, as those, too, have been and are produced in high-grade editions. A pre-1940 Grade IV Browning Auto-5 is elaborate, and can be quite a find for the collector, especially if well preserved. I would throw out one caveat: the various organizational shotguns sold at fundraising banquets. Ducks Unlimited is a prime example. It's a wonderful organization—I'm a member and laud the work they do. However, the idea that these banquet or dinner guns hold some high-grade value is a myth.

They are regular production guns and carry a value only slightly higher than a standard field gun. That being said, many Winchester Model 12s carry fine wood and engraving that enhance their value and collectability and make them truly high-grade shotguns, so we'll certainly not ignore repeating shotguns.

In the final analysis, what constitutes a high-grade shotgun does lie with the owner, in the eye of the beholder, if you will. While some of the above criteria may seem hard-hearted on my part, it is because many shotguns are perceived as high-grade but are really not. There are sleepers out there that show up at club swap meets and yard sales, but in reality, high-grade shotguns are a special breed. It isn't hard to see that the high-grade shotgun market suffers from a great deal of confusion, mainly because in today's world any side-by-side is deemed by someone to be a high-grade shotgun. But it's obvious that this is a great oversimplification, just as it is to assume that because a repeater is engraved beyond the decoration given an ordinary, off-the-rack field gun, it is of high grade. Maybe it is, maybe not. That's what this book is about, and by its end hopefully the definition will be more exact, and the waters less muddy.

CHAPTER 2

The Shotgun—A Brief History

Who discovered gunpowder is still debated, just like who invented spaghetti. Gunmaker and author W. W. Greener in the ninth edition (1910) of his book, *The Gun and Its Development* (Bonanza Books, New York, Ninth Edition, 2002) writes, "There seems little doubt that the composition of gunpowder has been known in the East from times of dimmest antiquity. The Chinese and Hindus contemporary with Moses are thought to have known of even the most recondite properties of the compound. The Gentoo code, which, if not as old as was first declared, was easily compiled long before the Christian era, contains the following passage: 'The magistrate shall not make war with any deceitful machines, nor poisoned weapons, or with cannons or guns, or any kind of fire-arms, nor shall he slay in war any person born a eunuch . . .'"

So firearms aren't exactly new, at least according to Greener's research. There seems to be something of a gap, and then the story is picked up some centuries later. Initially, game was shot sitting. The crude matchlock firearms of the day simply took too long for the match to drop into the pan, igniting the priming charge at an undetermined time and finally setting off the main charge and the shot leaving the barrel. Early paintings show aristocratically dressed individuals shooting at birds sitting on the ground over a hedge the gunners were using as a hide. A chapter titled "The Fowling Piece and the Stalking-Horse" in *The Gentleman's Recreation*—published in 1671—describes a fowling piece as best having a barrel "five feet and a half or six feet long," and further, in 21st-century language, instructs shooters to keep their powder dry. As an aside, *The Gentleman's Recreation* also mentions, "Enticement; by pipe, winning or wooing the fowl unto you by pipe, whistle or call," so duck calling didn't start in Arkansas, it was just perfected there. Even earlier, Gervase Markham mentioned shooting in "Hunger's Prevention, or the Whole Art of

Fowling," and in *The Merry Wives of Windsor,* written circa 1597, Master Ford is said to be "a birding," although no mention is made of by what means. Shooting birds on the wing had to wait for a more reliable ignition system, one that would provide a nearly instantaneous and predicable shot.

It is fact that during the early 1600s, the French were shooting flying birds with early muskets. When King Charles II was in exile in France, he, too, shot flying birds, and

when Charles II returned to the throne and the monarchy was restored in England in 1660, he most assuredly continued shooting flying birds.

When the flintlock arrived in the late 1700s, shooting flying birds became even more possible. Although this ignition system was still relatively slow, and sensitive to moisture, it provided a relatively immediate shot compared to the matchlock, where the glowing wick nestled in the priming powder until the weapon fired. It wasn't perfect, but a quantum leap. Soon not only were game-birds and waterfowl being shot on the wing, but shooting competitions using pigeons began to proliferate. Called "old hats," these flyer competitions used old top hats of the day, under which a pigeon was placed, and at the command "pull" a cord attached to the old hat was pulled, tipping the hat and releasing the pigeon. Thus the flintlock, where the priming mixture is held in a pan covered with a striker called the frizzen, became a true sporting arm. The pan was connected with the main powder charge in the barrel by a small hole drilled in the breech. The hammer carried a sharpened piece of flint which, when the trigger was pulled, struck the upright part of the frizzen, pushing the cover back and sending a shower of sparks into the pan. The sparks ignited the fine-ground priming powder, and the fire passed through the hole into the breech and

« Three side-by-side shotguns: Clayblough, Wm. Evans, and AyA showing the three styles of action.

This workman's bench at the over one-hundred-year-old Holland & Holland factory overlooks the graveyard in which Joseph Manton is buried.

ignited the main powder charge, firing the gun. Although we consider today's sidelocks "new," they are simply refined, hammerless versions of the locks used on flint shotguns.

By 1770 reliable Damascus shotgun barrels were readily available, and by 1790, double-barreled flintlock shotguns were available. During this time, Joseph Manton (1766–1835), acknowledged as the "father of the modern shotgun," was making guns. Manton brought together all of the facets of shotguns into what is the form of the modern double shotgun. Although it would have been only a matter of time until the modern shotgun took form, it was Manton who did it. Soon percussion ignition replaced flint, to be rather quickly replaced by the self-contained cartridge. When the cartridge developed, it was only a small step to breechloading. Remarkably, 1909, when Boss introduced the over-and-under, marks the last major development of the modern shotgun.

One might ask, what about the pump and semiauto? Christopher Spencer and Sylvester Roper developed a pump-action shotgun, for which Roper was granted a patent in 1882, and this led to the production of their Model 1890 pump-action shotgun. The Spencer pump was heavy, ill-balanced, and clunky to operate. In 1893, Winchester introduced the John Browning–designed Model 1893 pump that was designed to shoot blackpowder. The frame was open on the top, and the action was found to lack the necessary strength to fire the new smokeless powder. Winchester quickly followed with the Model 1897, later named simply the Model 97, and offered to replace any 1893 with a new 1897 action if it would be returned to the factory. Both Winchester pumps outperformed the Spencer, despite a lawsuit declaring patent infringement—the Roper patent was very broad, perhaps even vague, but given Winchester's status in the firearms business,

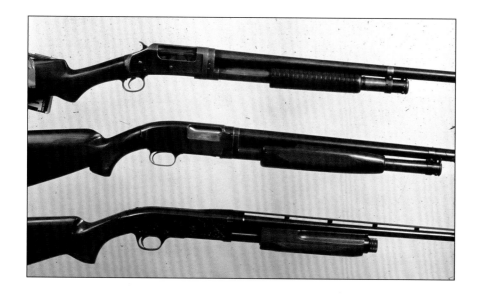

« Three pump-actions that were all produced in higher grades: (top to bottom) the venerable Winchester Model 1897, the Winchester Model 12, and the bottom-ejecting Browning, the third variation of the pump made on an early John Browning design.

scant hearing was given Roper's suit, and it was dismissed by the courts. In 1912, Winchester began manufacturing and warehousing its Model 1912, whose name would also be shortened to the Model 12, and the modern pump-action shotgun's form was defined.

John Moses Browning was a prolific firearms designer. From his inventive genius sprang the Winchester 1893. As he became interested in the machine gun and other weapons that operated without assistance from the operator other than pulling the trigger, the recoil-operated, semiautomatic shotgun took form in Browning's mind. Browning initially designed firearms for Winchester for a set fee; Browning designed the gun, and Winchester bought the design outright. This time, Browning saw a potential good seller, and demanded not only a design fee, but an ongoing royalty on each shotgun sold. Winchester wouldn't budge, so Browning took his design to Remington. On January 8, 1902, as John Browning and his brother

Matthew sat in the waiting room, his prototype shotgun across his lap and a semiautomatic rifle prototype across Matthew's, Remington's president, Marcellus Hartley, suffered a massive and instantly lethal heart attack. It is rumored that at the moment Marcellus Hartley's secretary George Bingham announced Hartley's death, John said to Matthew, "What do we do now?" Matthew Browning, the businessman of the pair, said, "We can accomplish nothing here. We must go to Belgium and see what we can do there."

So was established the relationship between the Brownings and Fabrique Nationale in Herstal, a suburb of Liège, Belgium. From this partnership quickly sprang the first of the Browning Automatic-5 semiautos that hit the dealers' shelves in 1903. Although the Browning brothers struck a deal for the manufacture of their firearms with Fabrique Nationale, upon their return, they also struck a deal with Remington to produce a simpler,

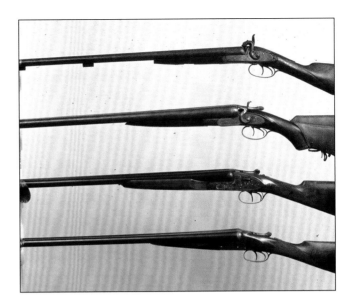

The development of the » double shotgun: (top to bottom) a muzzle-loading percussion double, an exposed hammer breechloader, a sidelock placed the hammers inside the action and a boxlock.

less expensive version of the Auto-5 on these shores. So was born the Remington 11, which stayed in production through World War II.

So it was that by 1909, the shotgun as we know it was established in its final form. The exterior shape was finalized by the Winchester Model 12, semiautos by the Browning Auto-5, and the only refinement left was the development of the gas-operated semiauto, first by High Standard and then by Remington, but its shape was that of the Model 12's gracefully sloping receiver.

In the process we've altogether glossed over the reason that breechloading doubles, pumps, and semiautos work: self-contained shotshells. As firearm development gained momentum, the flint system of ignition gave way to percussion ignition. Percussion ignition was fully developed by 1820, and by the time of the American Civil War, percussion ignition was in full use by the Union and Confederate armies. The battlefield is a great crucible for the development

of arms, and as that conflict evolved, breechloading rifles using self-contained rimfire and centerfire ammunition came into being. Shotguns followed a parallel line of development. The pinfire cartridge was developed in 1846, making possible early breechloading shotguns, and in a relatively brief 35 years the centerfire shotshell was fully developed. By 1870, the breechloading shotgun was perfected, and during an additional short 10-year period, the hammerless double was perfected. Hammer guns lasted well into the 20th century, finally falling by the wayside during World War II. Some hammer guns are still made, primarily for live-pigeon shooters who feel they are more reliable.

Although the development of the shotgun was relatively brief, and amazingly complete at a very early time in history, it is the period from the perfection of the breechloading shotgun in 1870 through World War I that presents the greatest confusion. During this time, the Indian

Wars were being fought, mostly to displace the Native Americans to open the vast prairies to settlers. Settlers faced the ever-present need to feed their families as they cleared the land and grew their crops; meanwhile, cities needed sources of protein to feed their ever-growing populations. The need for inexpensive shotguns to shoot the then-abundant waterfowl and prairie game thus gave rise to a vast sellers' market for shotguns. Into this market came a flood of side-by-sides, along with Winchester's pumps and Browning's semiautos.

Perhaps the greatest area of confusion in separating high-grade shotguns from the chaff comes from guns made during this period. Vast numbers of double guns were produced, mainly in Belgium, but also in Britain's major gunmaking center of Birmingham. Selling for from $10 to $20 each, these shotguns were designed and proofed for blackpowder. European gunmakers are required to submit their products to the rigors of their national proof houses, and therefore much can be learned from simply looking at the proof marks (Appendix B) that are stamped on the barrel and action flats. If gun owners and buyers would familiarize themselves with proof marks, they would be much wiser about their shotguns. Be that as it may, the majority of these shotguns were made for resale by various hardware, sporting goods, and gun shops under trade names. It should come as no surprise that many of these trade names are very similar to those of top-quality gunmakers. For example, the fine Parker Brothers shotgun was made in Meriden, Connecticut, so what did Sears, Roebuck & Company do? They located a firearms factory in Meriden and used the name Meriden Firearms Company, very close to the Parker Brothers' original 1865 company name, The Meriden Manufacturing Company. More direct imitators were E. D. Parker, T. Parker, Thomas Parker, W. Parker, and William Parkhurst. The similarities of these names to that of the original Parker company founded by Charles Parker and made famous as Parker Brothers are sufficient to confuse all but the most educated gun collector.

The problems don't stop there. How about W. Richards? I've answered several letters regarding W. Richards and W&H Richards shotguns, both of which bear Belgium proof marks, and which bear no relation at all to the vaunted British manufacturer whose name, Westley Richards, is *always* spelled out. Many expecting that their W. Richards was worth big bucks have been disappointed to find it is worth $200.

Certainly, there were many high-grade shotguns manufactured during this Golden Age. From 1870 through about 1939, driven bird shooting was enjoying its zenith in Great Britain, and during that time, many high-grade shotguns were made for the aristocracy and well-to-do who could afford them. And there were many who couldn't afford them, but spent their entire family fortunes pursuing and hosting these lavish shooting parties—and who ordered nothing but the best London could offer. These shotguns are perhaps the true foundation of the guns of glory. Makers such as Purdey, Holland & Holland, Henry Atkin, Boss, Charles Lancaster, Lang, Dickson, and

Some of the great mystique of high-grade shotguns is their heritage. This Watson gun was made for royalty, in this case His Imperial Majesty, The Sultan of Turkey, and the owner takes extra pride in knowing the history of his shotgun.

Westley Richards are synonymous with great guns, yet the firearms themselves appear, on the whole, to be somewhat plain—plain, that is, when compared with guns featuring gold and/or silver inlays and elaborate decorations, made for czars and sultans.

In the Unites States, prosperity grew until the stock market crash of 1929, and during that Gilded Age, bankers, businessmen, physicians, attorneys, and others ordered lavish shotguns. All American shotgun makers of this time offered high-grade shotguns in ascending grades of lavishness. Some were for the gun cabinet, others for the field.

Recently, more and more elaborately engraved and inlaid shotguns are being commissioned. Some are great works of art, while others are eccentric, often bizarre shotguns that appeal only to their owners. Subject matter ranges from gamebirds and animals—often apropos to the gauge and intended quarry of the shotgun—to automobiles, scenic vistas,

and even erotic subjects. I understand that an Arab potentate commissioned a shotgun featuring highly erotic engraving, then canceled the order, leaving the gunmaker holding an essentially unsalable gun. Many shotguns have appreciated in value because of their names, the engraving and finely grained wood, or their association with a historic figure, either famous or infamous. Regardless of their quality, those guns that are bizarre or perhaps even offensive have little value, or at the very least are difficult to sell, and then not at a premium, unless an equally bizarre buyer can be found.

Association with companies or individuals often makes the ordinary extraordinary. For example, Beretta recently repurchased Ernest Hemingway's Beretta SO3 over-and-under, complete with its leather leg-of-mutton-style case with Hemingway's address in Cuba written in ink by "Papa," for an undisclosed price. Shotguns that are clearly associated with prominent people, and whose provenance can be clearly substantiated, often take on value far beyond their practical worth. I suppose that's why the Boss with which Hemingway took his life was chopped into scrap. Not only must the shotgun be typical of the guns of the era when the person lived, but receipts, bills of sale, photographs, references in family documents, wills, and other documentation must also substantiate the ownership. Without real provenance, it's just another shotgun.

We'll get into fakes and nonvaluable shotguns in a later chapter, but one variety that keeps cropping up, and which is a fraud in almost every case, is the shotgun used by Wells

Fargo company guards. In any Western movie depicting a stagecoach carrying valuables, the person in the "shotgun" seat always carried a double-barreled shotgun. The only substantiated shotguns made for and used by Wells Fargo, the most famous historic name in transporting valuables, were a group of about 50 made on contract for Wells Fargo by the Ithaca Gun Company. Any others are highly suspect, and most likely fakes.

Throughout the development of the shotgun, there have been those made to higher grades of workmanship and decoration. Of these, some are high-grade shotguns simply because of the maker, others because of the decoration applied to either top-of-the-line best guns or regular production guns with all manner of engraving and inlays lavished on them. The Parker A-1 Special is just such a shotgun. The common Parker actions and barrels were finished with extra care, then engraved and stocked with the highest-grade wood. Certainly, the value of any Parker has accelerated over the past several decades, but unique shotguns such as the Parker Invincible, of which only three were made, assume extremely high values. A genuine Joseph Manton in good condition, for example, would command a high price to a collector interested in the first shotgun to gather all the facets into a whole that has seen little change in design, save for breechloading, in two centuries. Shotguns owned by the great, near great, and infamous also command a premium, although the guns themselves may not be even close to being high-grade shotguns.

Shotguns are wonderful objects. Few others can match the look and feel of a fine double or the sleek Winchester Model 12, and that's why we're so strongly drawn to them. A fine shotgun points as if it were made for the user, and many are. Even if previously owned, a fine shotgun is a joy to behold and to shoot.

CHAPTER 3

Great Names, Great Guns

To the ardent Parker or Fox collector, one need look no farther than our own shores for high-grade shotguns. To the casual observer, only those shotguns displaying lavish engraving and precious-metal inlays may constitute his idea of high-grade shotguns. Some feel that shotguns from the name British makers are the only true high-grade guns in the world. Others would point to Italy and Spain. As beauty is in the eye of the beholder, so are high-grade shotguns.

If one were to be truthful, the difference between British Best guns and their American counterparts is both in weight and manufacturing methods. By the turn of the 20th century, the breechloading double had assumed its present form. At this time robust gunmaking industries flourished on both sides of the Atlantic, yet each had its challenges and traditions. The game shot, the ammunition in common use, and other factors deeply affected how shotguns were made. Too, World War I had a far more profound effect on Britain and continental Europe than it did on America. While the youth of Britain, France, Germany, and Austria-Hungary were slaughtered on the fields of Flanders and elsewhere, the United States entered the war relatively late, and while we suffered losses, they paled compared to those of the initial combatants.

Returning soldiers found a recovered economy that would boom for a full decade, making fine guns available to the masses, and while the relatively new repeaters, pumps, and John Browning's Automatic-5 perhaps made sense to many, the production of the great American doubles continued. Although the Winchester Model 21 came along later, during the Great Depression, most American gunmakers were well established, and while their production perhaps didn't flourish—many, if not all, were struggling financially—from 1880 until World War II could very well be called the golden age of American shotgun

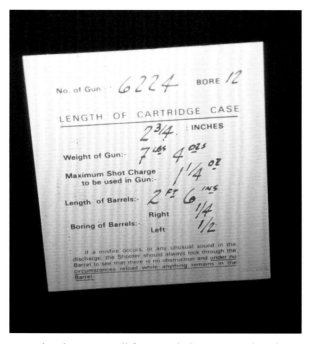

Bespoke shotguns will frequently have a card such as this that indicates the pedigree of the gun including chamber length, maximum shot charge, barrel lengths, overall weight, and chokes.

manufacture. While that era also continued in Britain and Europe, it was perhaps more subdued than in America.

British shotgunners ordered their shotguns for specific game, principally driven grouse, pheasants, and partridge. British cartridges have been and remain relatively mild compared to American ammunition. The normal chamber length of a bespoke British-made shotgun is 2½ inches, the shot charge 1 or $1\frac{1}{16}$ ounces, and velocities are in the range of 1,100 to 1,150 feet per second (fps) with pressures running 6,500 to 9,000 pounds per square inch (psi). Using these parameters, British shotguns tend to be lightweight. W. W. Greener, the British gunmaker and author, formulated his "Rule of 96," which states: To be comfortable to shoot, a shotgun should be

96 times the weight of the shot charge fired from it. Doing the math (1 [ounce] x 96 = 96 ÷ 16 [ounces] = 6 lbs.), a 1-ounce shot charge requires a shotgun of 6 pounds. It's a valid rule, and remains a good measure today. Typically, British shotguns, including those of lesser price, came with cards indicating the load and shot charge for which they were made, and intended, and virtually all reflected Greener's rule of weight to shot charge. In view of this philosophy, British cartridges tend to be loaded to about the same pressure and velocity to match the lighter shotguns intended to shoot those cartridges from the British Isles.

America, by contrast, was a dynamic civilization on the move westward, where the promise of land and abundant game waited. Game ranged from quail to prairie chickens

A fine hammer gun in action at the Vintage Cup.

Great American-made shotguns (top to bottom) A. H. Fox, an 1895 hammer Parker, Winchester Model 21, Ithaca NID made by Classic Doubles, and a Winchester Model 12 pump.

and grouse to ducks, geese, and turkeys, and even to big game such as deer, which were shot with buckshot (as was the occasional black bear). The spectrum of game available to the American sportsman and hunter seeking to provide for his family was broad, and so was the ammunition. The big duck clubs of the day ordered stiff duck loads by the thousands, and every general, hardware, and sporting goods store, and gun shop stocked a variety of loads. While our British gunmaking cousins could pretty well predict and even dictate to their customers what loads to fire in their shotguns, such a thought was folly on these shores. Hence, American-made shotguns were heavier, tending toward 7 and 8 pounds rather than those of slighter build from across the

sea. To be sure, lightweight shotguns could be and were ordered. A. H. Fox offered barrels in weights indicated by numbers. For example, No. 1, 30-inch, 12-gauge barrels weighed from 4 pounds, 2 ounces, to the lightest No. 4 barrels weighing 3 pounds, 6 ounces. The difference was more dramatic in the 20-gauge, where No. 0, 30-inch, 20-gauge barrels weighed 4 pounds, 2 ounces, down to No. 4 barrels that tipped the scales at a slight 2 pounds, 14 ounces.

Factory records indicate many light-weight shotguns being produced by the great American makers, yet the majority were heavier shotguns made to shoot whatever flew or ran by, and whatever load the user could find at his local source. Too, it's an American trait or phenomenon that bigger is better, and I suspect a no less universally held trait in 1920 than in 2010. Hence, heavier loads *must* be better than light loads for general use, so it was necessary to build heavier guns to accommodate our American philosophy.

The durability and reliability of American-made shotguns is unquestionable. A. H. Fox called his shotguns "The Finest Guns in the World," and to some they truly are. So what is the big difference between the two philosophies of shotgun construction? Essentially there are two: guns made for the individual and how they are made.

A London Best shotgun is almost always made for a particular individual. The stock is meticulously fitted—as is the balance, choking, rib, triggers, engraving, and other aspects—to the customer's exact specifications. American shotguns could also be ordered with specific stock dimensions, choking, etc., but still most came over the counter with factory stock dimensions, choking, and engraving appropriate to the grade.

The traditional manner of manufacturing a bespoke shotgun began with two barrel tubes and several blocks of steel. From these, the gunmaker cut the action and forend iron, along with all the other parts. Beginning with a lump of steel, and using only files and other hand tools, he carefully filed the action to its final form. The process was labor-intensive and expensive. American shotgun manufacturers used more modern techniques, beginning with forged steel billets already in the rough shapes of the action and forend iron. Doing what took a patient British gunmaker hours

The legendary Holland & Holland instructor Ken Davies compares the dimensions of a shooter's shotgun to those he set on his try gun.

and days, milling machines and other production methods took away all the excess metal in minutes. American production was fast, but the quality of materials was extremely high. While a British gun was produced in a straight line from raw materials to the finished gun, in America, once actions and all the other parts of a gun were made, they were placed in bins, and when a shotgun was to be completed, the fitter made the rounds of the bins, collecting the various parts that he would then assemble into a finished gun.

While British and some European shotguns were and some are still handmade, Amer-

Assembling a pair of barrels. This Beretta worker is applying flux to one of the ribs that hold a pair of barrels together.

ica's finest shotguns were machine-made, then hand-assembled. Granted the tolerances might be slightly greater on an American shotgun than on a British-made double, but for the given purposes and intents, each is a noble statement of the gunmaking art.

Whether a shotgun was bespoke and handmade in London or Birmingham, or machined and assembled in New England, there are other differences. Shotguns from Britain tend to be lighter with shorter chambers and are intended to be fired with lighter loads than Americans use. The most common 12-gauge field load on these shores is the 1¼-ounce 3¼-dram-equivalent field load with a muzzle velocity of about 1,250 fps. An Englishman would consider that a very heavy waterfowl load, and uses instead a 1- or 1⅛-ounce load with a velocity of 1,050 to 1,100 fps for the majority of his shooting. In short, American shotguns are heavier and more robust than their English counterparts, and there's good reason for this. A British maker dictates the load for

which a particular shotgun is proofed, and users are obliged to use that load. In America, shotguns were and are proofed to be safe with the highest-pressure shotshells commercially loaded, and the user is free to choose whatever load he feels will get the job done. Hence American shotgun makers favor robust shotguns to shoot heavy loads.

All firearms made in Europe and Britain must be submitted to their governments' proof houses. Even before a shotgun is accepted for proofing, it is carefully examined by the proof master or his assistants. If there is any discrepancy in bore diameter, barrel wall thickness, chamber length, or other aspect, it will be rejected and returned to the gunmaker for correction. Once past the careful eyes of the proof house staff, it is then subjected to firing with cartridges that overload it to about one-third to one-half more pressure than the highest-pressure load to which it will be exposed.

Actions waiting to be joined to a pair of barrels.

21

The Proof House of the Gunmakers Company of the City of London, where all British firearms must undergo their final inspection

Once the gun is proofed, the gunmaker is careful to specify the proper cartridge length and load to be used in that particular shotgun. It's different in America.

Proof is less formal on these shores, as there are no federal proof laws and no federal proof house, but rather every firearms company is responsible for proof testing its own shotguns. Certainly, ethics and the specter of a lawsuit for damages from a defective shotgun were and are sufficient to ensure that manufacturers produced safe firearms, but once the gun was out the door, they had no control over how it would be used. To be sure, American gunmakers exercise as much care as their overseas counterparts, and shotguns produced on these shores are equally inspected and fired with proof loads to ensure their safety when used with the highest-pressure loads for which a particular shotgun is chambered. Still, Parker, Fox, Winchester, etc., could not be sure what their customer would stuff into their shotguns, hence the majority were made to digest the heaviest loads available, and American shotgunners liked it.

High-grade shotguns are wonderful pieces of practical art, and their origin makes little difference when it comes to appreciating them. Certainly, a Purdey or Boss over-and-under will elicit oohs and ahs, but so will an exquisite Parker or Fox, or a German or Italian masterpiece. The greatness may be in the name, and we all have our favorites, but regardless, all high-grade shotguns deserve their place. How they get to greatness differs, but that's also what makes them so interesting.

CHAPTER 4

America's Best

One of my biggest regrets is the loss of my great-uncle's Parker. An ill-informed, antigun aunt, and a local police gun turn-in combined to take Uncle George's Parker from me. Yet, from my father's description, it was a rather plain Parker with a straight-hand stock, splinter forend, and Damascus barrels. Still, it would have been a revered gun in my collection. I suppose that sums up a great deal of America's appreciation for high-grade shotguns. Much value is placed on the name, followed by the wood and engraving. The truth is that virtually every American-made, high-grade shotgun is built using a common action, the upgrades being in the exterior and interior finish of the action, barrel material, engraving, and grain of the wood. While a London maker's name automatically makes his gun a high-grade, that isn't so on these shores.

America need never hang its head when it comes to shotguns. Ours are more durable and more heavily built than their British counter-parts. John Olin, father of the Winchester 21, had one taken from the warehouse along with several other top-grade shotguns from various manufacturers, foreign and domestic, and had them repeatedly fired with proof loads. Most gave up after fewer than 100 rounds. A couple went 150 rounds, but the 21 digested 2,000 proof loads with no measurable damage or wear. There aren't many American-made high-grade shotguns: L. C. Smith, A. H. Fox, Parker, Lefever, Ithaca, Winchester, and Remington constitute the lot. Virtually all of these are doubles. The Remington 32 is the lone over-and-under, and, of course, there are repeaters from Winchester, Remington, Ithaca, and perhaps another one or two manufacturers that are considered high-grade shotguns by virtue of their finish and deco-ration. The John Browning Superposed over-and-under was the product of American genius (Browning's), but was produced by Fabrique Nationale in Belgium, so it is consigned to being neither fish nor fowl, neither fully domestic

Four classic American-made shotguns: (top to bottom) A. H. Fox, Parker, Winchester Model 21, and Ithaca.

nor fully foreign. Certainly Browning shotguns, especially the Superposed, are high-grade shotguns, but like their American cousins, they are made on a common action, the decoration making the difference.

Any firearm can be decorated with engraving and fancy wood, but the quality of these additions must be also be considered. Following World War II, when our soldiers, sailors, and Marines were stationed around the globe, and especially during the Vietnam conflict, many were exposed to the inexpensive engraving readily available in the Far East. Many a Remington 1100, Browning Auto-5, and Winchester Model 12—as well as other models—was brought home with engraving and silver or gold inlays from Okinawa and

other, to quote the old song, "faraway places with strange-sounding names." Line up a rack full of shotguns and intermingle one of these, and it sticks out like someone's grandmother playing fullback in an NFL game. If there's a watchword for high-grade shotguns, it's *quality*. Quality of expression, quality of execution, and quality of materials sing to the observer. So does the "does it belong?" rule. Recently, one of our club members put a rather nice shotgun by one of the lesser-known English makers, but a quality shotgun nonetheless, on the consignment rack. Drawn to it like a June bug to a zapper, I immediately caressed its flowing lines, and noted the rather good refinish. It all crashed when I turned it over, and there on the bottom of the action, like a painted lady, was a pheasant in flight over a field of grain. Original? Absolutely not. In good taste? No! A good value? No! Had the Asian "artist" who desecrated this gun not cut the frightened rooster so deep into the action, judicious polishing might perhaps have eradicated the ghastly bird. But no, and lost to someone's gauche taste was an otherwise nice shotgun. At $4,000—a fair price for a good refinished boxlock, minus the gauche engraving—it sat for weeks and was eventually withdrawn. Too bad, because without the startled, cackling ringneck, it would have been a good buy at that price. So all engraving isn't beauty personified.

Highly figured wood can be a beautiful addition, provided it fits the gun. All too often, shotguns are restocked, often for valid reasons of fit, but unless this is done properly, following the original manufacturing style, it can be as gauche as poor engraving. For example, any quality gunmaker will leave the wood proud, or very slightly raised above the surface of the metal. If you spot an otherwise nice shotgun with the wood level with the metal, one of two things has occurred: Either the wood has been refinished at least once, or it has been restocked by someone who isn't aware of original styles. This may not be grounds for dismissal, but certainly the red flag should wave that this particular shotgun has been around the block more than once.

All these things will reappear later in more depth, but I bring them up here because American-made shotguns seem to be more afflicted with these aftermarket flaws than shotguns from Britain and Europe.

PARKER

If any American-made shotgun has gained in price and collector interest, it is the

This Parker uses the » familiar Scott spindle top lever that is synonymous with double guns today.

Parker. Frequently, I receive letters from readers of magazines to which I contribute inquiring about a shotgun the writer owns, often a family heirloom, whose name is some variation of Parker. There's E. D. Parker, Parker-Hale, T. Parker, Thomas Parker, W. Parker, and probably a few more I've not heard of, but there was only one Charles Parker, who, with his brother John, founded Parker Brothers in Meriden, Connecticut. Established as the Meriden Manufacturing Company in 1865, the firm was renamed Parker Brothers in 1868.

Charles Parker was born in Cheshire, Connecticut, on January 2, 1809. At 18, he went to work for a button factory near Cheshire and later switched to making coffee mills in Meriden. Soon Parker, at the ripe age of 20, with $70 in savings, began manufacturing coffee mills on contract. By age 35, Parker had become a hardware manufacturing giant whose factories made everything from clocks to pumps to silverware. When the Civil War broke out, the Union turned to the industrial and manufacturing might of New England to produce armaments for its forces. Parker produced two repeating rifles that, though innovative, saw little service in the war. Following the war, Parker owned a large inventory of rifle barrels and parts, which he soon converted to shotguns for the civilian market. At this same time, as Americans began moving west, came the development of the breechloading shotgun. Parker saw this rapidly advancing technology, and although he wasn't a designer, but rather an entrepreneur, he envisioned that a high-quality shotgun could be produced, not wholly

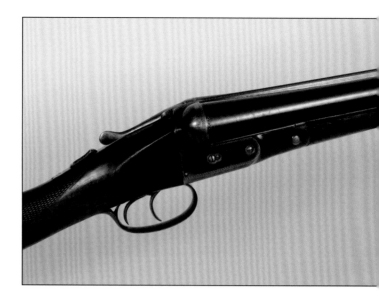

by hand, but by machine, with the parts hand-assembled.

In 1868, with Charles Parker overseeing production, his sons Wilbur, Dexter, and Charles Jr. began gunmaking in earnest. Wilbur was the head of the endeavor, and eventually his son, Wilbur Fiske Parker Jr., would become head of Parker Brothers, all under Charles Parker Sr.'s overall supervision.

The earliest Parker shotguns were fitted with a nipple for a percussion cap that supplied the ignition for a transitional cartridge that was only a refinement of the Lefaucheux pinfire breechloading system. These shotguns were chambered for 8-, 10-, 11-, 12-, 14-, 16-, and 20-gauge cartridges that were made of brass and contained the powder, wad, and shot, but relied upon the conventional percussion cap for ignition. These were marked "Meriden Manufacturing" and "Charles Parker, Maker."

Once past this transitional cartridge, and following the adoption of cartridges as we know them today, Parker shotguns took on the appearance with which we're familiar. Early Parkers used a lifter-style opener that consisted of a button or plunger in front of the trigger guard that was pressed upward, or lifted, to open the breech. When the breech was closed, the button popped out. When the more familiar top-lever opener appeared, Parker changed to this style of opener, and the top-lever-style action remained throughout production.

Perhaps two elements set Parker shotguns apart from others: the indented hinge-pin heads at the knuckle and the doll's-head that mates into a matching recess on the top of the action.

Several American-made shotguns, such as the Lefever and A. H. Fox, lock the barrel to the action by means of a rib extension, and it's an extremely solid lockup. Parker shotguns lock up by means of a Purdey-style underbolt that engages slots in the barrel lumps, and holds the barrels as tightly as any system. However, Parker

decided to incorporate their distinctive doll's-head rib extension into the action as an additional fastener. Unnecessary, and difficult to fit properly, the doll's-head remained a distinctive identifier on all graded Parkers. The stripped-down, economy, bargain-priced Parker Trojan didn't have the doll's-head, although in truth it is every bit a Parker, just without the frills.

Parker shotguns started with the Trojan, which came in 12-, 16-, and 20-gauge, with the same action minus the extra finishing of the graded shotguns, standard chokes, barrel lengths, and plain walnut with utilitarian checkering and a varnish finish. The Vulcan Grade started the graded guns, and for the most part these shotguns were made without ejectors, although barrel lengths and chokes were options. Most Vulcans, which came in 12-, 16-, and 20-gauge, were stamped VH, standing for Vulcan-grade hammerless. Vulcans with the optional ejectors were stamped VHE,

Hammer Parker.

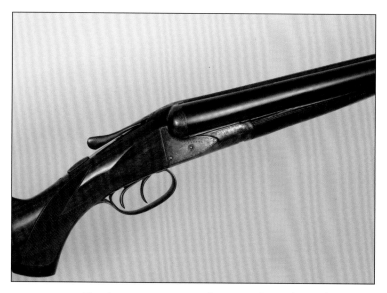

The A. H. Fox was made in grades A through F and E, like Parker, indicated ejectors. The plain Sterlingworth was ungraded and direct competition with Parker's Trojan.

as was every graded shotgun with E, standing for ejectors. From the VH or VHE—the most commonly found Parkers—grades ascended from P to G, then D, C, B, and the rarest of all, the AH—more probably AHE—and the exquisite A-1 Special. Each ascending grade of Parker included increasingly more elaborate engraving, higher-quality wood, and checkering. Each grade also had its own grade or name of barrel steel: Vulcan, Whitworth, Acme, and so on.

One of the great attractions of the Parker is the fact that the company used a variety of frame and action sizes; each was appropriate to a gauge, and some were scaled to the weight of the gun. One of the singular differences between many American-made shotguns and their British- and European-made counterparts is the use of gauge-appropriate actions.

Frequently, 28-gauge and even .410-bore shotguns are built on 20-gauge actions. Certainly, you have a 28-gauge or .410 shotgun, but made on a much larger action than is necessary or even desirable.

Parker made three action sizes—small, medium, and large—and the proper size action was selected to match the finished weight of the shotgun. The barrels were also made to match the action size. Heavy barrels for heavy actions meant that the heavier tubes were thicker at the breech end; consequently, the larger, heavier actions had the firing pin holes located farther apart to accommodate the larger-diameter barrels.

Starting in about 1877, the frame or action size was stamped onto the bottom of the barrel lug. However, because Parker gladly accepted custom orders, and a great number of their shotguns were built to customers' wishes, there may appear strange combinations of barrels and frames.

Parker faced considerable competition from repeating shotguns, and ultimately, like most of its competitors, succumbed to the economy. Nearly bankrupt at the tail end of the Great Depression, the company was sold on June 15, 1934, to the Remington Arms Co. Remington continued to make Parker shotguns, mainly from finished parts acquired from the sale. Few Parkers were made following World War II, however. Evidence points to the last Parker leaving the factory in 1947, although some were made as retirement gifts for high-ranking Remington employees as late as the 1960s.

A. H. FOX GUN COMPANY

Ansley H. Fox was a top-notch trap shot, and a visionary designer. He established, sold, and lost several companies, and even designed and produced a luxury automobile. Born Ansley Herman Fox in Decatur, Georgia, he spent his life making things, but if he has a supreme accomplishment, it is the shotgun named for him. His early shotguns, manufactured under the name Philadelphia Arms Company, look for all the world to be Parkers, with distinctive recessed hinge pins, and are called "pin guns" by Fox aficionados. This design was quickly dropped. In 1904, Fox resigned from the Philadelphia Arms Company, citing business differences, and in 1906 he founded the A. H. Fox Gun Company. Fox dubbed his new shotguns "The Finest Guns in the World." His claim is still argued mightily among gun enthusiasts. Fox's shotgun is latched using a revolving top hook that engages the barrel extension, and provides for a very solid lockup. Internally, there are only three parts: the hammer with an integral firing pin, the sear machined from forged steel and carefully hardened, and a coil spring that drives the hammer. Fox guaranteed his guns against breakage, and unlike a folded or V spring, a broken coil spring will often continue to function. Because of the integral firing pins, a Fox could be dry fired without

The author regularly shoots his HE-Grade Super-Fox using bismuth, Tungsten-Matrix, or Classic Doubles. These ducks were bagged on historic Beaver Dam Lake in Mississippi where the late Nash Buckingham also shot with his Super Fox.

breaking, unlike shotguns with separate strikers that will break from stress when dry fired without snap caps in place. It did not hurt Fox's reputation that Theodore Roosevelt took an F-Grade Fox shotgun on his famous African safari. According to Roosevelt, "No better gun was ever made."

Like Parker, Fox began making a low-priced shotgun, although not of low quality. In March 1910, the Sterlingworth appeared on the market. With the exception of the snap-on forend, all Sterlingworths are fully Foxes, using the common Fox action, but with a single wavy line of engraving around the action, and plain walnut. Made in 12-, 16-, and 20-gauge, these real workhorses sold for $35.

Perhaps one Fox—and there were elaborately engraved grades—that is really the stuff of legend was the rather plain HE-Grade Super-Fox. During the early 1920s, guided by John Olin, the Western Cartridge Company began using progressive-burning powder that provided more space in the case, which could be used for an increased shot payload at a higher velocity. So was born the Western Super Speed and Super X: the 3-inch magnum. An inquisitive attorney, E. M. Sweeley, and Captain Charles Askins began experimenting using a Fox action and single barrels bored by a Fox outworker, Burt Becker. The trio discovered that long, gradually tapering forcing cones and a bore widened from the standard .729 to .740 produced superior patterns with the new Super Speed and Super-X ammunition. Becker made some custom shotguns for luminaries such as Nash Buckingham, perhaps the most influen-

tial outdoor writer of the day. Buckingham all but deified Becker, but the rank and file bought HE-Grade Foxes, which were initially guaranteed to shoot 80-percent patterns at 40 yards. What the Fox spinmasters forgot to point out was that those patterns were guaranteed only with Olin's Super-X ammo. It wasn't long before "Barrels Not Guaranteed" was found stamped on the barrel flats, because Fox could not guarantee the pattern percentages with other than Super-X. This has nothing to do with the quality of the Fox Chromox barrels, which are among the best.

L. C. SMITH

Lyman Cornelius Smith was not much of a shooter or hunter, and he didn't design guns, but he did have a knack for financing enterprises. In early 1877, Lyman, his brother Leroy, and a gunmaking genius named William Baker formed a partnership and founded W. H. Baker and Company, to manufacture Baker's shotguns. In 1880, Leroy Smith and William Baker sold their interest in the company to Lyman C. Smith. Smith needed a designer, and in 1878 Alexander T. Brown joined Smith's company, which still manufactured Baker-designed guns, as a machinist. In March 1883 Brown had a patent issued to him for a lock and breechloading shotgun; it was the design of the L. C. Smith, America's only sidelock shotgun.

Brown's design included a basic sidelock and a top fastener that was very similar in design to those used by Fox, Ithaca, and Lefever. Using a rib extension, a hardened steel cylinder rotates horizontally, and a slot cut into

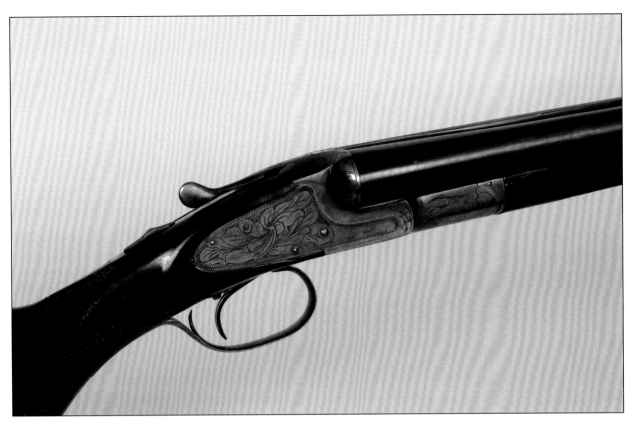

An Ideal-Grade L. C. Smith. In this case it's a Long Range model made to compete with the A. H. Fox Super-Fox.

the cylinder engages the cut in the rib extension. As solid a lockup as there is, this was nothing new—the sidelock was.

All American doubles are boxlocks except for the Smith, which is a somewhat unrefined sidelock, but a sidelock nonetheless. Top-quality sidelocks incorporate an intercepting sear that provides an important internal safety. The engagement of the sear of any firearm involves two very small metal edges that must be set so that they do not slip, yet the trigger that moves the sear from engagement with the hammer must be set sufficiently light to enable good marksmanship. This delicate interplay between the sear and the sear notch in the tumbler can be upset by a sudden jar to the gun. When

an intercepting sear is present, the tumbler is grabbed and held; without a second sear, the gun fires. The L. C. Smith lacks this basic part, and as a result is a pretty crude sidelock. One of the corollary problems with sidelocks is in heading up the stock. Contact between the flat portion of the action and sufficient yet very subtle clearance or relief between the wood and the sidelocks must happen. Otherwise, checking or cracking around the head of the stock is guaranteed. Smith stocks were machine-made, and fitting was carefully done, but heading up a sidelock stock requires much more time than was allotted to the lower grades. Too, the sideplates on which the sidelock mechanism rode were machined square, not beveled as those on the best British or European guns would be. When the sideplates were tightly fitted to the wood, splitting was almost assured as the stock expanded and contracted with the weather. Despite this, the L. C. Smith remains a classic American shotgun.

In 1890, Lyman C. Smith sold his interest in the gun company and turned his attention to typewriters, which garnered him an immense fortune. John Hunter had been seeking a shotgun to produce, and when he heard that Smith was getting out of guns for typewriters, a deal was made. In February 1890, the Hunter Arms Company came into being, with the L. C. Smith already in production. The majority of L. C. Smith shotguns were made by Hunter Arms.

Like its competitors, Smith manufactured graded guns, from the Field Grade to the Monogram, Premier, and Deluxe. Eighty percent of Hunter Arms's production was the Field Grade, which sold for $40 in 1913. Many Ideal Grades are found, which were the lowest grade among the graded guns, and sold for $10 more than a Field Grade.

LEFEVER

Perhaps the most innovative American shotgun was the Lefever Automatic Hammerless, which was built on what Daniel Lefever called a "compensating action."

Lefever was a firearms genius, the equal of John Moses Browning. He was born in 1835, and while not much is known about his early years, by 1857 he had purchased a gunmaking business in Canandaigua, New York. From this shop, he produced fine rifles

The adjusting screw at the front of Lefever action that enables tightening the barrels to action with nothing more than a proper fitting screwdrivers.

that were carried into the Civil War by the New York State Company of Sharpshooters. By 1884 Lefever had incorporated as the Lefever Arms Company, and in 1885 his revolutionary Automatic Hammerless was a reality. The new design used the opening of the barrels to "automatically" cock the hammers—hence the name. It locked up much like the Fox and Smith, using an extension of the rib. What was so revolutionary was that the entire gun was adjustable for wear with nothing more than a screwdriver. The barrels are joined by a ball-and-socket joint that can be tightened by a hardened screw in the end of the action bar. It fits into a matching socket in the barrel lump,

An Ithaca NID made by Classic Doubles.

and should the barrels loosen, a slight turn of this screw will tighten the barrels and action. Although the Lefever Automatic Hammerless has sideplates, they serve only as access plates to what is actually a boxlock action. Lefever shotguns went through other changes, becoming simpler as time progressed.

In 1921, the Ithaca Gun Company bought Lefever, and brought out the Lefever Nitro Special, a functional and sturdy but plain-looking shotgun that is more Ithaca than Lefever. These are seen frequently, and to the unwary buyer seem to be bargains, but such a shotgun is no more a Lefever than a Fox Model B is an A. H. Fox. At one point not long ago, the Ithaca Classic Doubles Company, which made wonderful reproductions of the Ithaca, planned to make an equally excellent reproduction of the Lefever. Steve Lamboy, who tried valiantly to build a classic American double yet

succumbed to lack of capital, owned the rights to the Lefever, and while I was visiting the ill-fated factory in January 2003, he showed me the preliminary plans for the Lefever. Sadly, the banks and bean counters intervened, and the Lefever remains a classic.

ITHACA

The name W. H. Baker, from L. C. Smith, runs through the New York gunmaking trade just as the stream, Fall Creek, runs through Ithaca, New York. In January 1883, Baker bought a lot on the bank of Fall Creek and set up the W. H. Baker & Company Gun Works. Perhaps because of the association of his name with his previous guns and/or to emphasize that his guns were of a new design, the company's name became the Ithaca Gun Company. In the 1885 catalog, Baker describes the gun as "The strongest, simplest and best

American gun manufactured." The illustration on the cover shows an attractive shotgun with a doll's-head rib extension, hammers, and a nicely shaped Prince-of-Wales grip. In the 1886 catalog, Baker makes the point that "The Ithaca gun has a top lever . . . an entirely new arrangement of locks and construction, making it more desirable in every respect . . ." This "New Ithaca Gun" stayed in production in one form or another until the last double was produced in 1949. Between 1888 and 1948, no fewer than four designs were produced in various grades—from Field Grade through the rare and exquisite Sousa Grade—including single-barrel trap guns, of which the Sousa Grade was the pinnacle.

The various versions of the Ithaca were all improvements that had similar outward appearances. They were the Crass, Lewis, Minier, and Flues models, all named for their designers: Frederick Crass, Frank Lewis, David Minier, and Emil Flues. Considerable mystery surrounds the first name of Minier. It was never clear who Minier was until Walter Claude Smith researched his extensive book about the Ithaca Gun Company, and discovered that Minier was originally a machinist living in Ithaca, New York. He worked for Ithaca Gun from 1886 until about 1907. In 1890, he was listed on a photograph as "assembly foreman," a position that would have enabled him to influence design. The New Ithaca Double, or NID, is the most common of the Ithacas, billed as having the fastest lock time of any double, and was made from 1926 until the company discontinued doubles in 1948.

Perhaps the most famous person associated with Ithaca shotguns was John Philip Sousa. Enlisted in the United States Marine Band (The President's Own) as a boy bandsman at age fourteen, Sousa eventually became the leader of The Marine Band, then resigned to form his own professional concert band that toured the United States and, indeed, the world. In those pre-radio and pre-television days, a visit from The Sousa Band was a major event throughout America. A great musician who possessed perfect pitch, and the ability to recognize any note played, Sousa could compose without the aid of a piano. "The Stars and Stripes Forever," for example, was composed on the Atlantic, as he was returning from Europe. Sousa was not only a noted musician, but a constant advocate of hunting and trap shooting. "A gun, a girl, a horse and music on the side," was one of Sousa's mottoes. Sousa shot a Charles Daly trap gun. Imported from abroad, Sousa's was probably made by the Prussian gunmakers Linder or Schiller. New York sporting goods dealers and firearms importers Shoverling, Daly and Gales took Daly's name as having the best customer appeal, and when Sousa's Ithaca was ordered, the stock dimensions were taken from his Daly. It was noted, "Duplicate forearm on Daly on account of small hands." Engraving was specified on the work order as "High Grade, but no gold or silver. Great deal of engraving." And so Sousa's Ithaca Grade, 7-E, 32-inch, single-barrel trap gun was born. It is now proudly displayed in the Amateur Trapshooting Association's (ATA) museum, which is soon to be relocated from Vandalia, Ohio, to Sparta, Illinois.

Contrary to Sousa's wishes, the "production" Sousa Grade, Ithaca's highest, had gold inlays, including a gold mermaid on the trigger guard, reportedly being Sousa's favorite. Apparently it wasn't, but the Sousa Grade is a thing of beauty.

Although doubles were Ithaca's first firearms, repeaters—and, in particular, the Model 37—became the company's mainstays. Based on the John Browning–designed Remington 17, with some patented improvements, the Model 37, released in 1937, was a bottom-ejecting pump gun. Also produced in high grades with extensive engraving and gold inlays, the Model 37 was Ithaca's flagship gun for generations, and remains a classic to this day.

In the 1970s Ithaca branched out to import Italian Perazzi clay-target guns, acquired 10X Clothing, produced the first 10-gauge semiauto, and in the process went bankrupt in 1986. Rising from the ashes was Ithaca Classic Doubles, a company formed by Stephen Lamboy, who purchased the rights to manufacture the NID and licensed the name. Lamboy set up shop in Victor, New York, and worked out an arrangement with an Italian firm for producing the barreled actions, with the intent of stocking and finishing the guns here. The Italian firm failed to deliver the agreed-upon quality, and Lamboy lost a good deal of capital. Still, he persevered, and began manufacturing the entire shotguns from forgings and barrels imported from Germany. The new Ithaca doubles were excellent and things of beauty. All the work, save the forgings and rough machining, was done in the Victor

shop. Even the engravers worked in a part of the shop. One of only two or three gunmakers in the United States—the others being Tony Galazan's Connecticut Shotgun Manufacturing Company and Rigby in California—Lamboy balanced on the tightrope of making guns and stretching for capital to satisfy everyone. Finally, admitting that it cost far more to make guns here than he ever imagined, Lamboy closed the doors of Ithaca Classic Doubles in 2003.

Ithaca doubles were never as racy looking, and save for their single-barrel trap guns, not as well finished as their competitors Parker, Fox, and Lefever. Still, the NID and its predecessors were rugged shotguns that served their owners well.

WINCHESTER

Oliver Winchester was an enterprising Connecticut shirtmaker who became a gunmaker. As the lever-action rifle forged westward, Winchester looked to shotguns, and using a design by John Moses Browning, began manufacturing the pump-action Model 1893. Christopher Spencer and Sylvester Roper already had a pump-action shotgun on the market, but it was clumsy to operate and carried and swung like a rock. Winchester's slide-action carried like an extension of the shooter's arm, and swung like a well-balanced double. Made to shoot blackpowder, the 1893 action proved too weak to safely shoot the newfangled smokeless powder, which also appeared in 1893, so Winchester modified the gun's action by closing the top to make it stronger, and renamed it the 1897. The 1897, later renamed

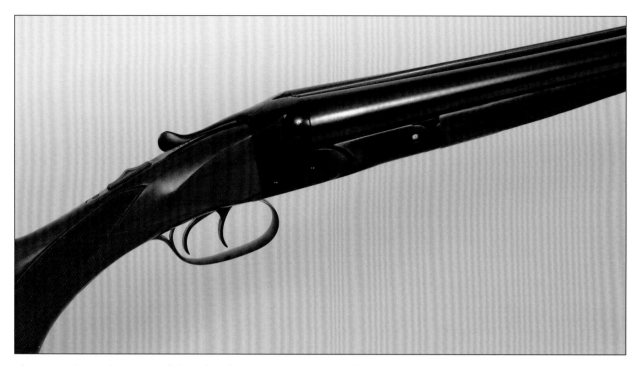

The rugged Winchester Model 21 that the Great Depression all but killed had the Olin family not bought Winchester at a sheriff's safe.

the Model 97, stayed in Winchester's inventory until discontinued in 1959. More than a million rolled off Winchester's New Haven assembly line.

By 1912, Winchester further defined the pump-action shotgun when the company introduced the Model 1912, first in 20-gauge, then in 12-, 16-, and 28-gauge. Something over two million Model 12s in the three gauges and in various grades were produced. Of these, the 28-gauge is the rarest. Winchester dealt with the .410 bore, which came into being to promote Winchester's 3-inch .410 cartridge, with a wholly different gun, the Model 42.

The Models 12 and 42 provided broad canvases for the engraver's art. Slab-sided, the pumps had sleek lines without excess curves, which provided large areas that could be outlined, and partially or completely filled with engraving and inlays. Although the Ithaca 37 and Remington 31 and 870 offer the same broad canvas, of the repeaters, the Winchester Models 12 and 42 top the list of desirable high-grade shotguns.

Winchester's fortunes didn't continue to go smoothly, however, as the company decided to expand into the world of hardware and recreational equipment. This, ultimately, would be their undoing. The 1926–1927 Winchester Product Catalog offered hundreds of items, including lead pencils, store signs and window decals, hoes, oyster knives, footballs, and basketball goal nets. It was during this period that the Model 21 side-by-side was born. Perhaps the most durable double gun ever made, the Model 21 went into production in 1929, and the warehouse received the first gun in March 1930, just as the Great Depression and the collapse of the stock market hit home. There is little doubt that the Model 21 would be but an asterisk in side-by-side history if it weren't for Winchester's crash. At the end of 1930, the first full year following the stock market's crash, Winchester was $8 million in the red and headed into bankruptcy. So severe were the financial problems that it fell into receivership, and on December 22, 1931, Winchester was auctioned on the steps of St. Louis's federal courthouse. At the auction, John M. Olin, whose family owned Western Cartridge just across and up the Mississippi River in East Alton, Illinois, laid out an immense check for $8.1 million and bought Winchester.

Olin moved quickly—he had to, as his outlay of over $8 million needed to be amortized quickly to keep both his new company and Western Cartridge afloat—to cancel out the washing machines, skates, baseballs, footballs, screwdrivers, and all the excess Winchester had brought on themselves, and quickly pared down the company to what it did best: making firearms. Still, fancy shotguns were not at the top of many individuals' lists during the Depression. In fact, if it weren't for John Olin's love of fine shotguns, the Model 21 might have perished with the roller skates, hoes, athletic supporters, and children's wagons.

Olin had good reason to like the Model 21. Plain compared to other doubles, it used immensely strong chrome-molybdenum steel in its actions and barrels, which were joined by a unique dovetail system that employed soft, lead solder that did not affect the barrels' molecular structure. In addition, the action

employed a very long water table that provided immense strength. When a side-by-side is fired, the barrels want to fly open. There is also torque: When the right barrel is fired, for example, it wants to push away from the breech face and twist to the left. By using long action flats, gunmakers can ensure that these forces are spread over a larger area.

John Olin continually sought new ways to promote the 21. In one advertising stunt, Olin took a Model 21 from the warehouse and several other doubles of U. S. and foreign manufacture and subjected them to the most extreme torture test ever attempted. Firing from a cradle, Olin's lab technicians repeatedly fired proof loads with pressures about one-third higher than the hottest sporting loads through each of the guns until they failed or became unsafe to shoot. (The current highest pressure allowable in a 12-gauge, 2¾-inch load is 11,500 psi, while proof loads run between 19,000 and 20,200 psi. When Olin performed his test, proof loads ran about 17,000 psi.) Most of the guns gave up before they had digested seventy-five proof loads, although one did get to 150 loads. The Model 21 soldiered on until 2,000 proof loads had been fired through it, and the test was stopped. Upon inspection by Winchester's engineers, who completely disassembled the test gun, no part showed any discernible wear or stress—not one.

Eventually, the Model 21 was made in 12-, 16-, 20-, and 28-gauge and .410 bore, and in numerous standard Winchester engraving and checkering styles and personalized engravings, all executed by Winchester's in-house engravers, some of the best in the business. Their work also graced the Model 12, and to a far lesser degree the Model 97.

Over its production life, the Model 21, when assigned its part of the manufacturing and material costs, never turned a profit, but it was John Olin's baby, and it remained in production. In the mid-1950s, when I peered across the counter at Bob Peters's Freeport Sporting Goods (in Freeport, Illinois), a new Model 12 pump cost $99.95, a Model 97 about $79, and a 21 ran $396, an astronomical amount. Also, in rural Illinois, doubles were considered effete. Why have only two shots when a Model 12 or Browning Auto-5 had three? By 1959, the Model 21 had been moved to the custom shop as a special-order-only item, and in early 1960, it became strictly custom, with only High-Grades available.

Winchester shotguns, save for High-Grade 21s and 12s, do not hold exceptionally high values. None are exactly cheap, but with the advent of steel shot for waterfowl hunting and a plentiful supply of relatively inexpensive pumps and semiautos that are design-specific for hard steel shot and every other load, complete with screw-in chokes, these wonderful shotguns have become more collector's items than used guns. With this comes the premium of new in the box, unfired, specially engraved and inlaid, and other embellishments that offer collector appeal.

Winchester no longer offers Model 21s from its custom shop; they are, instead, made in Tony Galazan's Connecticut Shotgun Manufacturing Company factory and sold through both Winchester and Galazan. Today, Winchester is best known for hunting guns; their current shotguns pale in comparison to those of the past.

BROWNING

When Browning introduced the first semiautomatic shotgun, the Belgian-made Automatic-5, in 1903, it was a big hit with the hunting public. It was subsequently offered

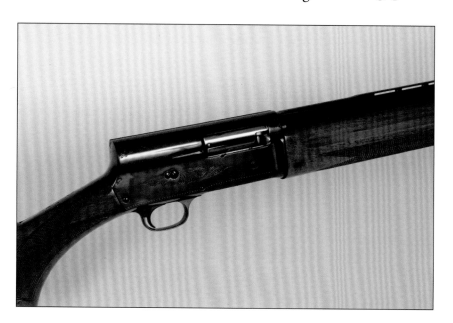

« An example of the ground-breaking Browning Automatic-5 that, in 1903, was the first semiautomatic shotgun released to the sporting public.

through the years in higher grades, with several degrees of engraving and wood. Similarly, the Superposed, John Moses Browning's last gun, one that was on his bench the morning he died, was also made in Belgium, at the Fabrique Nationale factory in Liège, a suburb of Brussels. Introduced in 1931, the Superposed was the first mass-produced over-and-under available off the rack to hunters and shooters. Well designed, it has undergone a simplification that first became the Liège, then the Citori, and is now manufactured in Japan. Like its predecessor, the Citori is available in various grades. Although some Browning shotguns, such as the commemorative Sweet 16, which came out in the 1950s, are sought after, for the most part the company's offerings aren't collected except by those who concentrate on Browning firearms.

ANTHONY (TONY) GALAZAN (CONNECTICUT SHOTGUN MANUFACTURING COMPANY)

A number of years ago, at the annual Shooting, Hunting and Outdoor Trades (SHOT) Show, where all the hunting and shooting equipment manufacturers display their wares for the gun trade and media, I saw a small booth that held some of the most beautiful shotguns I'd ever laid eyes on. The

The RBL made by Connecticut Shotgun Manufacturing was introduced in 2006 as a high-quality yet affordable side-by-side. It along with their much higher-priced bespoke Galazan are the only side-by-sides made in America.

name on the booth was Connecticut Shotgun Manufacturing Company, which is owned by Anthony Galazan. Striving to create the finest shotguns in the world, Galazan has succeeded.

Galazan currently offers superb reproductions of A. H. Fox's "The Finest Gun In The World," which are lavishly engraved, and feature a dark, black-blue, and case-hardened metal finish and bearing wood that is breathtaking to behold. Building shotguns to order only, Galazan has an inventory of parts that enables him to create a shotgun to the customer's precise demands, within several months.

I've been fortunate to visit Galazan's factory in New Britain, Connecticut. There, every facet of building a shotgun is done in-house. Skilled workers, predominantly from Europe, make each and every Galazan shotgun by hand. The hardening and bluing are done in a separate basement area, and the airy, open workrooms provide areas for fitting, stocking, and final finishing.

In addition to the A. H. Fox reproductions, Galazan, by agreement with U.S. Repeating Arms/Winchester, builds and services the venerable Model 21. Galazan has all the parts to repair any 21, and build to order any gauge in any grade.

Perhaps the flagship of the Galazan fleet is his over-and-under. Taking the best from the great over-and-unders—Boss, Woodward, Fabbri, Beretta, and Perazzi, to name a few—Galazan has produced an over-and-under that incorporates the finest features of each, yet is recognizable as none of them. The result is a sidelock over-and-under built to last. Every part has been designed to be rock solid, and the overall gun is not only a thing of beauty, but is made to be shot. Galazan has also designed and is building a sidelock side-by-side. As with the over-and-under, the buyer can select every aspect of this shotgun. From stock dimensions and wood to engraving to barrel length and choking, each gun is completely bespoke. The Galazan side-by-side is a true work of art.

In the mid-2000s, Galazan began making a truly affordable side-by-side that he called the RBL, which stands for Round Body Launch (Edition). Made using the American style of production—making parts then skillfully hand-assembling them—the RBL line represents real quality at an affordable price. In 2009 Galazan introduced his A-10 American over-and-under. A true sidelock over-and-under, this latest of Galazan's shotguns, like the RBL, represents top American-style gunmaking.

If you'd asked me in the late 1980s if someone could establish a high-grade shotgun manufacturing business in this country—and be successful at it—I'd have been very doubtful. Tony Galazan has done it, and while he doesn't make many shotguns each year, and none are off-the-rack guns, he has proved his critics wrong, and today is the sole manufacturer of high-grade double guns in the United States.

REMINGTON

Just as Beretta is the world's oldest gun manufacturer, Remington is this nation's oldest firearms maker, founded in upstate New York in 1816. The company's early production was confined to rifles and pistols. In 1873,

Remington began the manufacture of shotguns with the Model 1873 lifter-action hammer gun. Approximately 5,000 of these guns were made between 1873 and 1878. A succession of other side-by-sides followed, from lifter and top-lever models through the last hammerless side-by-side, the Model 1894, which was manufactured until 1910. Midway through the Model 1894's production, Remington started making a repeating shotgun, the Model 11, a recoil-operated semiautomatic built under license from John Browning.

The Remington 11's tale is a circuitous one. John Moses Browning had a longstanding deal with Winchester, wherein Winchester purchased Browning's designs outright. When Browning designed the Automatic-5, however, he thought the gun was so good that he demanded a royalty on each one produced. Winchester balked, so Browning went to Remington. As mentioned previously, he was in the waiting room of Remington's president, Marcellus Hartley, on January 8, 1902, awaiting his appointment, when Hartley died of a heart attack. Browning next sailed to Europe and approached Fabrique Nationale to manufacture his new Automatic-5, to be sold under his name in the United States. A deal was struck, with Fabrique Nationale using its own name on the gun in the rest of the world.

Remington's managers soon realized they had allowed a golden opportunity to slip through their fingers, and quickly made a deal with Browning to manufacture a semiautomatic shotgun under license. The result was the Remington Model 11, which remained

in production from 1911 through 1948. The Model 11 was succeeded in 1949 by the Model 11-48 which, while still a recoil-operated semiautomatic, had a rounded receiver that had come into vogue by that time.

Remington has always taken great pride in its Custom Shop, where high-grade firearms are produced. All Remington Custom Shop guns begin life as production actions and barrels. Once formed, they are taken over by Remington's top craftsmen, who carefully hand-polish, engrave, inlay with precious metals, blue, and finish the metal. It is then married to high-grade walnut that is shaped to the customer's specifications, checkered, and finished. In some cases, high-grade shotguns are produced using Remington's nominal stock dimensions, and cataloged as high-grade guns.

At one time, Remington offered its trap and skeet guns in A and B grades. The A grade had nice but rather ordinary wood. The B grades had nice figured walnut and were generally worth the extra $75 or so for the upgrade. Some guns were jokingly called A/B grades, whose wood was plain on one side and highly figured on the other. Other grades were the Tournament Grade, reserved for trap guns, and of course the Custom Shop graded guns. Remington can supply custom shotguns in both its gas-operated 1100 and 11-87 semiautomatics and 870 Wingmaster pumps, and with their excellent wood, fine engraving, inlays, and deep bluing, they are beautiful specimens.

In 1931, even as the Depression deepened, Remington introduced the wonderful Model 32 over-and-under. Different than

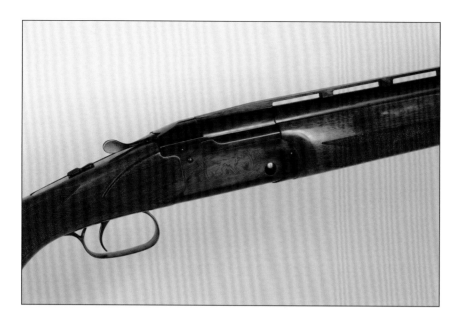

« The Remington 3200 that followed the lines of their discontinued Model 32. A much heavier shotgun than the 32, the 3200 was made for about ten years, until its production also ceased.

anything that had come before, although in truth partially designed after the British Boss and Woodward over-and-unders, this was a wonderful shotgun, one whose design has not been bettered. Introduced at the same time as the Browning Superposed, these shotguns were made for the common man, and designed to be manufactured from "to spec" parts, which could be hand-assembled with some fitting. The 32's price ($75) was within reach of the average working man. The Browning Super-posed, meanwhile, cost $107.50. Still, a standard Model 12 pump sold for $39.50, slightly more than half the price of a 32 and a third the cost of a Superposed.

The Model 32 was unique in not using a Purdey-style underbolt or a hinge pin, nor are the barrels joined with side ribs. The 32 is held shut by means of a sliding hood that completely encases the breech end of the upper barrel. This hood slides in two grooves in the top rear of the action, and when closed it rides on top of parallel rails on either side of the top barrel.

In recoil, the barrels attempt to move down, using the hinge as a fulcrum. This sliding hood holds them tightly to the face of the breech. In addition, should a round fail—something that almost never occurs with modern, plastic-cased shotshells—the shooter is protected by the hood. The barrels also pivot, not around a conventional hinge pin, but on a pair of opposing trunnions that engage cuts in the monobloc at the breech end of the barrels. The resulting action allows the barrels to lie very low, and the profile of the 32 is much lower than that of the Superposed. This allows the forces of recoil to push the gun straight back, lessening felt recoil. Overall, the Remington 32 is an excellent shotgun, and one that deserved to remain in the Remington line of arms. Regrettably it was discontinued in 1947, after approximately 6,500 units in various grades, mostly Field Grade, the lowest grade, had been produced.

In 1973 Remington brought out a much heavier but nonetheless excellent updated version of the 32, the Model 3200. Using the trunnion-hung barrels and hood-style locking system, the 3200 was very heavy, but gained some popularity with clay-target shooters, although the Field Grade proved to be more than most bird hunters were willing to lug around the uplands. A 3-inch-chambered Magnum 3200 was made with extra-heavy barrels that were built to shoot steel shot. Other grades included a rare live-bird version, trap and skeet models with upgraded wood, and so on. There were some early problems with the top tangs cracking, and if the throughbolt that held the stock to the action was overtightened, the sears could come out of engagement with the trigger, causing the gun to fail to fire. All these minor problems were fixed. The sideplates of early 3200s were engraved with a pointer on one side and a setter on the other. When these models were recalled when the tangs began to crack, the replacement actions had each dog enclosed in a wreath. If you see a Remington 3200 without the pointer and setter surrounded by wreaths, the action was not returned during the recall, and a very careful examination should be made of the top tang. The crack will appear as a line across the tang. Because Remington has

long since dropped the 3200 from production, no replacement actions remain, and this gun should be deeply discounted. The 3200 met its end not so much because it was too heavy, but rather because it seemed that everyone who wanted one had bought it, and sales slumped. Over-and-under guns produced following the discontinuation of the 3200 are not of the quality of their predecessors, and while they are nice shotguns, none measures up to the 32. As a tribute to this innovative shotgun, Krieghoff (located in Ulm, Germany) began making a copy of the Remington 32 in the 1970s, and named it the Krieghoff 32 (K-32). It has become a favorite of clay-target shooters. An updated—but little changed, mechanically and visually—version of the Krieghoff 32, called the K-80 (12-gauge) and K-20 (20-gauge), has replaced the K-32. In this guise, the Remington 32 lives on.

LOOKING ELSEWHERE

Entire books have been dedicated to Parker Brothers, Ansley H. Fox, L. C. Smith, Ithaca, Lefever, Browning, Remington, Winchester, and other gunmakers, and I'd refer you to those whose titles can be found in the bibliography.

CHAPTER 5

Britain: The Great Makers

The argument can be made that one need look no farther than the United States to find a shotgun of glory, but the truth is that whenever fine-gun aficionados gather, the talk always turns to those shotguns made across the pond. We've seen that American-made shotguns are heavy and, while hand-assembled, are not really handmade, and both are distinctions that separate two people already separated by a common language.

During the Golden Age of shotgunning in Britain, from 1880 to 1939, British shooters preferred to have their guns custom-made. Those of lesser means most likely bought a shotgun for rough shooting, shooting game while walking cover behind a pointer or setter. A British shooter may also have needed a pair of shotguns for shooting driven birds. Although it was essential to have two guns if a loader was used, many of the shoots didn't use loaders, and then a single gun sufficed.

In the case of fine shotguns, British, Scottish, and Irish craftsmen built shotguns just as tailors made fine suits. The shooter was carefully measured, and then the gun created for him. Included in this was the choice of cartridges, with the chokes being bored and patterned to exact percentages, using only those cartridges. During the Golden Age, shooters routinely purchased their shells—more properly, cartridges—from the gunmaker who made the shotgun. Many gunmakers loaded the cartridges they sold, while others simply got them from Eley or another ammunition company, with the gunmaker's name on each shell and on the box. Whatever the source, the standard British cartridge is 2½ inches long and loaded with ⅞, 1, and at the most 1 1/16 ounces of lead shot. Heavier loads of 1¼ and 1½ ounces of shot were intended for waterfowl hunting. In either case, the bespoke shotgun was designed and made around whatever cartridge the gunmaker suggested or the experienced game shot requested. Because these cartridges were predictably light, British guns are also light in construction and weight. American gunmakers weren't so lucky. Although some manufacturers offered proprietary cartridges, the average American shotgunner stuffed his shotgun with whatever ammunition he could get; hence, American-made shotguns are heavier and more ruggedly constructed.

Lest one feel that these lighter British guns might not be up to the task, I own a Henry Atkin that shoots as well today as it did when Mr. H. B. Duryea, Esq., took possession of it in 1900. It's all a matter of the care and feeding.

The list of British gunmakers is extensive, and no attempt will be made to cover each and every maker here. The late Geoffrey Boothroyd's extensive reference book, *Boothroyd's Revised Directory of British Gunmakers,* lists hundreds of individual gunmakers. Some were simply suppliers of gun parts, including the incomparable Joseph Brazier, whose locks are found on Purdey and Henry Atkin shotguns, and many other fine guns. Even so, the fact is that there are hundreds of gunmakers, and one cannot possibly touch on them all.

The British gun trade is divided between gunmakers in London and Birmingham, and those in Scotland and Ireland. One of the problems with British guns that can catch the unsuspecting buyer off guard is the difference between a London-made shotgun and one made elsewhere in the Empire but carrying a London address. It's an easy problem to overcome, since London-made guns are proofed at the London Proof House, and those from Birmingham and elsewhere in the Birmingham House, and each has its own unique proof stamps. I once owned a William Jackman Jeffrey shotgun whose rib bore the prestigious 13 King Street, St. James, London, address, but the proof marks showed that it was made for Jeffrey in Birmingham. The same occurred with a composed pair of Mortimer & Son shotguns. The address was Edinburgh, but the guns, as the proof marks showed, were made in Birmingham.

If you think I'm attacking the Birmingham gun trade, I'm not. The truth, however, is that London-made guns bring higher prices than those from Birmingham, and the address on the rib must be corroborated by the proper London proof marks. In use, and in practical terms, there probably isn't one bit of difference in how guns from either place shoot, but having a London-made gun does possess a certain panache.

JAMES PURDEY

Perhaps no other name in the gun trade possesses the charm and allure of James Purdey. The company's shotguns are all handmade, and have a unique delicacy that is attributed only to the very best. Certainly a devout Holland & Holland man would throw down his gauntlet and challenge that assertion, but regardless of personal opinions, James Purdey is probably the most respected name in the business. If it were not, it would seem superfluous that William Evans and Henry Atkin would have gone to the extra expense of adding to the engraving on their shotgun "From Purdeys." The Purdeys

The entrance to James Purdey & Sons on South Audley Street in the fashionable Mayfair district of London. Said to be the makers of the world's finest guns, upon examination, there is little to refute this claim.

took exception to their name being added to competitors' guns for the purpose of self-aggrandizement, but that's how is was. Purdey even sued Evans, but the judge determined that since William Evans had in fact worked at Purdey's, he could rightly say that he was indeed "From Purdeys." That lore aside, the fact is that practically any James Purdey shotgun will retain more value than virtually any other.

Although one can order any amount of embellishment, most Purdey shotguns are very restrained, in true British style. The standard engraving pattern is exquisitely executed, tight rose and scroll against beautifully case-hardened sidelocks, all set off against deeply figured, dark-finished English or French walnut.

It all started in August of 1798, when James Purdey entered into an apprenticeship under his sister's husband, Thomas Hutchinson, a stock marker. When his 7-year apprenticeship to Hutchinson was complete, young Purdey took a job with Joseph Manton, the father of the modern shotgun. It was Manton who perfected the double shotgun, and by the time James Purdey joined Manton in 1805, Manton was considered England's premier gunmaker. There is some question about exactly when James Purdey acquired his own premises—Purdey's states it was 1814, other evidence indicates it was 1816—regardless, it was the beginning of a dynasty whose reputation for making fine shotguns and rifles is uncontested. The company

Purdey's famous Long Room that was once the office and was open down the middle so one of the Purdeys could observe the workmen below. It is here that clients receive preliminary fittings and specify their requirements for a bespoke Purdey's shotgun. On the walls are photographs of famous clients and other ephemera from past decades.

was ruled with a firm hand from the earliest days. The author Michael McIntosh once noted that "A similar intolerance for anything less than perfection would characterize every Purdey generation." That intolerance has led to Purdey's reputation for being the very best. There exists the notion that Purdeys are less than hospitable to those simply looking and not seriously buying. At one time that was true, but in September 2009, my wife and I dropped by Audley House, and we were warmly received. We were shown several beautiful Purdey side-by-sides and over-and-unders, and were told that today the sporting guns, mainly over-and-unders, were made so that they could be delivered in a few weeks from stock. Without our prompting, we were then led to the historic Long Room where portraits of noted sportsmen hang along with mounted birds and other trophies. It is in this Long Room that customers are taken to order their bespoke shotguns and rifles, and at one time it was strictly off limits to mere mortals. In earlier days the center section of the Long Room was open and overlooked the workroom below, and it's company lore that members of the Purdey family more than occasionally looked down to be sure the workers were diligently working. Nigel Beaumont, the current managing director, dropped in and cordially greeted us, and later in a chance meeting on the street recommended a fine pub for our lunch.

HOW BRITISH GUNMAKERS OPERATE

On a tour of the existing London gunmakers, one would see workers filing, fitting, polishing, and machining various parts and partially finished guns. Yet it has been common practice from the earliest days of the British gun trade to acquire parts from various sources, then meld them into a finished gun. Few companies bored their own tubes; they were instead acquired in rough form, both inside and out, from noted companies such as Whitworth, Bohler, and Krupp. Actions were often filed in-house, but could have easily come from another outworker, as they were called and paid under that category. In many instances, stocks were made by one craftsman, actions by another, and the barrels filed by another, as the gun was shuttled back and forth across London by messengers until nearly complete. It was finally finished in the workrooms of the gunmaker whose name would be engraved on its action and barrels. Joseph Brazier is perhaps the best known of these outworkers. He and his descendants made top-quality locks for virtually every premier gunmaker, and they appear across the board on quality sidelock guns.

HOLLAND & HOLLAND

Joseph Manton died in 1835, but his legacy was safe. In that same year, Harris Holland opened his tobacco shop at 5 King Street, Holborn, London. He was a tobacconist and excellent shot, his shop was frequented by shooters, and many urged him to become a gunmaker. In 1840, Harris Holland became a "gunmaker," but in name only. Holland in reality became a contractor who worked with the multitude of London's outworkers to build his guns. Although this arrangement would seem to be open to the retailing theory of volume over quality, the fact seems to be that Harris Holland insisted on the highest quality, leaving the dross to others.

Over the nearly two centuries that Holland & Holland has been in business, their shotguns and rifles have been compared to and held in the same esteem as those from James Purdey as representing the epitome of the gunmaking trade. To be sure, there are others whose shotguns are Holland & Holland and Purdey equals, and some feel even better, but when fine guns come to mind, these two are the premier names.

Today, Holland & Holland makes traditional side-by-sides and a very popular over-and-under sporting-clays shotgun. Although you can purchase an off-the-rack side-by-side or over-and-under in one of their galleries in New York, Paris, or London, for Purdey and others, bespoke guns are still their stock in trade. Purdey attempted to establish a gun room in New York, but due to issues between Purdey and the landlord surrounding the installation of a secure room for the guns, the agreement ultimately collapsed, and their presence in the United States was short-lived. On

The entrance to Holland & Holland's London Bruton Street shop.

the other hand, Holland & Holland has dwelt in New York for the better part of a decade. In 2004, they closed their gun room on 57th and Madison Avenue, one that shared space with several floors of very expensive clothing, and moved to a gun room–exclusive premises at 10 East 40th Street, Suite 1910, where they have a large inventory of new and used shotguns. It is here that those visiting New York, or who have a specific question or need, can go. Their inventory of shotguns runs from relatively inexpensive used boxlocks to pairs of London bests that can be ordered as bespoke shotguns.

Holland & Holland's factory on Harrow Road was built for gunmaking and constructed during the era of gaslights. The workbenches are arranged so that each workman's bench is illuminated by natural light. At the time the Harrow Road factory was built, actions and barrels were made by outworkers in Birmingham, then finished and assembled at Harrow Road. In that age, the work was done completely by hand. Today, much of the rough work is done by computer numeric control (CNC) machines and by electric spark erosion machines. Although Purdey still hand-files their actions, Holland & Holland uses these work-saving methods, stating that it matters little how the extra metal is removed; rather it is the finishing that matters, and this is still by hand. These modern methods result in production-cost savings that are partially passed on to the customer, hence a Holland & Holland shotgun is priced slightly less than a Purdey.

CHARLES BOSWELL

Charles Boswell (1850–1924) apprenticed to Thomas Gooch at age fourteen. His apprenticeship finished, he became a sight-filer at the Royal Small Arms Factory at Enfield Lock. He began his own business in 1872, later establishing himself in fashionable London at 126 Strand. What is interesting is not the rather ordinary story of the Charles Boswell firm, but its most recent development.

The London gun trade—and the Birmingham trade too, for that matter—suffered greatly as a result of the Great Depression and

Holland & Holland still hand-fits their shotguns to the thickness of smoke.

World War II. (World War I didn't do the trade any good, but it rebounded during the Roaring Twenties.) During the Second World War, many gunmakers' shops were bombed out during the German blitz. By the end of the war, Britain's economy was in a shambles, and a period of heavy taxation followed. The heaviest burden fell on the landed gentry, who supported much of the gun trade. As portions of estates were sold to pay taxes, and heirs were forced to sell estates to pay the exorbitant inheritance taxes, shooting began to fade. Through the 1950s, '60s, and '70s, the British gun trade contracted and contracted, until once-famous names became parts of consolidated companies. Churchill, Atkin, Grant, & Lang was one of those, and even in such a consortium could not survive.

With the prosperity of the 1980s and '90s, fine-gun aficionados began to believe that a market for fine shotguns existed in sufficient force to make the revival of some of the best-known names feasible. Sir Edward Dashwood, Bart., is one. He bought the rights to the E. J. Churchill name, and now operates a manufactory in the English countryside.

More recently, well-known shooting instructor Chris Batha purchased the rights to the Charles Boswell name, and has begun making exquisite over-and-unders under that name. How Batha operates is indicative of this new era of London Best shotguns.

Batha purchases top-of-the-line barreled actions in Italy, then the finishing is done in Britain, including proofing at the London Proof House. The engraving and hardening

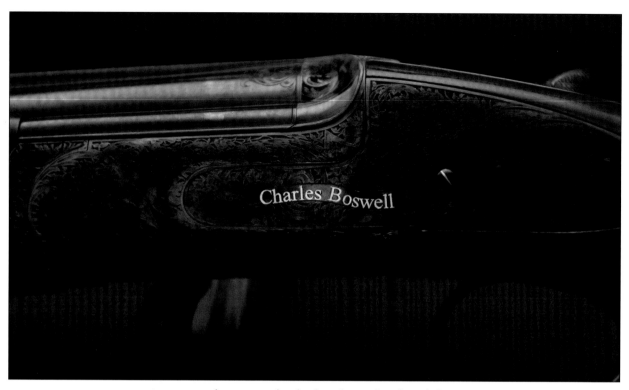

An exquisitely engraved, inlaid and case-hardened shotgun.

are done by British masters, and the resulting shotguns are of the highest quality and in the true restrained British style. The finished guns are breathtaking. I saw No. 1 at the Vintage Cup in September 2004, and Batha's work was beautiful to behold.

Although Purdey and Holland & Holland continue to produce their shotguns in the factories their ancestors built, many of today's "Best" guns are produced in the grand British style of using outworkers, each adding his or her expertise to the final product. Provided the basic materials are of the first order, the results meet expectations.

Today, one can expect to pay $100 to $250,000 or more depending on wood choice and engraving for a Purdey, a trifle less for a Holland & Holland—about $60,000 for their Sporting over-and-under and a shade under

$100,000 for a Royal side-by-side—while a Churchill or Charles Boswell will run about $40,000. Granted, Purdey and Holland & Holland guns retain a higher used price than those from the lesser-known makers, but the newly revived names are beautiful examples of gunmaking, so perhaps it's not all in the name.

BOSS & COMPANY

Although Boss made exquisite side-by-sides, their over-and-under is reason enough to mention them in regard to high-grade shotguns. Introduced in 1909, the over-and-under's design was so exquisite that it is embodied in the designs of many contemporary over-and-unders. Its design essentially shared the market with the 1932 Browning Superposed design and the variations of each.

It was Robert Churchill who set down in writing his formula for proper shotgun marksmanship, although he wasn't alone as is attested to by these and other books.

The brainchild of Boss actioner Bob Henderson, the design is the first to hinge the barrel on opposing trunnions that fit into matching cuts in each side of the barrels, just forward of the chambers. The cuts are not in the barrels but in the metal surrounding them. The barrels are locked to the action by means of bolts that project from the face of the breech and engage bites on either side of the lower barrel. Slim and sleek, the action is barely higher than the stacked barrels themselves. This arrangement allows the barrels to lie in the shooter's hand very much like those of a side-by-side, and provides for the recoil to be directed into the shooter's shoulder and away from the face. Furthermore, the hands lie on the same plane, which enhances the pointing aspects that good shotgun marksmanship relies upon.

E. J. CHURCHILL

Although Edwin John Churchill founded E. J. Churchill in 1891, it was his nephew Robert Churchill, who wasn't a gunmaker but was a good businessman, who promoted the Churchill name. Churchill shotguns are beautiful specimens of the finest of the London gunmakers, and Robert Churchill saw to it that his products maintained that provenance. E. J. Churchill produced both sidelock and boxlock guns in several grades, but even the utility-grade guns were top-notch. What Robert Churchill contributed was both controversy and a system of shooting that bears his name.

Robert Churchill was a squat man, rather resembling a bowling ball with legs. He preferred shotguns with short barrels, and developed one with 25-inch barrels—named the XXV—that carried a very high tapering rib that was so narrow at the muzzle that it resembled a knife blade. Churchill's theory was that, when shouldered, the high, tapered rib would appear to be much longer. Great controversy ensued from the other, more traditional, gunmakers and raged in the sporting papers of the late teens and early 1920s. By the mid-1920s, Churchill's XXV shotguns were in great demand. Whether or not his XXV shotguns are the right guns for someone or anyone is a personal matter, but the fact is that they sold like hotcakes, and generated good income and cash flow for E. J. Churchill.

Churchill's system of shooting is less controversial. Throughout the Golden Age of shotgunning, from roughly 1880 to 1939, all gunmakers maintained shooting grounds where their customers could practice, be fitted for a new shotgun, and, most important, receive instruction. Victorian society was deeply rooted in correctness, and hence it was correct for gentlemen and ladies who wished to shoot to receive instruction. Furthermore, one would scarcely think of starting the new shooting season without a refresher course to sharpen skills before the first shooting party of the year.

Victorian shooting parties were very much a part of the fabric of the nobility and upper reaches of British society. Americans also shot, but in canvas coats behind dogs, or in blinds with guides. The English gentry made a performance of shooting, with great emphasis on rules, etiquette, and good marksmanship. Dukes, earls, princes, and others who hosted shoots were known to stop the shoot if their guests didn't perform up to their expectations. Any breaches of etiquette often brought a strong rebuke from the host, with the violator often sent packing, and, in the words of Robert Churchill, his copybook forever blotted in the eyes of high society.

It was in this rarefied atmosphere that shooting schools prospered. All had their methods of instruction, but Churchill's system seemed the best articulated. Certainly Churchill

Historically, fine gunmakers had their own shooting grounds. Holland & Holland still maintains theirs northwest of London. Here the author's wife, Peggy, takes a lesson in the grouse butt with H&H instructor Roland Wild.

wasn't the first to publish a book on how to shoot. Charles Lancaster first published *The Art of Shooting* in 1889, and Colonel Peter Hawker preceded that with his *Advice to Young Shooters* in 1859, but it was Robert Churchill who put it all together for the reader. The system was based on a smooth, consolidated move of the shotgun, from a level starting position to the shoulder, as the muzzles constantly tracked the target. As the gun hit the shoulder, the muzzles would be timed to be sweeping through the bird and the shot fired. Churchill maintained that no lead was necessary, but rather that the shooter fire right at the bird, and the momentum of the swing would provide the necessary lead. Most contemporary instructors discount this simplistic approach and acknowledge that some lead or daylight is necessary, but for better or for worse, Churchill marketed his XXV shotgun and shooting system. Both survive to this day. Of the two, the Churchill system of shooting is the most famous. That Holland & Holland still teaches this system of shooting with little modification at their prestigious shooting grounds just outside London bears testimony to its solid style and equally solid results.

One could go on for hundreds and hundreds of pages outlining maker after maker of London Best shotguns. The bibliography provides numerous sources to broaden anyone's knowledge about these guns, and I direct you there.

BIRMINGHAM

There is little doubt that when comparing two shotguns of equal condition, one from a London maker bearing London Proof House marks and the other bearing Birmingham proof marks, the London gun would command the higher price. However, and it may be heresy to say so, the quality of one to the other may be undetectable. London was known for making a few guns a year by hand, while Birmingham names turned out many guns. They did this by using greater numbers of outworkers, who could each do their bit to several pieces a day. The guns were then put together into larger subassemblies, with everything finished either in the factory or by still other outworkers. Many

of these Birmingham guns found their way onto the racks of big-name London gunmakers as lower-priced guns, yet still bearing the names of the London firms. The name on the rib does not always tell the story, and only an examination of the proof marks can tell the tale, and often then only part of the gun's history. The bottom line is that while London guns are the prima donnas of the gun world, their less illustrious Birmingham cousins are often of equal quality.

Among the most famous of the Birmingham gunmakers are W. W. Greener, W & C Scott, and Westley Richards. Greener is now located in Hagley, England, and Westley Richards remains in Birmingham, although they have opened a U.S. agency in Bozeman, Montana. W&C Scott was bought by Holland & Holland in 1956, and production dwindled until the division finally shut down in September 1991. At one time, Holland & Holland made a series of boxlock guns, the Chatsworth, Bowood, and Kinmount, in the Scott factory. Those were among the last shotguns produced by Scott.

I equate guns from Greener, Scott, and Westley Richards to top-of-the line American shotguns. High-grade though they might be through engraving and highly figured wood, these are rugged, solid, workaday shotguns that seldom fail. The Greeners are quirky, in that many are fitted with the Greener side safety. Instead of the safety catch being conveniently located on the top tang, it's on the side of the action, projecting from the stock immediately behind the action. Greener's side safety is awkward to use until you get used to it.

« During the Golden Age of shotgun making, many variations existed such as this Greener Side Safety.

One constant problem of identification is that of Westley Richards. Numerous cheap shotguns were manufactured in Belgium during this era using variations on the Richards name, most especially W. Richards. Only shotguns bearing the name Westley Richards and the correct proof marks are genuine, as the real McCoy always has "Westley" spelled out.

British guns can occupy entire volumes, and we've not even touched on shotguns from Scotland. John Dickson in particular made rounded-action guns that are things of beauty, and are copied by several contemporary makers. Irish shotguns can also be great treasures, if you are able to locate any.

TODAY'S BRITISH GUN TRADE

Some years ago, I was engaged in conversation with a gentleman whose passion was British guns. Becoming ever redder in the face, he proclaimed the gathering scandal of well-known British gunmakers buying Spanish actions around which to build their guns. For better or worse, many of the guns currently produced in Britain indeed use actions, and often barrels, from Spain and Italy. It's not a major crime. In fact, many of the guns currently produced in Spain and Italy are of top quality. They lack the provenance of a London name, but are certainly wonderful shotguns. One only has to look at Chris Batha's spectacular Charles Boswell over-and-under to understand that a London gun made on an Italian barreled action isn't to be disregarded.

Although there are traditional gunmakers operating in and around London, the truth is that many guns are built on actions coming from elsewhere, but the fit and finish are in the hands of the maker whose name is engraved on the barrels and action, and that is in the greatest tradition of the British gun trade.

CHAPTER 6

On the Continent— Belgium, France, Germany, and Austria

Among the most difficult questions to answer are who made shotguns that originated in these four countries, and where they were made. Belgium is easiest, since many shotguns were made in or around the Brussels suburb of Liège, the most significant being those from the giant Fabrique Nationale plant. France had few gunmakers, but Germany and Austria had many. Those are the bright spots. The two highly destructive wars fought back and forth across most of this territory obliterated many records, and sometimes entire businesses. Certainly, the London gun trade suffered during the blitz of World War II, but as the Allies waged both a ground and air war against the Nazis, little was spared, and many small gunmakers and their shops disappeared without a trace—some to the Nazi tyranny, others to the U.S. Eighth Air Force. These factors make identifying and tracing shotguns from Germany, and sometimes from Austria, difficult if not impossible. That said, there are numerous great guns from these countries.

BELGIUM

The Belgian city of Liège is strategically located at the junction of the River Meuse and River Ourth. The land holds great deposits of coal and iron ore. It is not difficult to imagine how this municipality, situated on major trade routes, became a major manufacturing center. Somewhat geographically isolated and equally somewhat independent from the heavy hand of national government, Liège became a major supplier of arms to the warring nations of Europe. Since those early years, Liège has continued to be home to many of the great sporting arms manufacturing companies of Europe and the world, their guns rivaling those from the great houses of Britain, Italy, Germany, and the United States. Some of the world's greatest shotguns have come from Belgium— so, too, have many substandard shotguns.

From 1880 through about 1910, thousands of double shotguns were manufactured in Belgium, specifically for export to the United States. Sold through hardware wholesalers and retailers, gun shops, sporting goods stores, and mail-order houses, these shotguns were inexpensively made using twist, laminated-steel, and Damascus barrels. Made to a price, always extremely low, but often bearing a fancy-sounding name, these shotguns exist wherever shotguns are found. As a contributing editor of the National Rifle Association publications *American Rifleman, American Hunter,* and *Shooting Illustrated,* I answer members' letters regarding shotguns. Invariably, 70 percent of these letters involve questions regarding one of these types of shotguns. Roughly half those letters inquire about shotguns made in the United States by Crescent or Crescent-Davis, while the other half inquire about cheap Belgian guns from this era. During that time period, these shotguns were perfectly safe with blackpowder-loaded ammunition, and were affordable to a less-than-wealthy population. In today's market, they're simply wall hangers, and worthless from any other aspect. As we'll see later, it is possible to shoot many shotguns of this era, mostly with modifications, but the cheap, Belgian-made doubles of this period are worthless, since many really good shotguns are available for modifying into shooters.

Although Belgium was the birthplace of many marginal shotguns at the turn of the 20th century, many fine guns have come from there, and continue to. Among the current Belgian manufacturers, most of whose lineage goes back into history, are Fabrique Nationale, Auguste Francotte, and Lebeau-Courally & Cie.

Fabrique Nationale

Fabrique Nationale, located in Herstal, a suburb of Liège, is best known as the manufacturer of all Browning shotguns before a shift in manufacturing of many of the production guns to Miroku in Japan in 1976. Today, many custom models, including updated versions of the Superposed, are still produced in the custom shop in Herstal. Over the years, Browning-designed shotguns were sold in the United States under the Browning name and under the name F. N. or Fabrique Nationale elsewhere throughout the world. The proof marks are the key, and those Browning guns that bear Belgium marks are from the Fabrique Nationale manufacturing complex; otherwise they bear the marks of the Japanese plant.

Auguste Francotte

Auguste Francotte was founded in 1805 in Liège. Initially producing military weapons, Francotte soon felt the competition from Fabrique Nationale and realized he needed to change course. The result was best-quality sporting arms. The firm's shotguns and rifles were so good that Auguste Francotte owned a retail store in London's fashionable West End near other fine gunmakers, including Holland & Holland, Purdey, and Boss & Co., from 1877 through 1893. Throughout the 19th and 20th centuries, Francotte produced fine guns, many of which were sold through such prestigious U. S. firms as Abercrombie & Fitch, Von

Lengerke & Detmold, and Von Lengerke & Antoine. From lesser-priced boxlocks through top-quality sidelocks and Boss-style over-and-unders, Auguste Francotte shotguns were produced in much larger numbers than those of their British competitors, yet one seldom hears of a Francotte failing, and for the most part gunsmiths see them only for refinishing or restocking, and only rarely for mechanical repairs.

Lebeau-Courally & Cie

Lebeau-Courally was founded in 1865 by Auguste Lebeau. A skilled master gunsmith, Lebeau built the normal run of sporting guns, including shotguns and drillings. In 1876, he won the first prize at the Philadelphia Centennial Exposition. Lebeau also won Le Diplôme d'Honneur et La Medaille d'Or at the 1878 Paris Exposition, and in 1897 La Grande Médaille d'Argent de Saint Petersbourg. So it is obvious that Auguste Lebeau knew how to make a best-quality gun. In fact, Lebeau's guns were in high demand at the court of the Russian czar.

In 1896, Lebeau was joined by Ferdinand Courally, himself a master gunmaker, and the firm became Lebeau-Courally, the name it bears today. The firm prospered, winning gold medals at expositions and being designated as gunmakers to the royal courts of Spain, Italy, and Russia. When Lebeau died later that same year, Courally became the sole owner.

In 1902, Courally signed an agreement with the British firm Webley and Scott to produce large-bore revolvers for the British army. This agreement was not only financially sound for Lebeau-Courally, but part of it gave them a place in Webley and Scott's London showroom, and guns sold there bore the name Webley-Scott-Courally. When Courally retired in 1919, Philippe Reeve became the head of Lebeau-Courally, a position he held until 1956, and although the firm continued to produce firearms, the numbers of workmen and guns produced dwindled. Upon Reeve's death, the company was bought by Joseph Verrees, who was an excellent businessman, and whose vision and ethic returned the company to respectable production. Upon Verrees's death, the company passed to his niece, Anne-Marie Moermans, who still runs the company.

Lebeau-Courally builds excellent, top-quality guns, mostly sidelock side-by-sides and Boss-style over-and-unders.

FRANCE

Although not commonly thought of as a shooting society, the French are, indeed, avid shooters and hunters. Their gunmaking tradition is not especially strong, especially since the gunmaking kingdom of Liège in the Walloon region of Belgium and the city of Suhl in Germany are so close. Certainly, the French maintain the proof house at St.-Étienne, and shotguns are encountered with those proof marks, but in general France does not have a strong gunmaking culture, preferring to import, although there are a couple of notable exceptions.

When muzzleloading was the norm, a Frenchman named Casimir Lefaucheux was instrumental in the development of the breech-loading shotgun. One of the first modern loading systems was the pinfire, a self-contained cartridge whose primer was a thin straw that projected from the shell's rim. The pin fit into a corresponding notch in the barrels, and the hammer struck the pin, firing the gun. Carrying these cartridges was problematic, since a hard knock on one of the pins could fire a cartridge carried in a pocket. Though Lefaucheux did not invent the pinfire, he certainly made shotguns that used this technology, and thereby gave the breechloading shotgun a great push forward.

Darne-Bruchet

Of the French shotguns, those made by Granger and Vouzelaud are wonderful guns based on their British cousins' designs. But if France is known for any one shotgun, it is the Darne.

Established in 1881 by the brothers Regis and Pierre Darne, the Darne Company experimented with several new breechloading shotgun designs, and finally settled on one that is both unique and excellent. The Darne has especially sleek lines that are broken only by an unobtrusive pair of flattened ears, about where the conventional top lever is located on more traditional shotguns. To open the breech, one need only grasp these ears and pull them up and rearward, sliding the breech back; push

An elaborately French-made Darne that uses a unique sliding breech. Lavishly inlaid with gold and cased with gold-plated accessories, this is a true fine shotgun.

them forward, and the breech closes. When the ears are pulled back, the breech extracts both the fired and unfired shells. A slight tip of the gun to the right or left allows the fired hulls to drop off, and with equal ease, unfired shells can be dropped into an open hand.

I've seen a couple of Darnes at gun shows, and nearly bought one that had a loose buttstock (I didn't because it was cracked). At any rate, it was repairable, but the owner wanted too much and refused a fair—at least I thought it was fair—offer, and I moved on. As with any quality shotguns, Darnes could be had with best-grade wood and all the engraving a customer could want.

In 1980 Darne closed, and Paul Bruchet, their production manager, bought the company and moved it in 1984 to 25 Rue des Armuriers in St.-Étienne. With this move came several of the Darne workers, as well as Bruchet's son. Early production was under the Bruchet name, but eventually Paul Bruchet bought the Darne name, and today the guns are manufactured, one at a time to order, under the original name.

GERMANY AND AUSTRIA

If any word defines German gunmaking, it is solid. Germans have for centuries been known as excellent engineers, and this trait certainly carries through their gunmaking. "Overengineered" is an equally apt description, since German guns often have several locking bolts and others features that make them lasting testaments both in theory and fact. Names such as Merkel, Sauer, Heym,

Krieghoff, Hartmann & Weiss, and Johann Fanzoj may be familiar or strange. Certainly Krieghoff is recognizable to the clay-target crowd, as their over-and-unders are common on clay fields. Merkel currently has a vigorous U.S. presence first through Gun South (GSI) and also now by its part owner, Heckler & Koch. Heym and Sauer are well known because many of their guns were liberated by GIs fighting in Europe during World War II. Many of these shotguns are now being discovered by sons, daughters, nieces, and nephews, as these wonderful veterans pass away.

Older German shotguns typically come in 16-gauge, although there are many 12s as well. Still, the 16-gauge was and is highly popular in Europe, and hence it seems the majority of these shotguns were built in that gauge. In addition, most are choked extra-full. In terms of wood and engraving, German guns are aesthetically heavier in execution of both wood and engraving, and can often be identified at 100 yards. Buttstocks were traditionally made with cheekpieces and often accompanied by elaborate, deep carving, like a shootable Black Forest cuckoo clock. In addition, German-style engraving is normally deeply carved, all making for a unique and readily identifiable shotgun.

Merkel

In today's gun world, Merkel has, perhaps, the most complete catalog of fine shotguns. They don't make repeaters, but their side-by-sides, over-and-unders, and combination guns are of the highest quality. Furthermore, they're readily available in this country.

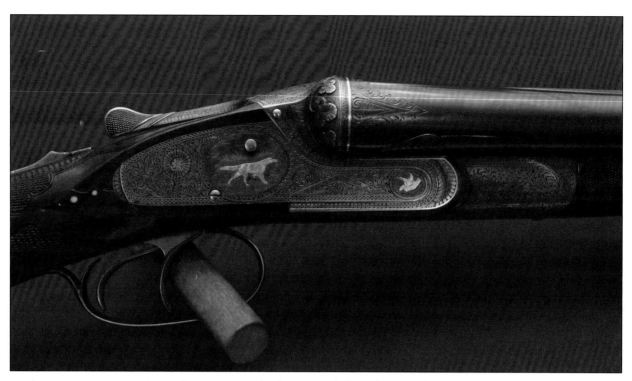

A typical German-made shotgun with heavily carved engraving.

Founded in Suhl, Germany, in 1898, Merkel, manufactured by Suhler Jagd-und Sportwaffen GmbH, suffered through both world wars and Soviet occupation. During the time Merkel was in the communist bloc, their firearms were subject to a 65 percent non-favored-nation tax, and imports were but a trickle. With the reunification of Germany, Merkel shotguns have become much more plentiful in this country.

Prior to World War II, Merkel shotguns were winners of many international prizes, and the guns made for those exhibitions are rare and valuable. Many a returning World War II GI brought home a Merkel as a souvenir. I shot with a retired Air Force colonel who had a liberated Merkel over-and-under, and he enjoyed shooting it immensely.

There have been few design changes, and much of the manufacture is now done by high-tech machinery, but high-grade Merkels are still handmade.

Krieghoff International

It is likely that on any clay range at any time there will be a Krieghoff K-32 or K-80 over-and-under. The firm was founded in 1886 as Sempert & Krieghoff. Sempert became interested in electricity, and left Germany for America to work for Thomas Alva Edison, leaving the sporting arms business to Ludwig Krieghoff. Ludwig and his son Heinrich continued to make sporting arms until the outbreak of World War I. Drafted, young Heinrich eventually gained a discharge in 1916, with orders to return to Suhl and help in the production of military weapons for the war. Between the world wars, Krieghoff continued making sporting arms until the Nazi takeover of Germany, at which time they were directed to make military arms. At the height of World War II, Krieghoff employed more than 6,000 workmen. When Germany collapsed in 1945, Suhl fell into the Soviet zone, and the Krieghoff family fled to West Germany, eventually setting up shop in Ulm.

At the end of the Second World War, Remington decided to revamp its shotgun line, and probably the first casualty was the Model 32 over-and-under. The only American competition for the Browning Superposed, the

A rack of German-made Kreighoff shotguns.

32, launched during the Great Depression, sold fairly well to clay-target shooters, but in total only about 6,000 were manufactured. In the mid-1950s, a group of American shooters purchased the rights to the Remington 32 design, and approached Krieghoff as a potential manufacturer. The 32 had several attractive attributes: The sliding top-locking breech was very strong, and because this shotgun also used the low-mounted trunnions of the Boss-style over-and-under, the design lent itself to being adapted to the interchangeable barrels so necessary to skeet shooters. (Multigauge inserts or tube sets were years in the future.) The mechanical trigger was also a plus, negating the need to alter it to function with very light shells, especially the 2½-inch .410. In 1957, the Krieghoff 32 became a reality, and met with a ready market in the United States. Since that time, the K-32 has been cosmetically and slightly mechanically altered to better adapt to American clay-target shooters' wishes, but essentially remains the basic 32, be it German or American.

In addition to these familiar clay-target guns, Krieghoff now produces breathtaking side-by-sides and over-and-unders for the field. At the 2004 Vintagers Shoot at the Orvis Sandanona grounds near Millbrook, New York, Krieghoff entered their new side-by-side game gun with case-hardened sidelocks in the juried concours. The gun was breathtaking.

As with any fine gun from a fine maker, the list of possible embellishments is endless, and bounded only by the imagination of the individual who orders it. Krieghoff, like so many German gunmakers, suffered from the two wars and very nearly ceased production, yet their perseverance has paid off.

Blaser

Originally known for their straight-pull bolt-action rifles, Blaser began making shotguns in 2004 in their modern factory in Isny im Allgäu, Bavaria. Designed to have a low-profile action, the lock-up is with a Purdey-style underbolt, and the ejectors are actuated by the action, not ejector hammers located in the forend. The striker arrangement is adapted directly from rifles, providing a very fast lock time. Because of their computer-driven machining techniques, barrels are interchangeable without fitting. Blaser USA, now in San Antonio, Texas, has been very attentive to the preferences of American shooters, and have consequently added state-of-the-art trap guns to their line of sporters and field guns. Because of their innovative design, Blaser shotguns are taking hold worldwide.

Johann Fanzoj and Peter Hofer

Historically, the area surrounding Ferlach in Austria was a leading arms producer. At one time a major military arms producer for the royal houses of Austria and the Austro-Hungarian Empire, Ferlach was world-renowned for fine sporting arms. Today, sadly, the trade is represented by a mere handful of gunmakers. Of these, Johann Fanzoj and Peter Hofer are among the finest, turning out twenty or thirty shotguns a year, all on special order. However, gunmaking thrives in the Ferlach area through its gunmaking school and apprentice programs. Ferlach-trained gunsmiths and gunmakers are at the top of the trade, and many have immigrated to this country and are employed by individuals such as Anthony Galazan or have started businesses of their own.

CHAPTER 7

Spain—Olé

Located in the Basque region of northern Spain, the seat of endless political turmoil, the Spanish gun trade is a vibrant industry that turns out quality guns at relatively modest prices. Popularized in the 1930s by Ernest Hemingway's *The Sun Also Rises*—set partly in Spain—the Basque region has always been a region of craftsmen. Its gun industry was mostly overlooked until the 1990s, when Americans awakened to the fact that quality shotguns were made there. Prior to that time, many low-grade shotguns had been imported from Spain. Made of inferior materials—Spain under the Franco regime was a Fascist nation and suffered for years under an embargo—many of these guns were 20th-century versions of the dross imported from Belgium from 1880 to 1910. Despite this, there were still a few good ones.

For a dozen years until his death on his sixtieth birthday on June 16, 1989, I hunted and fished with Charles Henry Mohr. Charlie was a foreign correspondent for United Press International, *Time*, and *The New York Times*. He reported actively from Vietnam, where he was awarded, as a civilian, a Bronze Star for valor by the U.S. Marine Corps for rescuing a wounded Marine under fire during the Battle of Hue. Later he was *The New York Times* bureau chief in Nairobi, Kenya, just prior to the cessation of hunting in that country. It was during this time that Charlie passed through Madrid on his way to the United States with his family for home leave. While in Madrid, he went to Diana, the top sporting shop in Madrid, and ordered a Pedro Arrizabalaga, considered then and now to be the "Purdey of Spain."

A naive young writer who grew up in Illinois, I had had little contact with double guns—Model 12s and Browning Auto-5s were the order of the day in my neck of the woods—so I knew little about them. Coming in from an Eastern Shore hunt, Charlie showed me his Arrizabalaga in the Mohrs' kitchen. Charlie was thinner than me, but we were both of the same height and arm length, yet when I mounted his Arrizabalaga, I thought it too long and the stock too high, and wondered how I'd ever shoot it. He then told me of being fitted for this gun, and how it took almost a year for it to be made and then arrive in Nairobi. I'm sure his widow would have given it to me when Charlie passed away, but with tears streaming down my face when I picked it up, I couldn't consider that, and it was sold for a good price, one I couldn't afford, through a fine gun room.

Later, I was invited to Spain in 1985 to see the Spanish gun industry's latest idea, DIARM, short for Desarrollo de Industrias Armeras, S.A. Supposedly the answer to the languishing Spanish gun trade, DIARM was a consortium formed of twenty, mostly small, family-owned gunmakers, who would all use a new factory filled with CNC machines, and would retain only Aguirre y Aranzabal, better known simply as AyA, as their flagship. They should have known better. In an area where tempers flare red hot, the consortium lasted only about a year and a half. The good part was that I was able to buy two AyAs at an unbelievable price from their gun vault—the bad part was that DIARM almost destroyed the Spanish Basque gunmaking tradition.

AyA survived solely because of the personality and drive of the late Imanol Aranzabal,

Called the "Purdey of Spain," this handmade Pedro Arrizabalaga is considered the top shotgun produced in Spain; fit and finish are superb.

The original Aguirrey Aranzabal (AyA) plant in Eibar, Spain. Until the end of World War II, most shotgun manufacturing plants were small, but AyA became a worldwide shotgun provider, and used this large factory until its amalgamation into the Spanish government's experimental DIARM that dissolved within three years of its founding in 1985.

nephew of the founder of AyA, and it was the only one to survive. Fortunately, Arrieta, Arrizabalaga, Grulla, and Ugartechea had chosen not to participate in the DIARM experiment, and remain, along with AyA, the backbone of today's Spanish gunmaking industry.

It is said that imitation is the sincerest form of flattery. So it is that the Spanish gun trade essentially makes excellent copies of established British shotguns, mostly Holland & Holland–style sidelocks and Anson & Deeley–style boxlocks. The fact that upward of 80 percent of Spanish-made guns go to the British gun market speaks volumes, and when the British gun trade severely lacked workers in the 1960s, it was to Spain that their headhunters turned.

As with a bespoke British gun, one can order a Spanish gun with any kind of engraving and grade of wood he or she wishes. For the most part, off-the-rack guns come with excellent engraving, often in the style of their British counterparts.

At one time, Spanish guns suffered from the notion, put forward by a few gun writers, that they were made of "soft" steel, and would not last. Certainly, single triggers remained a mystery for generations of gunmakers east of Cape Cod, but to condemn an entire industry based on poor single triggers and parts breakage is wrong. My colleague Michael McIntosh has a No. 2 AyA 12-gauge, made to his dimensions, that he says has digested 70,000 shots with only a broken striker. My No. 2 AyA 28-gauge has been shot a lot, with only the top lever spring being replaced; and my 53E AyA has also been shot a great deal, with only a single broken mainspring. Because most Spanish guns have hand-detachable sidelocks, replacing a mainspring—provided you have one—takes only a few minutes.

My dentist, Myles Digennaro, is a double-gun aficionado, and recently ordered two pairs

Six hand-made high-grade AyA shotguns, made in 1985 for a Madrid banker for use by his guests and himself for shooting driven red-legged partridge at his estancia.

of guns, one from Arrieta and the other from Grulla. Both are beautiful guns with excellent wood-to-metal fit. The finish on the metal is top-notch, and the overall finish and fit as good as anyone could expect or, for that matter, want. Digennaro took advantage of a trip to Spain to visit the factory and order his guns in person. English is now so universal that one can count on at least someone at any of the Spanish gunmakers being fluent in both language and gun talk. However, if you're contemplating ordering a Spanish shotgun, it's best to go through one of their agents in this country. Spain uses the metric system (as does Italy), and converting millimeters to inches and so on must be done carefully. Such agents are also familiar with the various models and extras, and can better guide the customer to the best gun for the money.

British-trained gunsmith Jack Rowe with an AyA 28-gauge.

CHAPTER 8

O Italia

When you talk glorious Italian guns, look no farther than the Val Trompia, which the Mella River has carved on its way out of the Italian Alps. As the world has turned, gunmaking has evolved, and while great centers such as Ferlach, Suhl, London, Birmingham, Eibar, and the American Northeast have contracted to bare representations of their former greatness, Italy has prospered. For example, one cannot believe the extent of the giant Beretta Due plant in Gardone Val Trompia.

Brescia is a dichotic town, combining the Old World with its narrow winding streets with broad multilane highways and the presence of industry everywhere. It's the north of Italy, and specifically Brescia, that drives a good part of the Italian economy. Brescia is a factory town, and it is there that Perazzi, Bosis, Fabbri, and Marrochi are located. Head north, up the Val Trompia, and you'll find Abbiatico & Salvinelli, Beretta, Rizzini, Ferlib, Siace, Caesar Guerini, and several other small gunmakers.

Italian gunmaking probably began here because, like other centers such as Ferlach, there was water power and natural resources. Brescia became Italy's gunmaking center as the country found itself embroiled in wars against invaders from the north. From the 1500s through both world wars, military orders were good for business. After World War II, however, much of Europe lay in ruins, with many gunmaking businesses destroyed. Fortunately the Italian industry survived, and now flourishes.

What set Italy apart was the ability to quickly grasp modern technology at the end of World War II. Certainly, handwork is omnipresent, and some guns are handmade, but while the British gun trade eventually learned that a CNC machine can remove the excess material from a forging in minutes, but by hand in hours, the Italians embraced it immediately.

Italy also possessed some of the world's greatest engravers. One is hard-pressed to take anything from the Ken Hunts and others of engraving that is nearly photographic—is done. It's whatever the customer wants.

Italy also lies close enough to Turkey to take advantage of the beautiful walnut grown there. While standard Italian walnut is unmistakable with its honey to dark brown color with only a hint of longitudinal dark streaks, high-grade Turkish walnut is breathtaking. Often more understated than American black walnut, European walnut has a beauty all its own.

Casa Beretta, the centerpiece of the enormous Beretta Due factory in Gardone Val Trompia, Italy. When work slackened in the 1930s, the Beretta family kept their factory workers employed building this beautiful mansion until firearm orders increased.

Using a hammer and very sharp chisel, Beretta's master engraver Giulio Timpini executes an engraving in the Beretta engraving studio at the Beretta Uno facility in Gardone Val Trompia, Italy.

this world, but it seems that Italy has a corner on them. In the Beretta Uno plant, just off the main drag of Gardone, where the high-grade guns are produced, is that company's engraving salon, where seasoned artists sit next to apprentices, teaching them the art. Beretta officials state that they don't care if their graduates stay with Beretta, so long as they continue the art. Along the benches, every kind of engraving, from tight British scroll to Germanic deep relief to bulino—that wonderful "banknote" style of

View of but a fraction of the stock blanks being dried at Beretta's Meccanica del Sarca facility. Here all of the walnut used by Beretta is dried and stocks for lower-priced shotguns are machine made.

to U.S. troops, and used by many police agencies, benefit all of Beretta's divisions, including sporting arms.

Beretta has built its family of sporting shotguns on tried-and-true, basic actions. One system forms the basis of their gas-operated semiauto shotguns, while another action is used for all of Beretta's boxlock over-and-unders. Over the years, Beretta has refined its gas-operated, semiautomatic system to the point that these shotguns are a leading force in competitive shooting and in the field.

The 686 over-and-under action forms the basis for all Berettas. A solid action that provides for user-replaceable trunnions and recoil lugs, it uses the Boss-style action with

A Beretta workman installing ejectors in the Beretta Due factory in Gardone Val Trompia, Italy.

BERETTA

The oldest family-owned manufacturing business in the world, Beretta is only a few years short of being 500 years old. Today, this firearms manufacturing giant produces everything from submachine guns to exquisite shotguns. The company's lucrative military contracts, including the M-9 semiautomatic pistol issued

≫ A Beretta sidelock over-and-under with magnificent engraving and gold inlays that is stocked with the highest-grade wood; a glorious modern shotgun.

« Cavaleri Ugo Gussalli Beretta (l.), patriarch of the nearly 500-year-old firearms manufacturer—the world's oldest family-owned manufacturing company—discussing one of their spectacular high-grade shotguns.

Touching up the checkering at Beretta's wood facility Meccanica del Sarca.

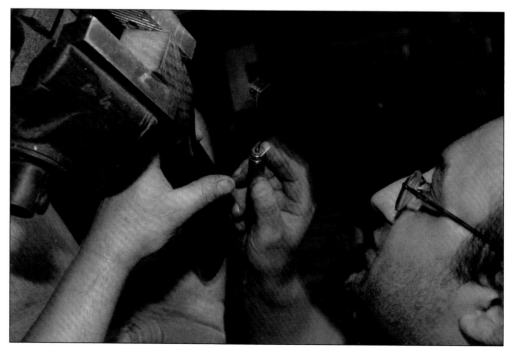

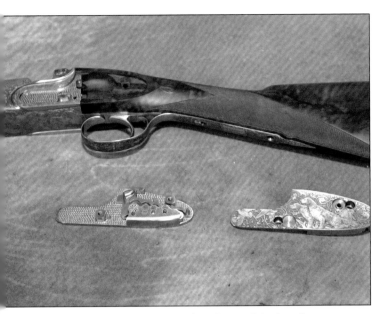

The stocked action and pinless sidelocks of Beretta's elegant SO-10.

trunnion-hung barrels and two locking bolts that project from the breech face. The barrels close with exterior projecting recoil lugs at the very end of the chambers that fit into matching cuts in the action. Should the gun become loose from extreme use, the trunnions and exterior recoil lugs can be removed and replaced with nothing more than a screwdriver.

Beretta makes wonderful sidelock over-and-unders with both Holland & Holland–style sidelocks that use folded or V springs, or an even more advanced Beretta sidelock using coil springs. Their latest top-of-the-line over-and-under, the SO-10, was released in late 2005 and retails for $90,000. Side-by-sides are also in the Beretta line, from their workaday 471 through exquisite, high-grade sidelock guns, produced mainly for the European market, but available in the United States on special order. Their newest side-by-side, the Imperial Monte Carlo, was released in early 2010, and retails for $130,000.

PERAZZI

Located in Brescia, Perazzi is the result of a far-thinking gunmaker and an Olympic champion. Daniele Perazzi was a Val Trompia–trained gunmaker who began business in partnership with Ivo Fabbri, with whom we'll visit in a minute. Perazzi saw the advantages of the Boss-style action, and it became the basis for his and Fabbri's guns. Enter Ennio Mattarelli, Italy's top Olympic (bunker) trap shot, who was seeking a gun for the 1964 Tokyo Olympics. Mattarelli had a number of ideas of what he wanted in a gun for this exacting discipline, and with Perazzi built a shotgun with which he won the Gold Medal. With Mattarelli as his partner, Daniele Perazzi began making specialized shotguns for target shooters. By the 1970s, clay-target shooters were looking for specialized guns to get them those extra birds, and Perazzi was on its way. High ribs, low ribs, wide and narrow, and screw-in chokes are all available from Perazzi, but perhaps one of their greatest features is the interchangeable triggers. Much like the Westley Richards drop-lock action, with a firm forward push of the tang-mounted safety, the rear of the trigger assembly is released and easily removed. Although one can order coil hammer springs, Perazzi prefers to supply V springs, which the company feels provide better and more uniform trigger pulls. However, these springs can break, not a popular thing to happen in the midst of competition. With a Perazzi, though, all that's needed is a few seconds to drop out one trigger assembly and slip in the other. Replacement springs and the appropriate tools are also supplied with all guns.

Here a Perazzi stocker verifies the stock dimensions on a single-barreled trap gun. Trap guns dominate the single-barrel niche of high-grade guns.

Today, Perazzi makes a full line of clay-target guns that almost requires a program for all the details. In addition, Perazzi's field guns are anything but plain. Made in sets of 12-, 20-, and 28-gauge, with a .410 to complete the set, plus 20- and 28-gauge, two-barreled combos, the field guns come with wood, engraving, and gold inlays that would appeal to a sultan.

ABBIATICO & SALVINELLI

The 1960s were great years for the Italian gun trade. During that decade, Perazzi, Fabbri, and Abbiatico & Salvinelli were all founded. Mario Abbiatico was a Val Trompia–schooled engraver and gunmaker, as was his business partner Remo Salvinelli. Together they formed Fanricca d'Armi Mario Abbiatico e Remo Salvinelli, and called their partnership FAMARS. Initially they made field-grade beaters to top-of-the-line, Boss-style over-and-unders and Holland & Holland–style sidelocks, and their first guns were not mechanically great—a problem traced to less-than-careful heat-treating of component parts—but their engraving was outstanding. Abbiatico was a bulino-style engraver who used a handheld graver to cut the metal without the use of a hammer. Called "banknote engraving" because of its realism and similarity to the engraved plates used to print currency—you can apply ink to a fine bulino engraving and make a paper copy, just as the U.S. Bureau of Engraving and Printing does with dollar bills—it is simply exquisite. Today Abbiatico & Salvinelli make three styles of high-quality guns: side-by-side hammerless doubles, self-cocking hammer doubles, and Boss-style over-and-unders.

FABBRI

I can vividly recall the first time I held a Fabbri over-and-under. It was at the pre-Olympic test games in Montreal in 1975. I was participating as part of the quickly organized U.S. team, and one of the bunker shooters had a Fabbri. Its balance and feel were extraordinary, but it was the engraving that caught the crowd's attention. It was perhaps the first really exquisite engraving I'd seen. But far beyond that was the feel of that shotgun.

Founded by Ivo Fabbri in 1946, the company started off using high-tech machinery, not to turn out complete shotguns with only a minimum of handling and handwork, but in support of the workmen, to streamline those gunmaking functions that require the removal of large amounts of metal. This allowed the workers to devote their time to the fine handwork that sets Fabbri apart. Made of the finest materials using the familiar Boss-inspired action, with some of the finest walnut in the world, a Fabbri can take several years from the time of order to delivery. The buyer can request engraving by the artist of his choice, provided he is willing to wait even longer. If it were mine, I'd leave it plain, because I'd sure like to have it to shoot right now.

SIACE

Pronounced See-AH-che, Siace is a small gunmaker located in Gardone Val Trompia, just down the road from the Beretta complex. I mention them here only because Siace not only makes guns under their own name, but supplies barreled actions, both side-by-side and over-and-under, to many small makers who then finish them in their own styles. In 2004, Dakota Arms of Sturgis, South Dakota, best known for its excellent rifles, entered into a business relationship with Siace to produce Dakota's Superlight side-by-sides. Having shot one and examined it closely, I can vouch that it's a nice shotgun, emblematic of the fine work accomplished in the Val Trompia.

Although we have spent considerable time discussing the great American and British gunmakers, the truth is that today the very best of the best shotguns are coming from Italy. It is telling that many British "Best" makers are using barreled actions from Italy as the heart and soul of their guns. In a country of constant labor unrest and strikes, the gun industry seems to be in a world of its own, intent on producing quality shotguns for the world.

CHAPTER 9

Locks and Actions

High-grade shotguns come in several styles: side-by-side, over-and-under, single-barreled, pump, and semiautomatic repeater. Some of these actions are elaborate; others have the same actions found on lower-priced guns but have better finishes and are enhanced by the engraving and inlays of precious metals.

SINGLE-BARRELED

The simplest action is that of the single-barreled shotgun, which needs only to provide methods of securing the barrel to the action and opening it for loading, and a firing mechanism. The most plebeian shotguns are single-barreled guns, many of dubious parentage, intended primarily as beginners' guns, or for those who can't afford anything else. From there, the atmosphere becomes rarefied.

While not really considered a proper field gun—one would hardly take one into a Scottish grouse butt—the single-barreled gun has become best known on the 16-yard and handicap trap lines.

Virtually every U. S. fine gunmaker—Parker, A. H. Fox, L. C. Smith, Lefever, and Ithaca—made a single-barreled trap gun. Winchester did not. Apparently the Olin family, who owned Winchester at the time of the introduction of the Model 21, felt that a single-barreled version of the 21 was not necessary. Be that as it may, the single-barreled trap guns by the big-name American makers are all great guns, and many are still seen on the line around the United States. At the 2004 Grand American trap shoot, the penultimate year before the Amateur Trapshooting Association (ATA) and the Grand American's move to Sparta, Illinois, I saw a young man shooting a beautiful graded Parker, a G-grade. It was his grandfather's gun, and he took great pride in shooting it.

Lest we think that single-barreled trap guns are solely American creations, I've seen numerous examples from Purdey and others of the great London Best tradition, all probably

A rack of single-barrel and over-and-under shotguns for sale at the Grand American. Although many inexpensive and crude single-barrel shotguns are sold for beginners, trap guns are considered high-grade, with many extensively engraved with inlays and stocked with exquisite wood.

Young John Philip hunted ducks with his father along the East Branch, which later became the Anacostia River, which cuts across the District of Columbia. Eventually, Sousa became the leader of The Marine Band, and then, in 1898, formed his own professional concert band. In those days before radio, Sousa was as famous as any contemporary star of motion pictures or music. Little known to those outside of music is that Sousa loved trap shooting and hunting. He was the first president of the ATA, and once said of his lifetime priorities, "A gun, a pretty girl, a horse and music on the side."

Sousa shot a Charles Daly, but on December 23, 1916, he ordered an Ithaca. It was a 7E-grade, 32-inch, single-barreled gun weighing about 8 pounds. He asked that the stock dimensions of his Daly be copied with a "very thick comb." Furthermore, Sousa asked for "[A] great deal of engraving," and "high grade but no gold or silver." This last statement is interesting, since when Ithaca introduced its special-order Sousa-Grade, the gun came with a mermaid inlaid in gold on the trigger guard. The legend grew that Sousa had ordered the mermaid for his personal trap gun, but in truth he hadn't. In fact, his gun on display in the ATA museum in Sparta, Illinois, has tight scroll engraving, and that's all. It is also worth noting that a 1917 advertisement shows Sousa dressed in a plain sweater holding his Ithaca, the printing stating, "Mr. Sousa knows the lightning lock of an Ithaca improves his shooting; it will improve yours." Until his death in 1932, Sousa remained an avid trap shooter, even shooting one-handed following a horseback

made for the American market, but built with the same pride and quality as a Best side-by-side for the grouse moor.

Perhaps the most famous single-barreled shotgun made is Ithaca's Sousa-Grade. John Philip Sousa was born in Washington, D.C. His father was a trombonist in the United States Marine Band. Antonio Sousa is seen in a photo from the day The Marine Band accompanied President Abraham Lincoln to Gettysburg, where he delivered his immortal address.

riding accident that severely incapacitated his left arm. It was tradition for Sousa to fire the first shot at the Grand American.

Plebeian though it might at first seem, in truth the single-barreled shotgun has a place in the world of fine shotguns.

DOUBLE GUNS

The Sidelock

The epitome of double shotgun locks, the mechanism that fires the cartridge, is the sidelock. Actually, it's a throwback to days of hammer guns. In those guns, the sidelock was a fairly simple affair consisting of a mainspring that drove a tumbler, the top portion of which was the hammer. The sear or sears that link the whole to the trigger are also carried on the sidelock. As breechloaders overtook muzzle-loaders, hammerless guns also eclipsed those with exposed hammers. When the hammers were moved inside, the form of the lock stayed essentially the same. However, bringing the hammer into the lock had its own problems. The tumbler, on the bottom, had to be made smaller, with the hammer and large striking surface remaining on the top. All this had to be done while keeping the entire assembly small enough so that a minimum of wood was removed to inlet the locks. This brings us to the fact that the terms sidelock and boxlock are used to describe two distinct actions, while in

Considered the world's finest shotgun, this early hammer Purdey was made before the turn of the 19th century, yet it still commanded a high price in 2005.

truth there are locks, i.e., firing mechanisms, in both guns, and the outward appearance denotes the difference. The problem is that there is a way to masquerade a boxlock action as a sidelock.

A true sidelock, with some rare exceptions, contains the tumbler/hammer, mainspring, sears, and sear springs. In the early days, the sidelock was built with the mainspring facing both rearward and forward. When facing rearward it was called a back action, wherein the rear-facing mainspring was behind the tumbler and was cut into the wood toward the wrist of the stock. The bar action is the more familiar sidelock, and in it the mainspring is in front of the tumbler and is accommodated in the

metal, or in the bar of the action, forward of the tumbler and hammer. The back action has a less appealing appearance, which is why the bar action is all that is seen today.

For the most part, a true sidelock will have the heads of the pins—the British term for screws—evident on the exterior faces of the sideplates that carry these parts. It is accepted practice that these screws, which hold all the parts, including the pin at the apex of the mainspring, all project through the plate. Some true sidelock shotguns do not show these pins. Beretta's SO-10 has concealed pins, as do other very high-grade shotguns such as the Fabbri and Galazan's new sidelock. The problem arises when a boxlock is dressed in a false sideplate. Absent the pinheads, and absent the corresponding price of a true sidelock—sidelocks are more expensive to make—these guns are not sidelocks and should be evaluated accordingly. The beauty of sidelocks, and to some extent boxlocks with false sideplates, is that they provide an extensive canvas for engraving.

Many feel that one of the biggest advantages of a sidelock is better trigger pulls. Since a shotgun's trigger is slapped and not squeezed, popular nonsense to the contrary, I feel little difference between a top-quality trigger in a sidelock or in a boxlock. So long as the let-off is sufficiently light and there is no slack or preliminary takeup, a good shotgun trigger is a good shotgun trigger.

Perhaps the best attribute of a true side-lock is in its intercepting, second, or safety sear. If you look at a sidelock, you will note that there are two arms that engage the trigger blade. In order for the tumbler/hammer to fall, firing the gun, both these arms must be pushed simultaneously. If the gun is dropped or otherwise jarred and the primary sear is taken out of engagement with the hammer, the second or intercepting sear will catch the hammer, holding it against falling and firing the gun. One of my criticisms of the American-made L. C. Smith is that its sidelock is crude—just look at one—and lacks this important safety sear. By and large, all sidelocks use a V spring as the mainspring. Some sidelocks use coil springs, including the Beretta SO-10. The drawback with V springs is that if they break, the lock is out of action. Often, though, a coil spring will continue to function even when broken.

Sidelocks are the epitome of fine guns. Side-by-sides and over-and-unders built with them represent the epitome of the gunmaker's art and provide the artist's canvas for the engraver.

The Boxlock

Although sidelocks are generally considered to be the top of the heap, one cannot hold that boxlocks are inferior. They don't give engravers the broad expanse for their art, and few carry intercepting sears. What boxlocks do have, however, is durability. They tend to be made using coil springs that will often continue to function even when broken. Break a V mainspring in a sidelock, and you're out of business until the spring is replaced.

Because the working parts are fully enclosed within the action, they are not as exposed to the weather as those of a sidelock. Too, boxlock actions tend to be very simple, containing few parts: the hammer, which includes the sear notch that directly engages the trigger and incorporates the striker, hammer spring, and cocking rod. Ansley H. Fox advertised the advantages of the simplicity of his guns, and the truth is that few Foxes ever visit a gunsmith. It is also true that because the parts are mostly contained within the action, more wood is available at the head of the stock, ensuring a more durable stock.

In terms of high-grade shotguns, all the high grades made by the great American makers are exquisite. My own Ithaca, made by Ithaca Classic Doubles just before their plunge into bankruptcy, is special, with unique engraving by the talented Jack Jones, high-grade American black walnut checkered by the incomparable

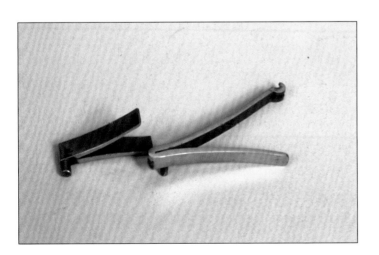

« Traditionally, sidelock shotguns use V springs. Quality V springs will provide long service, but are far more prone to break than coil springs.

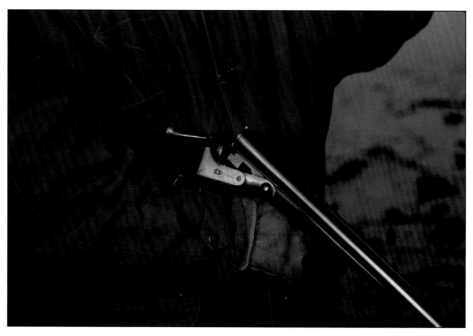

With the prevalence of bismuth, Kent Tungsten Matrix and Classic Doubles ammunition older shotguns such as this classic Parker can be used for hunting and clay shooting. Before shooting, older shotguns must be inspected by a competent gunsmith to ensure safety.

Ron Buck, and beautiful case hardening by Doug Turnbull. Gunther Frommer looked after the trigger and mechanical aspects, and in side-by-side comparison to my Henry Atkin with its Joseph Brazier sidelocks—there are none better—I can't tell any difference in the trigger pulls, as they're both good. My Ithaca was made for me, to my tastes, and hopefully my heirs will find a buyer whose opinions are like mine.

Sidelock and boxlock aficionados will argue the merits of each, probably until hell freezes over. The fact is that with some exceptions—Parker A-1 Specials and similar shotguns—sidelocks command higher prices, are harder to inlet, take more wood from the head of the stock, have marginally better trigger pulls, and provide for more extensive engraving. On the other hand, boxlocks are more durable, better protect the moving parts from the weather, have fewer parts, and lend themselves to the use of coil springs that, even if broken, can continue to work. The downside is that there is less area available for engraving. The differences between the two locks are significant, yet in truth one is as good as the other, and in the final analysis, each achieves excellence.

Regardless of the type of action, the mechanism by which the action is closed bears brief mention. Early breechloaders went through several permutations until the adoption of the Scott spindle and Purdey underbolt that are common on today's double guns. Any one of several locking systems was used. Parker's first guns used a lifter action that worked by pushing up on a projection in front of the trigger guard. The Jones rotary underlever is moved sideways to open the action. The snap underlever is pushed forward to open the breech, as is the side lever mounted to the side of the action. Virtually all of these provide for a solid lockup of the barrels to the action, and provide great interest to the collector.

Triggers, Selectors, and Safeties

The trigger is the link between the shooter and the gun. Triggers are an odd lot, from twin or double triggers to single and single selective. When the trigger is pulled, the blades that are on the top of the trigger push the sears out of engagement, allowing the hammer to fall. The sears are held in tight contact under the force of the mainspring. Most sear engagements are less than an eighth inch, and it is up to the gunmaker to ensure they are properly filed so that the engagement is firm, yet the triggers let off at a light three-and-a-half or four pounds. We all talk of "Lawyer's Triggers" that are set at very heavy weights to prevent, in theory at least, accident discharges, or more practically to use as evidence during litigation.

Typical of fine shotguns are double triggers placed in tandem beneath the action. The front trigger normally fires the right barrel of a side-by-side, or the bottom barrel of an over-and-under; the back or rear trigger fires the left or top barrel. Normally the front trigger is set about half a pound lighter than the back trigger, because the rear trigger is longer and hence applied more leverage and even though set heavier, will feel the same.

Shooting double triggers is an easily learned skill. Normally a round or two of skeet, shooting doubles at all stations, or just a run at a sporting clays course will teach the skill. My wife had never used a double-trigger shotgun until we took a couple hours of instruction from Roland Wild at the beautiful Holland & Holland Shooting Grounds northwest of down-town London. Within a few targets, with an occasional slip, she mastered shooting double triggers in a very few minutes.

Single triggers come in two varieties, selective and non-selective. Non-selective triggers are just that, they fire first one barrel, then the second with the shooter having no choice. Selective triggers offer the shooter the choice of which barrel to fire first. Because double guns almost without exception have barrels with different chokes, it can make a difference in certain situations which barrel is fired first.

Barrel selectors come in many styles, the most common being part of the safety catch mounted atop the upper action tang. Browning's selector slides to the right or left to select the first barrel to be fired. Most Italian double guns use a small slide set in the tang safety that is shifted to select the desired barrel. Many shotguns, including the Winchester Model 21, use a small gold-colored button set in the top of the trigger, that is hard to find, and if wearing gloves, darned near impossible. The very best safety-barrel selector ever made was on the old Remington 3200. It was a three-way lever mounted on the top tang: centered the gun was on safe, pushed to the left the bottom barrel was fired first, and pushed to the right, the top barrel fired first. Simplicity itself.

Single-selective triggers have been the bug-a-boo of gunmakers since someone thought them up. Notorious for not working, only in the 20th century have they ceased to be a problem. The Winchester Model 21 was the first to incorporate a truly functional single-selective trigger. It uses the little gold button, but it does select. I have an Ideal-Grade L. C. Smith Long Range that was their answer to the A. H. Fox Super Fox waterfowl gun. Mine has a Hunter One trigger that uses a small serrated slide at the front of the trigger to select the desired barrel. It selects so long as I want to fire the left barrel first. Most of these were replaced with Miller selective triggers (now owned by Doug Turnbull Restorations), and they were successful. European single-selective triggers have, until recently, been in the same boat as my Hunter One: unreliable. However all European manufacturers now make reliable single-selective triggers, but early guns so equipped may be a problem.

Safeties are mysterious to many, thinking that when on safe the gun won't fire of its own accord. And that's normally true. With few exceptions, and I can't think of any, shotgun safety catches only block the triggers from moving the sears. Unlike some rifles that lock the firing pin, shotguns do not. Therefore, unless it is a top-quality sidelock with an intercepting sear, a hard knock from a dropped gun can cause an accidental discharge. So the old adage is never more true that *safety is the responsibility of the person handling the gun*, and a safety catch is never to be trusted.

COMBINATION GUNS

My Swedish friend, Bjorn, called on New Year's Day, and during our conversation he said that on their hunting ground they had taken twenty-some roe deer, several predators, a couple dozen pheasants, plus some hares. It is for this mixed-bag type of hunting that combination guns were made. The typical northern European hunter—German, Austrian, Scandinavian—can encounter every kind of game, from moose to rabbits to pheasants, in a single morning's hunt. Hence, a firearm that provides an accurate rifle along with one or two shotgun barrels is a handy gun indeed. Here in the United States, we occasionally encounter one of these combination guns at gun shows, with most being souvenirs from the Second World War. But while they may seem rare here, such is not the case in Europe, where Krieghoff, Hofer, and others routinely produce combination guns.

Normally, we encounter three-barrel drillings (named for the German word for three *drei*, the proper pronunciation is *dry-ling*, not the common *dril-ling* as in Black & Decker) that are composed of two shotgun barrels and one rifle barrel. Commonly, the rifle barrel is chambered for one or another uncommon rimmed European cartridges. The trap in buying a drilling is in feeding the rifle. The only way to regulate accuracy is through bullet weight and velocity, provided one can locate

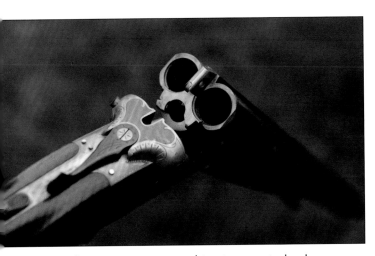

The most common combination gun is the three-barreled drilling that combines two shotgun barrels with a single rifle barrel.

ammunition. Certainly, the best remedy is to find some brass—there are several companies that supply obscure ammunition and brass—then handload until an accurate round is found. Because these guns are not built to withstand the very high pressures to which bolt-gun users are accustomed, great care must be used in cartridge selection. Frequently, it will require a skilled gunsmith to make a cast of the chamber to even determine the proper cartridge.

Shotgunwise, combination guns tend to be either 12- or, more commonly, 16-gauge. The latter guns are more common in Europe, especially those made prior to World War II. Commonly, 16-gauge guns are chambered for shorter cartridges than our regular 2¾-inch, 16-gauge loads. Again, a competent gunsmith must be consulted to check the chamber lengths. Many will measure 2½ or 2 9/16 inches, short of our 2¾-inch shells. Lengthening chambers is relatively easy, although I would recommend that a barrel specialist such as Briley Manufacturing in Houston be entrusted with this work.

While the gun is there, you probably ought to have the chokes checked. Most will be super-tight, extra, extra full chokes that don't shoot very well with our modern, plastic-wadded ammunition. Opened, they ought to pattern pretty well.

Combination guns are really neat, and I've always thought I'd like to add one to my collection. They are mechanically complicated, but there's something really fun about selecting the rifle barrel and having a rear sight pop up. Often, the precise and beautiful workmanship is worth the price of ownership. There are problems with shooting them, but none are really insurmountable, save a really oddball rimmed European cartridge, and even then, it may be possible to sleeve the rifle barrel to something that's at least usable.

REPEATERS

Repeaters, also infrequently called magazine guns, are the least expensive of high-grade shotgun actions. Pump-actions and semiautomatics comprise the repeaters, and over the years both types have been offered in ascending grades and commemorative issues by their manufacturers. Mass-produced, these high grades are normally hand-finished with top-quality polishing and bluing. The slab sides of pumps and semiautos offer broad areas for artistic engraving and precious-metal inlays. The application of high-grade wood, normally finished in dark red and brown tones, sets off the high finish of the action. When these types of guns are done with special engraving for an individual—provided the engraving and embellishments are tasteful—they can hold slightly more value than a simple high grade offered in one style. With very few exceptions, the provenance of being made for a famous person being the most prominent, these guns do not command the prices that double guns draw.

DINNER GUNS

Various conservation organizations such as Ducks Unlimited hold annual fundraising banquets. At these dinners, shotguns embellished with extra engraving, upgraded wood, and medallions indicating the organization are often offered for auction. Normally the same serial numbers are provided to each chapter each year, and individuals bid on these with an eye to collecting them. The hard truth about these guns is that they hold little more value than standard guns of the same models bought at a gun shop. One often sees collections of these guns for sale, even in new, unfired, in-the-box condition. Just be aware that the smallest number of Ducks Unlimited dinner guns made was 500 in 1973, and in recent years, 3,500 to 5,000 guns have been made and auctioned each year. The good news is that by purchasing these guns and all the other items at a banquet, we sportsmen and women directly support conservation efforts. The bad news is that you can't expect to retire to the Riviera by selling a collection of dinner guns.

CHAPTER 10

Hammer Shotguns

Despite the fast-growing use of hammerless shotguns, exposed-hammer guns remained in regular production until the outbreak of World War I, although special orders were built long after that war. Parker cataloged hammer guns until about 1920. And, until his death in 1936, King George V—the son of Edward VII, who defined the Golden Age of British shotgunning—shot exposed-hammer Purdeys, even though he could have bought and used any gun in the world. Other devotees felt the same way, and kept the hammer tradition alive as the decades passed. Recently, organizations such as The Vintagers (www.vintagers.org) have stimulated renewed interest in these guns among hunters and shooters. The august firm of Griffin & Howe, recognizing an emerging market, now sells new James Purdey hammer guns. Griffin & Howe's past president, Joe Prather, once told me that his firm sells several a year—because they are individually handmade, the production time is

long—and that 28- and 20-gauge versions will be available. Although some people consider hammer shotguns quaint and passé, the renaissance of the hammer gun seems here to stay.

In the simplest terms, hammer guns marked but a station along the road of shotgun evolution, and included both side-by-sides and early repeaters. Both the Winchester Model 1893 and the much stronger Model 1897 had exposed hammers, as did the Marlin 1898 pump. There was a feeling of safety in using a hammer gun, since one could quickly and easily see whether or not the gun was fully cocked and ready to fire, or resting safely at half cock. Many gun writers during this age took sides, advocating either the newer, hammerless guns or the older hammer guns. Certainly, seeing that the hammers are down at half cock provides a sense of security. Too, if the hammers were cocked and the shot was not taken, it was a simple matter to ease the hammers back to half cock. With hammerless shotguns, the triggers are blocked

A shooter swinging on a clay target shooting a vintage double loaded with very light loads that create low pressures. Alternatively, small-gauge tubes can be installed permitting firing target loads without problem in these old shotguns.

A transitional hammer to hammerless action, the external hammer performs no function in firing the gun, other than showing the user the gun is cocked.

from engaging the sears by means of a sliding safety on the action tang or located elsewhere such as the side-mounted Greener safety.

At one time, hammer guns were almost a dime a dozen—that's no longer true. With the renewed interest in these transitional guns, which bridged the gap between muzzleloading flint and percussion and breechloading shotguns, prices have risen considerably. However, while there are definitely some good guns out there, there is also an incredible amount of junk. Only a small number of the many hammer guns are worth the asking prices. Expect to pay close to $1,000 for a P-Grade, the lowest-grade, twist-barrel hammer Parker. Ascending grades command much higher prices, as do guns with steel barrels. For British-made hammer guns, the sky seems the limit. Even so, one can often purchase a hammer gun from a significant maker for far less than a hammerless gun. If including a Parker or Purdey in your collection is important, take a look at hammer guns, as there are still some bargains out there.

SHOOTING HAMMER GUNS

When I bought my first hammer gun, I searched all my reference books to learn how to properly handle my new prize. Look as I might, I couldn't find much at all. Here are the things I've learned.

Shooting black powder is fun; however, its clouds of smoke can all but obscure the targets. Black powder also leaves behind heavy fouling that takes considerable cleaning to remove.

Cocking: Depending on the strength of the mainsprings, it may be possible to cock both hammers simultaneously using the thumb. I've never been able to do this. I find that it is easiest to cock the left hammer first, then the right. That seems backward, but it works for me. Another dilemma occurs when hunting with a hammer gun. Certainly the safest and probably most proper way is to cock the hammers as you bring the gun to your shoulder. However, I can't cock both hammers simultaneously, so I cock the left hammer just as I reach the dogs, or as the ducks or geese make their last pass—then,

at the flush, I cock the right hammer. I *must* pay very careful attention to where the muzzles are pointing—as is true with any firearm— and should I trip, I shove the gun forward in a straight line so as not to harm the dogs. Hunting with hammer guns is really fun, and I've had several memorable duck hunts with an old 10-bore Clabrough Bros. that former general manager Chuck Webb at Briley Manufacturing fitted with 3-inch, 12-gauge chamber tubes. With their Vega steel choke tubes, I can shoot steel shot or any of the other nontoxic loads, and shooting ducks with it is very enjoyable.

CHAPTER 11

Pairs, Garnitures, and Specials

PAIRS

Perhaps no aspect of double guns is as misunderstood—save the values of obvious wall hangers—as paired guns. Though these are loosely called "matched pairs," there are actually three versions of pairs: a composed or composite pair, a matched pair, and a true pair. All of these consist of two guns, but how they become a pair requires some explanation.

A *composed pair* is a pair of shotguns, normally side-by-sides but also over-and-unders, that are alike in stock dimensions, barrel length, weight, and balance, but not made as a pair. Composed pairs are most frequently by the same maker, but in some instances, two separate guns from different makers but quite similar in weight, balance, and feel have been paired. Although not a matched or true pair, and certainly not of the value of either a matched or true pair, a composed pair can still serve a shooter very well in the field. I once

owned a pair bearing the name of Mortimer & Son of Edinburgh, Scotland, that were both made in Birmingham by the same maker but with two slightly different style actions. The stock dimensions, barrel length, weight, and balance were nearly identical, and I doubt if one could discern the difference in use, but they sure weren't matched.

A *matched pair* is two shotguns of the same dimensions, barrel length, weight, and so forth, which the gunmaker manufactured separately, years or perhaps even decades apart. An individual wanting a matched pair will return to the maker of a previously manufactured shotgun to order another of identical specifications. A matched pair is not a true pair, which consists of two identical guns made at the same time.

A *true pair,* almost always misnamed a "matched pair," is two shotguns with consecutive serial numbers, either side-by-sides or more recently over-and-unders, that the

gunmaker built at the same time to the exact same stock dimensions, overall weight, barrel length, balance, and often choke. Such guns are primarily for shooting driven gamebirds. Occasionally, guns of a true pair may have different chokes. In that case, gun number one normally has either a modified or full choke in the right barrel, with cylinder choke in the left. The second gun of the pair will then have cylinder

Two guns in action during a vintage 200-bird flurry that simulates shooting driven birds. The loader, Holland & Holland instructor Keith Lupton, keeps loaded guns rotating to this young lady as she concentrates on hitting as many as possible.

An example of a pair of fine, cased shotguns. Intended for driven bird shooting when two guns are fired in rotation with a loader recharging the guns, the two guns in a true pair are as closely matched as humanly possible.

or improved cylinder in the right barrel and a modified or full choke in the left. In practice, the hunter fires the first gun at the approaching birds, the first shot being taken farther away and the second shot closer to the gun. Then the hunter exchanges guns and uses the second gun first to shoot at the close, departing birds and then, using the left barrel, to fire at the last of the birds. Such a pair of shotguns normally shares a case, and as a rule the two are indistinguishable from one another in both feel and appearance, save for their different serial numbers. They are specified as number one and number two, inlaid in precious metal on both the corresponding barrels and actions. When building a true pair, gunmakers most often make the stocks from a fletch that is a stock blank of double thickness. Once this is sawed in half, the resulting wood will hopefully be of the same grain and color, making the finished stocks virtually identical. The metalwork, engraving, and other aspects of a true pair are in the hand of the gunmaker, but the wooden components are governed by nature, and an appropriate pair of stock blanks, or a fletch that produces identical blanks, are in the hands of nature, and very rare and hard to find.

GARNITURES

In the heyday of driven bird shooting, great shots of the day such as King Edward VII and Lord Ripon found that they could shoot faster and kill more birds if they had a third gun. King George V, Edward VII's son, owned and used three trios of 12-bore and one trio of 16-bore ejector, hammer Purdeys until his

death in 1936. When these were used with two loaders, the rate of fire could be quite fast.

Today, it's relatively easy for gun collectors to find pair guns in one form or another made by all of the Spanish, Italian, and British gunmakers, plus those by Anthony Galazan of Connecticut Shotgun Manufacturing Company. My dentist, Myles Digennaro, recently received two true pairs of guns from Spanish gunmakers Arietta and Grulla, and they're beautiful. If he desired, both companies would gladly have made him a third.

SPECIAL-USE SHOTGUNS

Over the centuries, shotguns have been called on to perform various tasks, from trench guns for war, to guard guns for stagecoaches and banks, and guns that worked equally well for both big game and birds.

Paradox Guns

Paradox guns were conventional side-by-sides, both hammer and hammerless, in which the last few inches of their smooth bores were rifled. In theory and use, a solid projectile fired through one of these guns would be spun when it engaged the rifled portion of the barrel, just as a projectile from a rifle would spin, and thus achieve considerable accuracy. When used with shotshells of the late 1800s and early 1900s, the wads would be spun out of the way, and not invade the pattern and disturb the shot cloud. I'm not sure paradox guns performed either mission well, but they are rare, and an interesting phase of firearm development.

Wells Fargo Guns and Others

Never, ever has the Latin phrase *caveat emptor*—let the buyer beware—been more important than when dealing with guns attributed to famous individuals or to Wells Fargo.

As the American West expanded to the Pacific, and gold and silver were found in abundant quantities, a means of securely shipping valuable cargos became critical. Wells Fargo became the namesake for all freight and passenger companies that used horse-drawn coaches to navigate the prairies in the face of hostile Indians and bandits. Although many different shotguns were used to guard these shipments, there are only a handful of true Wells Fargo guns. Prior to 1915, the Wells Fargo Express Company purchased a number of New Ithaca Gun models with exposed hammers from Ithaca. After 1915, Wells Fargo purchased another order of "new two-bolt hammer models" from Ithaca. In both cases, the guns are marked "W F & Co Ex." These guns are the real things. Guns with "Wells Fargo" carved or stamped into the stocks or elsewhere are probably frauds. No slope is as slippery as the Wells Fargo slope, and anyone contemplating the purchase of such a gun had better consult an expert before he plunks down his hard-earned money. Firm, written provenance detailing the use and ownership of a Wells Fargo gun is necessary, and even then care must be taken to ensure that the provenance is believable.

Guns that have belonged to movie stars, military officers, and other personalities always bring high prices—even if they're frauds. Anytime a firearm is offered as being the "personal gun of so-and-so," there ought be some kind of paper trail. Recently, a good friend and great gunsmith had a badly worn Fox Sterlingworth come in for a complete overhaul. The owner stated that it had belonged to General of the Armies John J. Pershing. However, there was no paper trail, and by the barest coincidence, I knew General Pershing's grandson, who was an avid hunter and shooter. I knew that he had learned about all of his illustrious grandfather's guns, and that they were mostly graded guns from several prominent makers. I asked my friend what provenance the Sterlingworth's owner had, and the answer eventually came back, "none." This is a rather benign example of a celebrity gun, and goes to show that unless there is corroborating evidence in the form of letters, photographs showing the alleged owner actually holding the gun, and other evidence, hearsay and family legend and lore are just that. There is no telling how many of Jesse James's pistols his mother sold to the unsuspecting, and that ought to be a lesson to all.

CHAPTER 12

Small-Gauge Shotguns: The Darlings of the High-Grade Guns

Small-gauge shotguns, 20- and 28-gauge and .410 bore, are not only more rare than guns of larger gauges, but also have a certain panache. Best and top-quality small-bore shotguns are typically built on frames or actions specially scaled to that gauge. Perhaps one of the criticisms of the Winchester Model 21 is that only two frame sizes were used, one for the 12- and another for the 16- and 20-gauge. The few 28-gauge and .410 guns were all built on the 20-gauge action. On the other hand, Parker used twelve different size frames for their shotguns. The diminutive .410 was built on a 000-size frame that was further lightened by cuts in the water table or action flats (the area of the action that projects from the breech face, against which rest the barrel flats when the gun is closed). Ought-size frames were reserved for 16- and 20-gauge guns and were scaled to those gauges. Twelve-gauge guns shared several frames, with the 1 size used for very light, 6½-pound 12s and the 1½ used

for standard-weight 12s. The No. 2 was used for heavy, 9-pound waterfowl guns. Ten-bore guns used No. 2-, 3-, and 5-size frames, with the No. 5 being reserved for 10-pound wildfowling guns.

Small-gauge frames are governed primarily by the distance between the firing pins. The greater the distance, the larger the frame. It is therefore easy to understand that when a 28-gauge or .410 is constructed on a 20-gauge frame, the breech end of the barrels must be quite thick to align properly with the frame. If the firing-pin holes are closer, then the barrels can be made thinner, and the appearance and aesthetics of the whole are far better. The Parker 000 .410-bore's frame's distance between the firing pins is $^{13}/_{16}$ inch; the distance for Parker 12-gauge guns in the light ½ and 1 sizes is $1^1/_{16}$; and the heavier actions have the pins located with $1\frac{1}{8}$-inch separation. The height of the standing breech also changes with the various gauges. The 000

The action on the right is a 12-bore, on the left a 28-gauge. Note the difference in the size and firing-pin placement of the smaller action.

breech stands $1\frac{3}{32}$ inches from the water table to the top of the bolsters, the 12-gauge's breeches hover right around $1\frac{1}{4}$ inches, plus or minus $\frac{1}{16}$-inch variation from lightest to heaviest. Shotguns by other makers either adhere to a similar formula for their small-gauge guns or they don't, and it's easy to spot those guns that are made on the proper-size frame for their gauge.

Perhaps it becomes too much of a technical exercise to evaluate small-gauge guns solely by the measurements of their frames. A properly crafted small-gauge gun is sleek and unmistakable. Although frame size is most important, because the lines of the gun are established by it, barrel length also makes a big difference. My AyA No. 2 28-gauge is built on a small action appropriate to the gauge, but it has

28-inch barrels. My 20-gauge Ithaca Special has 30-inch barrels. I have my guns to shoot and hunt with, and the barrel's length is selected for those reasons. Both guns look a trifle long in comparison to their girth, but if I plan to hit something, the barrels need to be that long.

The late Bob Brister, certainly the dean of American shotgun writers, made perhaps one of the best comments ever in the foreword to Cyril Adams and Robert Braden's book, *Lock, Stock & Barrel* (Safari Press, Huntington Beach, CA; 1996). When Brister approached Adams, seeking an opinion about a 26-inch-barreled over-and-under, Adams replied that "It was probably a pretty good gun for holding up convenience stores." My sentiments exactly.

Page after page of Winchester Model 21 skeet guns go unnoticed by me because of the company's penchant for making them all with 26-inch barrels. Even men and women of the shortest stature can effectively shoot guns with 28-, 30-, and perhaps even 32-inch barrels. The only use for 26-inch barrels is on repeaters, and that's because their actions all measure 6 inches or longer, and their magazines further add forward weight. If you're looking at a gun solely to collect and not to shoot, then barrel length is irrelevant, so long as it's the original length. But if you want to shoot it, look for longer barrels.

There is a myth that shooting a small-gauge gun is "more sporting." Nash Buck-

This AyA No. 2 28-gauge was a perfect match for Minnesota woodcock. High-grade small-gauge shotguns made on a properly scaled action bring a premium price.

ingham often repeated the old adage, "Never send a boy on a man's errand." The myth somehow equates to the philosophy that a small-gauge gun somehow gives the bird more of a chance. I assure you that it matters little to a truly good shot what gauge he's using, *so long as the birds are in range.* There is also a myth that the pattern from a small-gauge gun is smaller in diameter than that thrown by a large gauge. *Wrong!* The fact is that the patterns shot by a properly choked shotgun, regardless of gauge, are of the same diameter, only of decreasing density as the gauge, hence the shot payload, diminishes. The myth that a .410 bore is ideal for a beginning shotgunner is all wrong! The .410's small payload and lousy patterning provide almost no chance for the beginner to hit anything. The 28-gauge's pattern is sufficiently dense to score hits out to about 30 yards, the 20-gauge to 35, and the 12-gauge to 40 yards. With high-performance loads, these lethal yardages can be stretched. The facts are that small-gauge guns are fun to shoot, light, and easy to carry, but they're no more "sporting" than the heavier 12-gauges, and in fact outside of their useful ranges, less sporting, since wounding is not part of the true hunter's lexicon.

The value of, and market for, small-gauge guns are strong. For every dozen 12-gauge guns made, probably one small-gauge gun is made. Perhaps that is a little strong, since

the 20-gauge enjoys good popularity, but in terms of the 28-gauge and .410 bore, I suspect about one or the other is made for every ten or twenty 12-gauge guns. Twenty-four-, 32-, and 36-gauge guns are even more rare. These guns are made on order. At a recent Vintagers Cup at the Orvis Sandanona facility near Millbrook, New York, I overheard one individual state that he had spent a year finding either a 32- or 36-gauge gun for the competition. Obviously, due to the very limited number of these odd gauges, they command a premium. In an earlier chapter, I mentioned the Sousa-Grade Ithaca single-barreled trap gun. According to Ithaca's factory records, only eleven of these unusual guns were produced, including one .410 bore! Needless to say, the fact that only a single gun in .410 bore was produced makes that gun extremely valuable.

Small-gauge shotguns are very appealing and fun to use in the field. The fact that great gunmaking houses such as Holland & Holland, Beretta, and Perazzi have built commemorative sets of four and five guns, one in each gauge (12-, 20-, 28-, .410 bore, and some 16-gauges as well), for prices approximating the gross national product of a small nation, shows the artistry and beauty of all the gauges. However, when the guns are seen side by side, the subtle beauty of the small gauges becomes apparent, and illustrates why these guns command the high prices they do.

CHAPTER 13

Shotgun Stocks—Wood, Wood, Wood!

When talking about shotguns with fine-gun dealers and the gunsmiths who work with those guns, I always ask them what American shooters, collectors, and hunters tend to look for in shotguns. Without hesitation, all agree that fine wood is important to prospective buyers. Certainly, the name on the gun is more important, but the fact is that many Best guns from the late 19th and early 20th centuries have excellent English or French walnut, but not of the high figuration we Americans have come to expect from our native black walnut.

Gunstocks have been made from just about anything, from molded plastic, to aluminum, to hardwoods such as screwbean mesquite and oak, to God only knows what else. I once received a letter from someone looking for a part for an inexpensive gun, for which none existed, and he further stated that the previous owner had begun making a stock from hickory wood. At one time in the 1950s

and 1960s, maple was all the rage. Hard maple works well, but it takes a certain taste to like it on a shotgun. Be that as it may, walnut is and always will be the prime gunstock wood.

In the genus *Juglans*, there are more than forty different species of walnut found throughout the world. The finest walnut is *Juglans regia,* the royal form of European walnut that is grown throughout Europe. Called French, English, Spanish, Circassian, Bastogne, and several other names, it is the prime gunstock wood. Two world wars raged across much of the *Juglans regia* growing area, including the Ardennes Forest, where two vicious World War II battles were fought. Beyond that, trees were cut wholesale to make military rifle stocks during those wars, and it's not unusual to encounter a G98 Mauser with a AAA-special grade stock. While some high-grade walnut is still harvested in Europe, prime walnut today comes from Turkey and surrounding areas of Asia Minor. One of the

The wood room at the Griffin & Howe shop in Bernardsville, New Jersey.

selling points of guns made in Turkey is, in fact, their great wood.

In terms of usefulness for stocking, French or English walnut, regardless of where it comes from, is the best. It is lighter, more flexible, and more easily worked than American black walnut. Good English walnut shapes well and takes checkering more easily than any other wood, making it the choice for custom stockers. On the other hand, black walnut frequently has more spectacular grain, and while top-grade blanks are easy to shape and checker, lesser grades contain a great deal softwood or sapwood, which does not provide a firm working area and makes checkering difficult, as the diamonds cut in the softer areas slough off easily. When standing in Beretta's fine wood room in the Beretta-Uno plant in

A small sampling of the high-grade wood Beretta offers its customers.

Gardone Val Trompia, one could hardly say that French walnut does not have spectacular grain. Still, Americans tend to be influenced by black walnut, due to its prevalence here, and consequently compare other woods to it.

While top-grade shotguns are stocked in woods other than walnut, they are rare. I once previewed a large shotgun collection at the Holland & Holland gun room in New York. Among the various shotguns for sale were several stocked in maple. There were two or three maple-stocked Winchester Model 21s and two Model 21 trap guns. Their stocks were well executed, but that did not make much difference in their estimated values. Maple was extremely popular in the 1950s and 1960s, and many shotguns were restocked with it. The light-colored wood was normally filled with a dark filler, giving the stocks a golden look. Today, walnut rules the roost, and collectors scorn shotguns stocked with anything other than good French or black walnut.

STOCK FIT

There is no aspect of a shotgun more important than how well the stock fits the shooter. As little as $\frac{1}{16}$ inch can affect the point of impact of the pattern. Shotguns are pointed, not aimed. Any concentration on the front bead, be it metal or one of the fluorescent sights that are currently all the rage, will result in a miss: If you look at it, save the shell. A properly fitted shotgun should come first to the cheek, and second to the shoulder. At that point, with the shooter's vision locked onto the leading edge or beak of the target, the shot should be fired. When I shoot my best, I see only the target, and the gun is guided by my brain, through my eyes. Certainly, we see the barrel in our peripheral vision, and that information enters the equation that the brain computes, but the facts are that the better a gun fits, and the less the shooter has to attempt to fit himself to the gun, the better a shot he will be.

Arriving at a precisely fitting gun is problematic. Really good gun fitters are not found loitering on the corner. Sure, there are plenty of guys who hang around sporting-clays layouts who claim to be fitters, but most do not have the level of skill to do a really good job. Some retailers boast of fitting their customers, but the really good fitters are few and far between. Anyone who claims he can fit a shotgun without shooting it is a fraud. One guy who retails top-name clay guns claims to "fit" his customers by having them point at a paper target on the wall with a flashlight inserted in the muzzle of a shotgun. One year at the Vintagers Shoot, as my wife and I munched our overpriced hamburgers, we overheard a guy behind us ask his buddy, "Have you been fitted? You just have to go down to . . . and they'll fit you. It only takes five minutes [presumably using a flashlight]; it would cost you fifty bucks in England." Sorry, but any gun fitter in England worth his salt would charge you at least 50 pounds, and would not think of fitting a gun any other way than at a shooting ground. As with everything else about fine guns, *caveat emptor!* At the Grand American trap shoot, virtually all stockmakers offer "fitting." Trapshooting uses a shouldered gun, and perhaps a trap gun can be fitted fairly well without shooting, but any sporting gun, be it for clays or game, must be fitted while shooting.

Shotgun fitting is done by first firing at a stationary plate that is precisely 16 yards from the shooter. The shooter is first asked to mount his gun and fire, almost as one would when firing a rifle. Next the gun is mounted and fired as it comes to the shoulder. Provided the shooter has a good gun mount—it's virtually impossible to obtain a good fitting without having a good gun mount—he will place most of his shots one on top of the other.

Proper fitting of a shotgun requires shooting at a 16-yard target.

Once the shooting is finished, normally after four to six shots, the center of the pattern is compared to the point of aim. (I hate using the term "aim," as shotguns are pointed, but it is necessary here.) For each inch the center of the pattern deviates from the point of aim, the stock needs to be adjusted $\frac{1}{16}$ inch. For example, if the center of the pattern is consistently striking 2 inches low and 1 inch right, then the stock needs to be raised $\frac{1}{8}$ inch and

cast off, assuming a right-handed shooter, $\frac{1}{16}$ inch to center the pattern. Should the shooter desire a higher point of impact, which is highly recommended so that the target is never below the barrel, the stock will need to be raised even more. Once the impact is determined, the gun should be adjusted and shot again to ensure that the adjustment is correct.

When fitting a stock, it is typical to use a "try" gun. This is a shotgun with a fully articu-

Instructor Chris Batha checks the dimensions on a try gun, whose fully articulated stock can be altered to accommodate any shooter. Once satisfied with the point of impact, Batha measures the final settings then transfers them to a form the stock maker will use to alter or build a new stock.

lated stock that permits the user to adjust the buttstock for drop, cast, and length and degree of pitch. The drawback of try guns is that they are not particularly well balanced because of the extra hardware necessary to permit adjustment. Gun fitters will often choose to apply tape, strips of leather, buttpads, and other devices to adjust the customer's existing stock to

the new dimensions. The only problem is that cast off or cast on for lefties cannot be accommodated without using a try gun. Because the change of any one aspect of a stock affects all the other dimensions, and they often must be readjusted, the try gun best allows for this infinite tweaking. For example, lengthening a stock brings the face farther back onto the stock, where the drop is more. Therefore, as the stock is lengthened, the drop must also be adjusted upward to compensate.

Fitting using a plate takes time. I've seen Bryan Bilinski, a highly experienced gun fitter who owns Fieldsport in Traverse City, Michigan, take three hours with a single fitting. It's that precise, and shooters are often encour-

aged to shoot their gun with temporary pads and comb raisers, and then return for a further fitting in six months or a year—just to be sure—before a new stock is made.

A properly fitted stock ensures the best possible performance from any shotgun. Because a shotgun is pointed, the proper alignment of the shooter's eye with the barrels makes

Following several shots, Chris Batha evaluates the target. Consistent deviation from the point of aim indicates the necessity of changing the stock's dimensions.

the gun shoot where he is looking. The key to good shotgunning, in fact, is having the gun consistently shoot where the shooter is looking. Anything else is second-rate. Needing to take time to adjust your head to a stock so your eye is properly aligned wastes time and makes you rush the shot. Even worse, it can cause the shooter to look at his barrels, which almost always guarantees a miss. Spending money on a good fitting by a truly qualified gun fitter, and then restocking the gun if necessary, is a wise investment.

A high-grade stock sets off any shotgun, and almost always brings wows from onlookers.

Most high-grade shotguns are stocked in nothing less than top-quality walnut, although some owners will restock a gun to their dimensions, yet with a lower-grade blank. My gunsmith friend Greg Wolf makes the point, "The work is the same. Building a stock from a cheap blank or a high-grade blank takes the same time and effort, so always buy the best." That's not to say that restocking with a lower-grade blank is wrong, if it's all you can afford, but often it's not a major expense to obtain a truly exquisite blank. A well-executed stock with glorious grain sets any gun apart from all the rest, and is a joy to own.

CHAPTER 14

Fit and Finish

The art of fitting a wooden gunstock to the metal of the action and forend iron takes incredible skill. Anything but a precise fit is practically worthless.

The head of any buttstock must precisely fit the rear of the action, so that the maximum amount of wood is available to absorb the recoil when the gun is fired. If the fit is not uniform across the face of the stock, over time the wood will be compressed, causing the dimensions of the stock that govern point of impact to shift. Even more problematic is the fact that improperly fitted wood normally subjects it to higher than normal pressures and can lead to cracking and even breaking.

When a master stocker lays out a stock from a blank, he ensures that the grain running through the grip—the area that will be shaped to mate with the action—runs lengthwise to provide the greatest strength. Farther back in the stock he'll be looking for figure, but through the grip, the grain must run front to rear.

There is much to be accommodated with a sidelock action. Primarily, though, the stocker must ensure that the head of the stock squarely meets the rear of the action. A sidelock action offers less contact area than a boxlock action, and the heading of the stock must be very well done because of the smaller contact area. Once headed up, the top and bottom straps must be accommodated, then the locks. Because the locks are cut into the wood, they must be inletted precisely, with a minimal amount of wood removed. A well-inletted stock will have the parts of the locks outlined in reverse within the wood; even the screw heads are cut into the wood. The fine stocker leaves every scintilla of wood possible to support the action. Many lesser-priced sidelock shotguns are not precisely inletted, with the inletting either done by machine or done in such a way that all the wood is removed. This is a time- and cost-cutting measure that robs the action of proper support. Still, for

Block custom stocks that have been headed up or fitted into actions share a rack with a nearly completed stock. Once inletted into the action, the wood is then shaped to the customer's dimensions. All bespoke shotguns are stocked in this manner.

the price of these guns, hand inletting in the traditional manner would raise the price out of the bargain bin. Occasionally shot with light loads, it probably doesn't matter.

Inletting a boxlock action is less difficult, since all the parts of the locks are contained within the action. Without the extra wood removed, the action has more support.

Fitting the wood to these actions is a matter of high skill and ascends to the level of art when done precisely. In the case of less expensive shotgun stocks cut with computer numeric control (CNC) machines, the fit is quite good, considering that little handwork is involved. Once, while touring the Beretta factory, I saw an experimental CNC machine

One of Beretta's skilled stockers carefully working down the stock of a high-grade sidelock.

A Spanish stocker fitting the wood to the trigger-guard strap of a sidelock AyA.

The assortment of chisels and tools on the bench of one of Beretta's stock makers.

that produced virtually finished stocks. It was an incredible device. Less advanced machines in Mecanico Sarcha, Beretta's wood-processing facility, produced stocks for lower-grade shotguns that, while requiring a little handwork to attach to a gun, are nonetheless quite amazing. Because Beretta production shotguns are all boxlocks, machine inletting with just a bit of hand fitting provides a quality shotgun at moderate cost to the consumer. Their high-grade over-and-unders and side-by-sides are all hand-inletted to the highest standards.

Still, machine inletting will often produce less than precise results. In examining a shotgun, following the usual look-see through the barrels, the exterior metal, overall style—pistol grip, straight grip, beavertail, splinter forend, wood grain, engraving, etc.—the experienced gun man

A Beretta apprentice whose work is being monitored by a master stocker. Custom stocks begin as a block into which the action is inletted, then finished to the customer's dimensions.

will closely examine, with a loupe if necessary, how well the wood fits the metal.

The exterior fit of wood to metal can tell many stories. Virtually every new shotgun is finished with the wood slightly "proud" of the metal. Leaving a tiny bit of wood above the metal allows for contraction of the wood as it dries further. Beretta, for example, air dries its wood for months, then places it in a kiln for hours, and then allows it to air dry and stabilize. Even then, the wood will continue to dry and contract. The better it is dried and stabilized initially, the less the contraction. If the wood is not left proud, and slight contraction takes place, then the gun will have a poor fit. If the stock is refinished—and nearly all stocks on "shooters," as opposed to collector guns, should be at some point—then the wood should be left slightly proud at this stage, or at least left level with the metal. One way to tell if a stock has been refinished is to see how proud it is of the metal.

Winchester always finished its wood proud of the metal. If you come across a Model 12 whose wood is level with the contours of the action, then you can be certain it has been refinished.

Restocking often does not follow the lines of the original stock. Some folks like this idea, but if you're seeking to preserve originality, then the stock has to look like the original.

FINISHES

Although wood is the best and finest material for stocking sporting arms, giving usefulness and beauty to any arm, it must be protected. Some kind of coating must be applied to prevent water from invading the wood and making it swell, and to attempt to prevent the incursion of excess oil. Many contemporary gunsmiths apply a thin layer of fiberglass bedding to the breech-contact areas of their stocks. I know that this causes traditionalists to cringe and cry foul, but the fact is that if a gun is to be used in the field and presumably in rain, snow, and the gloom of night, then the more protection provided, the better. When I had my Super Fox restocked by custom gunsmith Greg Wolf, for example, I specifically asked him to seal the action end of the stock with bedding compound, to which he replied that he routinely does so when

The stock finishing area at the Beretta Uno plant in Gardone Val Trompia, Italy. Here the custom ordered stocks are finished or refinished when repaired.

a gun is intended for the field. His inletting is impeccable, and the bedding compound applied only to protect the vulnerable, unseen end grain.

A further benefit to the use of bedding compound is to increase the durability of the stock head, especially when heavy loads are to be fired on a consistent basis. Many lower-priced and even some high-ticket guns come from their factories with no finish whatsoever on the stock head, inviting the incursion of oil and water, and all their nasty results. This can ultimately lead to the wood either softening into mush, rotting away, or becoming cracked.

Automated Finishes—Lacquers and Synthetics

Currently, inexpensive to moderately priced production guns are finished with sprayed-on lacquer. Lacquer dries in seconds, so many coats can be applied quickly, and it provides the wood with a good level of protection. Moving up the scale are the epoxy-based finishes, which are sprayed onto the bare wood and then dried with heat, which speeds the chemical reaction within the finish. These finishes are tough as nails, and damned hard to remove. For generations, Remington, which was owned for decades by DuPont, best known for chemicals and paints, coated its stocks with an epoxy-based finish called RKW. This really protected the wood, but anyone wanting to refinish one had the devil's own time getting the finish off. Today, Remington still offers its familiar brilliant gloss finish, but has added

a satinlike oil finish with little decrease in protection.

Watching stocks move along a mechanical finishing machine is interesting, and the finish on production guns is tough and highly protective. In fact, when we move into the high-grade gun realm, stock protection actually diminishes when compared to the production stocks coated with epoxy and other synthetic finishes.

Oil Finish

The most highly valued stock finish is the traditional oil finish. There are as many finishing concoctions as there are stockers. Some use something as simple as Birchwood-Casey Tru-Oil, but in the main, each stock-maker and finisher has his own pet formula.

The traditional oil finish material is linseed oil, which is oil derived from pressed flaxseed. It is rubbed on in very thin coats, allowed to dry, then reapplied. Such a finish takes weeks, if not months, to accomplish. More frequently, a drier, often called a Japan drier, is mixed with the linseed oil to speed the process. Many commercially available oil finishes are simply premixed combinations of drier and oil. Tung oil is also a favorite. Quick drying, it can provide a hard, durable finish. Made of the oil pressed from the seeds of the tung tree, it provides some protection from moisture. When properly applied, it appears to be in the wood, as opposed to a sprayed-on finish that is obviously on the wood.

The different types of walnut vary in porosity. English or French walnut tends to have very fine pores and lends itself to oil finishing. More porous American black walnut usually requires some kind of filler to fill its larger pores. These fillers also often include a dye or color to enhance the grain. Winchester used a reddish-colored filler that gave its stocks their distinctive look. British stockmakers used alkanet root to color their stocks, and the red hue it imparts is beautiful. Some fillers are quite thick. When applied and allowed to dry partially, then rubbed

off with a coarse cloth or piece of burlap, the thickening agent, normally some form of silica or talc, remains in the pores. Many stockmakers do not like these fillers, since the silica or other filler quickly dulls their checkering tools.

The most traditional oil finishing method is to apply repeated coats of oil, with drying time and light sanding with very fine paper between each stage, until the finish completely fills the pores. Buy a Holland &

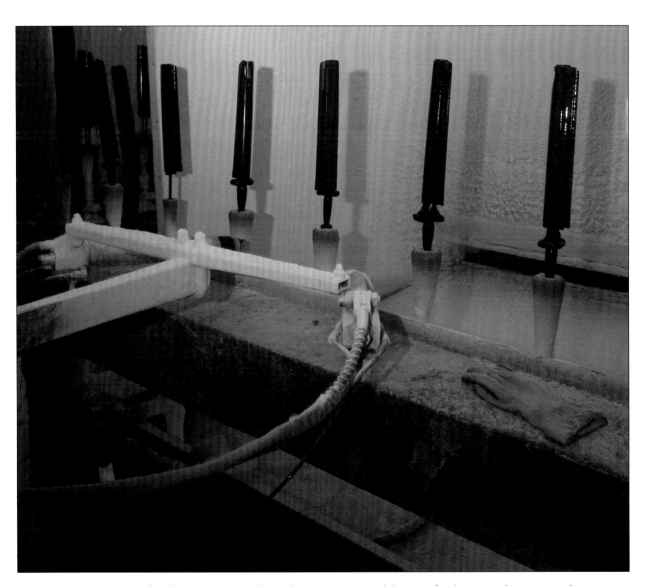

Robotic sprayers apply finish to Beretta stocks at their Meccanica del Sarca facility near the Swiss-Italian border.

Holland, Purdey, or other extremely high-grade shotgun, and that's the finish you get.

The drawback of a traditional oil finish is that, when used in or subjected to rain, it quickly loses its luster. I took a new Ithaca double to Argentina to shoot doves for five days, and by the time I'd run 1,500 rounds through it, the finish on the stock and forend had dulled considerably. A refresh with a drop of oil rubbed out as far as it would go brought the finish back to its factory-new appearance. I also picked up a couple of scratches, and using 800-grit paper with finish as a lubricant, it was easy to rub out the scratches lightly. Not as durable or protective as a synthetic, the traditional oil finish is the easiest to maintain.

Varnish

Varnish can be used to provide a very hard finish that's more impervious to weather than oil. Not quite as pretty, varnish can also scratch and be difficult to repair. When scratched, oil finishes can be repaired by simply massaging a small amount of oil into the damaged area, allowing it to dry, and then continuing until the finish is repaired. You can't do this with varnish, due to its hard, impenetrable surface.

Recently, traditional spar varnish and other oil-based varnishes have taken a backseat to synthetics, and as popular as these finishes were on older Browning shotguns, they have all but faded from use in favor of oil and synthetics.

REFINISHING

Restocking and refinishing jobs can usually be spotted when the wear on the stock does not equal that on the metal. A high-luster varnish or synthetic finish on a stock that ought to have a subdued oil finish should immediately unfurl a red flag that all is not right. Polishing and rebluing, or redone case hardening on an action, is often as easy to spot as an albino elephant in a herd of Black Angus cattle. Why? Because unless the polishing is done by a master, the engraving will lose its sharp edges, and the trademarks or stamping marks, patents, model numbers, and other information will be dull. On all but the most rare shotguns, refinishing the wood and metal will reduce the value significantly. If the gun has any collector value, a collector will want original finish, and nothing less. This extends to added ventilated ribs, extended stocks, recoil pads, and so on. Anything that didn't come on the original gun is taboo. In fact, Blue Book Publications has gone so far as to publish a book containing all the *known* factory information about the Parker shotgun, and a quick look at the serial number can bring you to the exact measurements, barrel lengths, and finishes of the original gun as it left the Parker factory in Meriden, Connecticut. Other shotguns don't have this ready reference, but a skilled eye can tell if the gun's been refinished.

The positive to this is if a buyer finds a shotgun he really likes, he can use refinishing as a lever to reduce the price. I bought a "shooter" Model 21 for $1,900, a fairly low

116

price for a 21, because one of its owners had cut the stock to fit a small man or woman. If that was not enough to knock down the price, the aftermarket Simmons ventilated rib was. And nice as these ribs are—the fact is that Simmons in Olatha, Kansas, reengineered the manner in which Winchester applied their factory ribs, and in the 1950s and 1960s actually installed ventilated ribs on all new Winchester shotguns under contract—in the case of this particular Model 21 it didn't increase the value, and instead detracted from it. Collectors want originals, while shooters can live with alterations, provided they aren't unsafe or poorly done.

When is a refinish in order? That's a touchy subject, because some shotguns ought to be left in original condition, while others might benefit from a restoration. A top-notch restoration is expensive, but on a gun that's been used hard, it might be worthwhile. Certainly a shotgun that is attributed to a famous person, provided the

provenance (with paper trail) is there, should be left as is. However, oftentimes a gun can benefit from a complete restoration. It isn't a half-measure kind of thing. Refinishing the wood alone is half the job. To do a complete job, the metal must also be redone: carefully polished, blued using the proper method originally employed on that particular gun, and the case hardening done by a master. Refinishing wood is easy, within the realm of the do-it-yourselfer. Refinishing metal isn't. The stripping, recoloring, and refinishing of a stock can make it look incredibly good, but unless the metal goes along, it's a half measure. On the other hand, if the metal is great, and the stock is scratched and dinged, then perhaps only a wood refinish is in order.

In short, if you have a potentially collectible shotgun or are seeking a collector specimen, then beware of possible refinishing. One need only watch *Antiques Roadshow* to understand that original finish is everything on a collector specimen, and that ought be the guide. As much as we like to make things just a little better, there is much to like about leaving things alone. Fine wood sets off almost any shotgun, and, properly finished and maintained, is a thing of beauty.

CHAPTER 15

Checkering

Checkering is twofold. Aesthetically, it can lend beauty and distinction to an already exquisite stock; functionally, it provides a firm gripping surface on the stock and forend. In truth, a splinter forend is not intended to be held, but without checkering it sure looks plain.

Two factors govern checkering: the number of lines per inch cut into the wood and the pattern used. Checkering patterns can be conservative, simply following the lines of the grip and forend, or elaborate, with the pattern having many curves and lines that cover a great deal of space. Checkering is measured by the number of lines per inch. The finer the lines, the more difficult they are to cut, but the results are beyond beautiful. On the downside, the finer the checkering, the less gripping power it provides. Normal checkering runs about sixteen lines to the inch. When it reaches twenty lines per inch, the tactility begins to diminish. Checkering at thirty-two lines to the inch is spectacular, but its value in providing a

firm grip is about nil. Before deciding on what type of checkering you want, you first have to decide if you want a decorative gun that will seldom if ever be shot, or a functional one that you're going to use.

Checkering patterns vary from simple to complex. Simple patterns follow the lines of the grip and forend. Unless you're willing to spring for extra checkering—a Purdey, Holland & Holland, or other bespoke shotgun will come with excellently executed checkering in the first place—the pattern on most guns will be pretty basic. Elaborate, or even larger, checkering patterns are priced additionally. Winchester offered something like eight stock checkering patterns, and would apply personalized patterns when requested, if possible.

Checkering is an art, done by craftsmen who specialize in it. Some use power checkering tools that allow them to fill in wide areas quickly. Others prefer the traditional handheld rasps. Perhaps one of the greatest feats of

An array of European walnut stocks that have been machined at Beretta's Italian wood facility.

checkering I've ever seen involved Rosa, AyA's top checkerer, whom I met when I visited Spain in 1985. I was the guest of the newly formed DIARM—an attempt to consolidate the entire Spanish gunmaking industry that failed within three years—and we were taken on a tour of the old Aguirre y Aranzabal factory in Eibar. On the top floor of the building, working only under natural light, was Rosa, carefully checkering the butts of special-order AyAs. Using a single-track checkering tool and a V-shaped veiner, she laid out the pattern using a brass template. Then, employing two guidelines she cut by eye, Rosa quickly cut the checkering lines, first in one direction and then in the other, using only her experience and left hand to space the lines precisely. It was perhaps the most dramatic display of checkering I've ever seen. Rosa's demonstration, all the while talking with us through our interpreter Imanol Aranzabal, the nephew of the AyA's founder, made it all nearly surreal. A great checkerer is a real artist. It takes artistic flair and excellent hand-eye coordination, plus a steady hand.

In the normal flow of building a stock, the stock is completely finished, ready for the customer before the checkering is cut. Once the checkering is cut and complete, the wood is treated with a very thin coat of oil, which is quickly brushed out of the checkering so that it does not clog the fine diamonds. Anyone refinishing a stock or repairing a scratch must take care not to clog the checkering.

Ordinary checkering, if executed to a high standard, can be very appealing. It is also important that checkering fit the grade of shotgun. Seeing an elaborate checkering pattern on a base-grade shotgun, say a V-grade Parker or Fox Sterlingworth, should raise a red flag. The chances are that the shotgun has been restocked, since it is often quite reasonable to upgrade checkering when a gun is restocked. There's certainly nothing wrong with a finely executed upgrade, but it's certainly not a

A single-row checkering tool is used in tight corners such as on this forend.

collector. High-grade checkering comes on high-grade guns.

Ever since I was a teenager, I've tried to checker various stocks. The results have been terrible, and my gunsmith friend Greg Wolf usually gives me a baleful look, and says, "Maybe you ought to leave it with me to kinda fix up." He really means, "Sand it off and do it over again." Fine checkering is obvious—poor work even more so.

Like engraving, checkering is a way to enhance a top-notch shotgun. Dollar for dollar, extensive and excellent checkering is far less expensive than engraving, and can really set off a great piece of wood.

A worker at Beretta's Meccanica del Sarca pointing up a stock following laser checkering.

CHAPTER 16

Butts

It is highly important that a shotgun's stock fits the shooter, and the butt plays an important role in this. Shotguns intended for collectors and perhaps never to be shot also need attractive butts. In the first case, how the butt fits the shooter's shoulder is important; in the latter, appearance is everything.

Recoil, especially when shooting heavy loads, can be the downfall of good shooting. It takes only so much recoil, sometimes just one shot, to cause the shooter—consciously or, worse, subconsciously—to cringe whenever the shotgun is discharged. Conscious fear of recoil results in shooters tightening their muscles and even closing their eyes as the shot is fired. Subconscious fear of recoil results in the shooter's greatest foe, the flinch. Flinching occurs when part of the brain says "shoot" and another part says "don't shoot." Shotgunners have suffered from these phenomena for centuries, and have constantly sought ways to soften recoil. We often think that the rubber recoil pad is a child of the mid 20th century, but it's not. Early large-bore rifles and shotguns had recoil pads made of gutta-percha, a resin, and rubber. Names such as Silvers were associated with early recoil pads, and those restoring shotguns from the late 19th and early 20th centuries seek reproductions of Silvers and other pads apropos of that period.

Today, we can choose from three basic styles of pads: reproduction, traditional, and high-tech. Reproductions are normally red rubber pads with smooth sides. Traditional recoil pads for specific shotguns, such as Winchester or Ithaca, are available from Tony Galazan's wonderful catalog (www.connecticutshotgun.com). However, these pads are not really great attenuators of recoil. That job goes to high-tech pads, typically made from Sorbothane or other space-age materials that not only absorb recoil, but do so very efficiently. As the years have passed, these high-performance pads have become more

Shotguns Butts: (1 to 4) Leather-coverered, rubber recoil pads, and checkered wood.

attractive. Their nearly universal drawback is that they are sticky to the touch, and make shouldering a shotgun difficult. The makers of Limbsavers recommend coating their pads with Armor All and allowing them to dry overnight. This provides temporary relief from the sticky surface. One more long-lasting cure is to detach the pad from the gun and allow it to sit in the sun on the dashboard of a car or truck for about two days. Frequent checks will indicate when the surface has sufficiently oxidized and skinned over. Not exactly high-tech, but effective.

Traditional pads combine semi high-tech with a classic appearance. These are easily worked by a stockmaker or gunsmith, and while they don't provide the ultimate recoil attenuation that the high-tech pads do, these soak up plenty of recoil, and really help when applied to a well-fitted stock.

Recoil pads come in a variety of colors. Red was the favorite of the Silvers, and when Frank Pachmayr introduced his pads—by which most others are still judged—he colored them brown and black. Some prefer something close in color to the wooden buttstock, others prefer the contrast provided by black. In recent years, inserting a smooth plastic horseshoe at the top radius at the heel provides an aid to mounting a pad-equipped shotgun.

The ultimate recoil pad is covered in leather. The sex appeal of a leather-covered pad sets off a stock like no other. Covering a pad with leather is no easy feat, however. First the rubber pad must be precisely ground so that it is slightly smaller than the mating wood of the stock. The pad is then coated in glue. Split calf-skin, goatskin, or pigskin is then stretched and coaxed across the pad. No wrinkles or puckers are allowed; covering a pad is a real art.

Of the leathers used to cover pads, pigskin is quite traditional, and many vintage shotguns sport pads so covered. Calfskin and goatskin are softer and more delicate leathers, but have smoother surfaces than pigskin. Leather can be dyed any color of the rainbow, and good taste should govern which color to use. Leather-covered pads are not cheap, running from $250 to $500, depending on who is making them, but to set off a fine stock, look beautiful in itself, and still provide recoil attenuation, a leather-covered pad is hard to beat.

Plebeian buttplates can be made of animal horn, steel, brass, or, most commonly,

Recoil pads come in a variety of colors to suit any taste. These are high-tech pads suited to competition shooting such as trap and skeet.

hard rubber. Recoil pads were traditionally special-order extras at additional cost. Parkers, A. H. Foxes, and Winchester 21s and Model 12s all came with plain, hard rubber buttplates. The ages of some of these shotguns can sometimes be determined by the buttplate styles. Today, Galazan does a brisk business supplying reproduction buttplates for Parkers, Winchesters, and others, and no collectible shotgun ought to show anything else unless the factory records indicate it was shipped with a recoil pad, and that had better be in the original style. Shotguns made in mainland Europe and Great Britain normally had buttplates of horn or imitation horn, which takes on a slightly greenish color with age.

Top-grade shotguns are often finished with hand-checkered butts. There is a sleekness and savoir faire to a shotgun whose stock seems to have no end; it just keeps going like an Impressionist painting. The butts of these are traditionally checkered using very fine line spacing. It is common to bore out the butt of a top-grade shotgun to create the proper balance. Once balance is achieved, fillers carefully matched to the grain of the butt are made and glued in. While it would be simple to cover these with a recoil pad or buttplate, the true craftsman's art is shown when the filler matches the grain and is then checkered so as to be invisible except under a strong loupe.

Further enhancement, as well as strengthening of a checkered butt to prevent the all-too-common breaking off of the toe of the stock, usually consists of engraved heel and toe plates that carefully outline the curves of the stock's heel and toe. Precisely inletted into the difficult-to-work end grain, they can be blued, case-hardened, engraved, or inlaid with gold. The space between the heel and toe plates is checkered. An alternative is to surround the butt fully with a skeleton buttplate that leaves the checkered center but outlines the butt. Frequently found on early American shotguns, skeleton buttplates are beautiful in execution. In a practical sense, skeleton buttplates and heel and toe plates provide protection for the delicate end grain. It is common to see shotguns with checkered butts with chipped toes. The wood is thin and, because the grain runs the length of the stock, breaking a chunk from the toe of a stock is all too easy. These chips can be repaired, but if a gun is to be used, and the character of a checkered butt retained, a skeleton buttplate or heel and toe plates are wonderful solutions.

The butt of a shotgun intended for shooting should definitely be protected. I've luckily not chipped the toe from either of my checkered-butt AyAs, but I'm particularly careful with them. One of the problems with shotguns bearing hard buttplates or checkered butts is that if they're stood on a hard surface, such as a wooden floor, a duck blind, or elsewhere, the chances of the gun slipping and falling are multiplied. Recoil pads tend not to slip as easily.

How you treat your butt is a personal matter. However, from plain to elegant, the wood of the butt of the stock is worth protecting or decorating.

CHAPTER 17

Barrels

The barrel is the oldest component of the modern firearm. Early guns consisted simply of a barrel with or without a wooden handle. They were loaded from the muzzle, then fired by placing a burning wick to a hole in the side to ignite the powder. Early examples of these hand cannons are found in Chinese history. Marco Polo brought gunpowder to Italy and, as a consequence, the Beretta family began making barrels in 1526.

Early shotgun barrels were made using the Damascus or twist process, in which strips of alternating iron and steel were wound together, forming a ribbon that was forged flat, then wound around a mandrel. Once the winding was complete, the barrel tube was welded to form a solid barrel. The interior was then bored and the chamber cut, then the rough tube's exterior was struck or shaped using a progression of half-round files and fine-grit emery paper.

Damascus-style barrels were not in themselves weak, as most assume. Fine, British-made and some American-made barrels, such as those used by Parker Brothers in their top-of-the-line shotguns, are immensely strong, and many will pass modern proof. The problem is that rust and corrosion easily attack the softer iron strips. Used during an age of highly corrosive primers and blackpowder whose residue soaked up moisture, few barrels built before 1950 do not show the effects of corrosive priming. If moisture or corrosive primers enter through a pin-size hole, it is possible for corrosion to honeycomb through a Damascus barrel, creating extremely weak areas. Although some people have conducted empirical tests on these barrels and declared them safe, the only way to be certain that they are safe is to have the gun submitted to proof, which is very expensive—and if the barrels burst, there's no recompense. Unless a Damascus-style barrel is in proof, the

An example of small-gauge, in this case 20-gauge, tubes being inserted into old and potentially unsafe Damascus barrels to make this 1875-vintage hammer Parker a joy to shoot.

best way to shoot these guns is to have a pair of small-gauge tubes—usually 20-gauge in a 12-gauge barrel—made by Briley and shoot it in the smaller gauge. Tubes add little weight, and have the additional feature of interchangeable chokes.

Damascus-style barrels varied in quality, depending on the number of steel and iron strips used to make them. The higher the number, the more elaborate the figure on the exterior surface of the barrel. To emphasize this figure, barrels were etched in an acid solution that darkened the iron, making it contrast with the steel. Once treated, the barrels were varnished for preservation.

Other styles of twist barrels are stub and laminated steel, neither of which is as expensive or as strong as Damascus. Made in essentially the same way, these barrels were used on inexpensive double guns, mainly made in Belgium for export to America and the colonies of Britain, France, and Germany. However, not all laminated steel went into cheap guns. Parker Brothers made guns very early in their existence using laminated-steel barrels.

STEEL BARRELS

Near the end of the 19th century, barrels were increasingly made of steel, or "fluid steel," as it was called in that era. Two methods were used then, and still are: boring and cold hammer forging. Shotgun barrels begin with a tube made of alloy steel that may contain nickel, molybdenum, chromium, or other elements in various percentages according to the wishes of the gun manufacturer. Some early steel barrels were named for the producer of the steel used, such as Bohler, Krupp, Siemens, or Whitworth. These barrels were normally reserved for higher-grade shotguns or for upgrades of lower-priced models. Parker used various names for

A worker in the B.C. Miroku factory in Japan, which manufactures the majority of Browning shotguns, checks a barrel for straightness by looking for irregularities in the shadows running down the inside of the barrel.

the barrel steel associated with the different grades of their guns, including Trojan, Vulcan, Acme, Titanic, Parker Special, and Peerless.

In the most traditional barrel tube manufacturing, a tube of steel is selected and then bored to close to finished specifications with a deep-drilling machine. Once the barrel is drilled, the exterior is then struck or shaped except for final finish polishing. Then the bore is lapped, and the chamber cut. During boring and lapping, material is left in the interior of the barrel in the choke area, awaiting final boring and shaping. Traditional lapping is done with a long bench that carries a cradle onto which the barrel is fixed. The lap is a steel rod with a lead sleeve at one end. This sleeve is coated with oil and abrasive. Then the barrel is moved back and forth by hand so that the lapping is done

Barrels are straightened using a barrel press. The barrel is supported at the ends and the large wheel turned to apply force in the middle, straightening the barrel.

with long, longitudinal strokes. Less expensive barrels are lapped with a rotary hone.

H&H Barrel Lapping

The other barrel-tube manufacturing method uses a short, thick section of steel about 18 inches long that is mounted on a mandrel that mirrors the interior of the barrel to be made in the hammer-forging machine. The tube is then subjected to thousands of strokes by very hard hammers that thin the metal, and in so doing stretch the metal along the mandrel, forming a tube. A faster and less expensive process, hammer forging makes barrels of good quality. In fact, most modern barrels, save those from makers such as Holland & Holland and Purdey, are made using this process. They still must be internally lapped and formed to completion, but the process is much quicker.

After barrels are machined and lapped, they are then straightened by a master barrel straightener. He places the barrel in a specially made vise with a large wheel that applies force on two sides as the barrel rests on a centrally located pad. Looking through the barrel with a light source, the barrel man looks at the shadows cast down the barrel and determines

Chopper-lump barrels machined and ready to be soldered together.

Barrel lapping at
Holland & Holland is by
the traditional method
of mounting the barrels
in a cradle that slides
back and forth as the
lap polishes the bore.

A pair of Holland & Holland chopper-lump barrels that have been regulated, wired, fluxed with solder added at strategic points, then heated in an even melting the solder, permanently joining the two tubes.

whether it is straight or not. If not, he rotates and positions the barrel so he can flex it a bit, gradually making it straight. I say gradually, but an experienced barrel straightener can true up a barrel in a few seconds.

Once the barrel tubes are formed straight and true, they must be joined or otherwise made ready to form part of a shotgun. In the case of repeater barrels, this entails threading the rear of the barrel to accept the barrel extension. Rib posts are soldered on, and the means of holding the barrel to the magazine is also attached by welding.

Double guns are more challenging. Traditional side-by-side barrels are made with a "chopper lump," which is a block of metal at the breech end that is forged integral with the barrel tube. When the two barrels are joined together, this lump, named for its resemblance to a meat cleaver or chopping device, is welded or silver-soldered to the mating lump of the other tube, solidly joining the barrels at the breech. The Winchester Model 21 is unique in that its chopper lumps are machined with male and female dovetails that are pinned together.

Double-gun barrels, either side-by-sides or over-and-unders, are held together by means of top and bottom or side ribs. Exceptions include the Remington 32 and 3200, and Krieghoff over-and-unders, which are joined at the breech and then, absent side ribs, joined at the muzzles by a hanger system that allows the two barrels to expand and contract singly, allowing less movement of the point of impact. This is particularly important to clay-target shooters, whose guns become very hot during extended shooting. Otherwise, double-gun barrels are joined by ribs that are silver-soldered in place.

At one time—and this still applies to bespoke shotguns—the barrels were joined at the breech via the chopper lumps, with wedges placed between the barrels and wired in place. The gun was then shot "in the white" and the wedges adjusted until both barrels superimposed their patterns. Chokes were regulated once the barrels were completed. Once the barrel man was satisfied with the pattern place-

Once fluxed, the ribs are laid on the barrels along with a strip of silver solder, then they are wired and clamped together, and sent through an oven that evenly raises the heat, melting the solder.

ment at the range, the wedges were soldered in place and the ribs were placed and soldered, normally with soft lead solder. That's why these and most double guns cannot be hot blued, because the heated bluing salt solution would melt the solder.

Modern production guns are assembled with jigs that position the tubes while the ribs are laid and wired in place. One aspect of barrel assembly endemic to the modern gun trade is the monobloc. This is the breech end of the barrels that contains the lump section, into which are machined the recesses that accept the locking device, the extractors, and the cuts that enable the barrels to pivot. Holes that accommodate the machined ends of the barrel tubes are then bored into this monobloc. It's an efficient production method, and very strong.

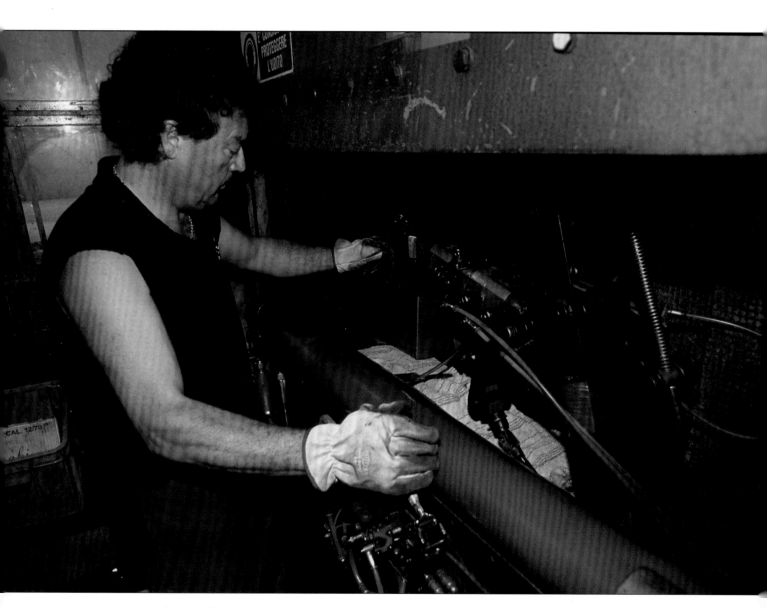

A Brescia, Italy, proof-house worker locking a shotgun in a cradle prior to proof testing. When ready, a safety cover is closed and the proof load is fired using compressed air.

I might add that when barrels are "sleeved" because of the tubes being damaged, or to revive a Damascus-barreled gun, the existing breech of the gun is machined to make a monobloc, and the new barrel tubes assembled as with a new gun. Once the side and ventilated ribs are wired in place, it's time for the soldering.

Using the monobloc at the breech end, the tubes are then cleaned and degreased—solder will not stick to dirty or greasy surfaces—and are then coated with flux, which prevents oxidation and allows solder to flow. The Miroku factory in Japan uses a hydraulic ram to seat the tubes in the monobloc, ensuring that they bottom out and are true within the machined breech. The ribs and barrel surfaces are also coated with flux—in the case of silver solder, a solution of borax and water—and then the barrels are held tightly together with wire to prevent warping when heated. The barrels are then heated red hot, either with a handheld torch or in an oven that heats the metal uniformly to melt the solder. Solder is wonderful stuff, because when the parts are clean and carefully fluxed, the solder flows just where you want it.

Following soldering, the barrels are cleaned and polished. Production guns are carefully soldered so that there is little excess to be removed. Soft or lead solder can be scraped off, but silver solder is very hard and difficult to remove from the exterior. The assembled barrels are now checked again for true, to make sure one isn't misassembled.

Sometimes when barrels are soldered, bits of solder will drop off into the void between the tubes. Age also allows these little globs of solder, called skeleton by the gun trade, to appear and rattle about. In order to remove them a small hole or holes are bored into the ribs in areas covered by the forend so that they can be shaken out.

Exterior polishing is done on a wheel in production facilities, but on bespoke shotguns it is done by hand with increasingly finer grits of emery paper. The polishing of a bespoke gun is simply amazing. Once polished, the barrels are blued, or "blackened," as the British prefer to say. For the most part, double-gun barrels must be rust blued, whereby they are coated with an acid solution and hung in a cabinet that has high humidity. This causes them to acquire a coating of red rust within just a few hours. The barrels are then polished off with a wire brush, and the process is repeated until the proper depth of blue is acquired. Rust bluing is much more expensive and time-consuming than hot bluing. Hot-blued barrels are suspended in a solution of hot salts that impart a blue color to the metal, the depth and color of which are determined by the composition of the steel and the bluing formula used. They are then rinsed in clear water and given an oil bath to kill any residual acid. Buffing with a soft cloth finishes the job.

Once finished, the barrels are sent for proofing. It is common practice in Britain and Europe to proof only the barrels, then return the completed shotgun for definitive proofing when fully finished. The reason is that should a barrel fail—and today that's a very rare occurrence—time has not been wasted joining it to an action, finishing, etc.

Good-quality barrels will last for generations, provided they are cared for. Anytime a dent occurs—shotgun barrels are quite thin and can be easily dented—the dent must be raised by a competent gunsmith. Leaving it would cause that part of the barrel to be constantly abraded and thinned whenever the gun is shot. I have a Henry Atkin (from Purdey's) Best, London-made sidelock produced in 1895. It has the original, German-made Siemens steel barrels, which are every bit as good as the day they were struck up and finished in Atkin's shop. With only a bit of care, they will last for another century.

CHAPTER 18

Finishing the Metal

The wood on a shotgun is only a start. The part that does the actual shooting, the metal, must also be finished. In the early days of gunmaking, back in the 1700s, it was found that if the exterior metal surfaces were allowed to oxidize uniformly (in other words, to rust) under controlled conditions, the metal surface was to a large extent protected from further oxidation. Various processes are used, but chemical rusting of the surface that results in a uniformly blued exterior is the most traditional and universally used method on high-grade shotguns.

In recent years, the use of stainless steel on utility shotguns for boaters and waterfowl hunters has become more and more common. However, unless the gun is covered with some kind of camouflage, it's more difficult to hide than a more traditional blued shotgun. The addition of a permanent camouflaged finish to special-purpose shotguns is a process wherein the metal of the gun is lightly etched, and the stock and forend, normally made of synthetic or plastic, are also lightly roughened to hold the finish. The entire gun is then lowered into a tank, upon which is floated a membrane holding the camouflage material, which bonds to the metal and stocks like an impervious skin. Camouflaged and with the metal surfaces protected from the weather—the interior still requires maintenance—these shotguns are primary tools for the rough-and-tumble waterfowl and turkey hunter, but, like bolt-action shotguns, hardly guns of glory.

Some shotguns are made with aluminum receivers or actions. These lend themselves to anodizing and etching. Although some shotguns with aluminum actions might be of interest to collectors, in the main they're not. One exception was the Browning Twelvette Double Automatic shotgun, whose action was made from duralumin, an aluminum aircraft alloy. Anodized in royal and light blue, gray, maroon, light brown, several shades of green,

A worker at the Connecticut Shotgun Manufacturing company is ready to dip a pair of barrels into a hot bluing solution. Because these barrels are joined using silver solder that melts at a high temperature, they can be hot blued.

gold, and jet and dragon black, these colorful shotguns remain lasting memories from my youth. Although some recent semiauto shotguns have aluminum actions and receivers, they stick pretty much to silver, blue, and black.

When Damascus, twist, and laminated steel barrels were in vogue (from the 1500s to their eventual phasing out in the early 20th century), they were browned by a rust process very much like rust bluing, and a properly cared-for shotgun of this era will display browned barrels. Restored specimens with Damascus barrels should also be browned. At

one time, Damascus barrels were polished and blued to disguise them, in a fraudulent and unscrupulous effort to disguise the barrels and make them appear to be fluid steel and sell what were then otherwise undesirable shotguns.

The finish on fine guns needs to be proper, as must the shape of the stock and other aspects of the gun. A double gun ought to exhibit a slightly softer polish than a repeater. A high-gloss finish on a fine double needs explanation. If the gun was ordered with an exceptionally high-gloss finish, that's okay. More likely, though, it was refinished without knowledge of the gun's original appearance. Restoring a fine gun requires that the individual doing the work be highly aware of how the original appeared, and then strive to make the restoration appear the same. Doug Turnbull of Bloomfield, New York, specializes in restoration, and his efforts, albeit expensive, reward the customer with a beautiful authentic job, and in terms of case hardening, even better than the original. The barrels of fine doubles are normally rust blued, which results in a softer appearance than a high-gloss blue job.

CASE HARDENING

When truly case-hardened, the parts—normally the action and forend iron—are completely finished and polished. Then the parts are packed in an open-top iron box with a mixture of bone or bone meal, charcoal, and possibly some bits of leather and other mate-

Two contrasting finishes: top steel left in the white and bottom case-hardened.

This Beretta workman is doing a final fit using a fine flat file with emery cloth that allows him to cut precisely and follow the contours of the action.

rials that the person doing the case hardening has found will deliver the proper degree of hardness and color. Every master case hardener has his own formula for what provides both hardness to the exterior of the metal and the attendant beautiful colors, ranging from deep blues to browns and grays. Once packed with the bone-and-charcoal mixture, the box is placed in an oven, and the temperature raised to a specified level, at which the box and its contents are heated red hot, then held there for a specific period of time. Next, the box and its contents are removed from the oven and immediately quenched in water, oil, or a mixture of both.

It is interesting that even today, at a time when many gunmaking procedures have gone high-tech, some gunmakers still use the same hardening procedures that have been used for centuries, employing crude ovens without thermostats or other controls, and relying on the expertise of the man doing the hardening to judge the heat and when to quench it—often in a shop without heat or air conditioning. For many, case hardening remains more an art than a science. For those who are successful at it, the specific methods are also closely guarded secrets.

What case hardening does is to harden the very thin top layer of metal, while the inner, and much heavier, core of steel remains flexible. The inner metal core's flexibility takes the recoil and the flexing of the action under the stresses of firing, while the hard outer surface resists abrasion and protects the action. One drawback is that, because the surface is so hard, a blow from another hard object can cause the case hardening to chip, and most older shotguns with case-hardened actions show this wear. Assuming that the metal of the action is of the proper temper and elasticity, chipping of the case-hardened action is only cosmetic.

HARD FITTING

When a firearm's action is properly case-hardened—not just colored by boiling it in a vat of cyanide, which often passes for case hardening, but is not—the parts warp. Because the parts have been previously finished and fitted, the warping of the action presents a problem. Not only are the individual parts heat-treated to the proper degree, the action is finished. At this point, the services of a skilled gun finisher, called the hard fitter, are needed. If the fitter is lucky, the action has warped only slightly. If not, he needs to file, bend, and refit the various parts so that everything works properly. Hard fitters are among the most highly skilled and experienced workers at any gunmaking firm, and when an action really goes out of whack during hardening, they earn their money. Once hardened and completely fitted, the action is then coated with a very hard varnish to protect it. This varnish can be purchased from Brownells or Galazan; when the original inevitably chips, it can be retouched.

BLACKENING OR BLUING

Almost without exception, the barrels and furniture, or component parts such as the triggers and trigger guard, are blackened or blued. There are several different processes that can be used to blacken or blue these parts. The primary difficulty is that each method produces a different appearance. Some are reasonably quick, others take longer, and none is particularly easy.

The key to good bluing is the polishing. A poor polishing job, especially on a refinished shotgun, sticks out like a sore thumb. One

Here a worker at the Connecticut Shotgun Manufacturing company is polishing a pair of barrels by the traditional method of longitudinal strokes with a file or emery paper folded over a file.

particularly telling place is the engraving and stamping. If polishing is not carefully done, the stamping on the barrels and action can lose its sharp edges. Poor polishing also does not preserve the sharp edges left by the original manufacturers' polishers. Of course, the current trend is toward bead-blasted finished metal, in which case polishing is rendered

moot. Proper polishing by hand with ultra-fine-grit paper over a flat file takes time, and the majority of the cost of a really good bluing job is in the polishing.

Bluing is actually the oxidation, or rusting, of the gun parts. By prerusting and then polishing off the red portion of the rust, gunmakers ensure that the metal is better able to resist rusting. There are three basic bluing types: charcoal or nitre, hot, and rust. Charcoal or nitre bluing occurs when the part is heated to a certain temperature, often gauged by the color of the part by a skilled workman, then allowed to cool. Using this type of bluing in a production setting requires a large oven whose temperature can be tightly regulated. This kind of bluing used to be used on Winchester Model 21 actions. If one of them appears to be purple rather than blue, that indicates that the heat-and-time combination was not precise. Charcoal or nitre bluing is frequently used today to blue trigger guards, and especially screws or pins.

The most frequently used method of bluing is by hot salts. In this method, and in fact in every method of bluing, the parts are carefully cleaned and degreased. Then, with the bluing solution at its proper temperature, the parts are immersed and allowed to remain for a specific period of time. When removed, the parts are washed to cleanse them completely of the bluing salts solution, then immersed in a special oil that completely stops the action of the bluing salts and prevents rust. Virtually all repeaters are hot-blued.

Prior to the universal use of hot bluing, rust bluing was the primary method. Again, the parts are carefully polished, then completely degreased. After that, the parts are swabbed with a solution of sulfuric acid and water, which causes them to rust. Once coated, the parts are hung in a cabinet that's set to maintain a high level of humidity. Soon the parts exhibit a nice coat of red rust. When the oxidation process is fairly complete, the parts are removed and the rust is polished off with a wire brush or wheel. The process is repeated until the desired depth of blue is achieved. Once the final rust-and-polish cycle is complete, the parts are carefully washed in fresh running water and then treated with oil to prevent further oxidation.

Rust bluing is the most labor-intensive method, and therefore the most costly. However, its use is absolutely necessary with double-gun barrels that are assembled using solder that melts at a relatively low temperature. Many is the inexperienced gunsmith who has dunked a customer's barrels into his hot-bluing tank, only to find them in pieces, necessitating their reassembly, and often reregulation to point of impact. Such gunsmiths should be avoided like the plague, as those who are at the top of their trade would know not to hot-blue double-gun barrels, and rust-blue them instead. The truly

conscientious gunsmith will even rust-blue the action so that everything matches.

Bluing protects the exterior of the metal, but it is still susceptible to rusting. When the gun is exposed to rain, it should be dried and coated with a water-displacing oil such as WD-40. However, do not use WD-40 on the mechanism, as the oil contains a wax that can mix with the dirt and carbon prevalent in shotgun actions, eventually freezing the action. If the gun is exposed to brackish or salt water, it must be thoroughly flushed with fresh water. Really pour it on, and keep at it until every vestige of salt water is flushed away, then continue with drying and applying oil.

Fingerprints are also enemies of fine guns. My fingers do not secrete much acid, but other people's hands carry so much acidic perspiration that they can rust a shotgun in minutes. Every time a fine gun is handled, it should be carefully wiped down with a cloth that's lightly moistened with a preservative, to ensure that all fingerprints are completely removed.

Bluing isn't as impervious as the modern dipped finishes, Parkerizing, or even a matte-blued finish that holds oil very well, but nothing else belongs on a high-grade gun than a well-done blue finish, contrasting, if appropriate, with a beautiful case-hardened action and forend iron.

Engraving

The consensus is that wood is the prime draw, but engraving is the frosting. Engraving can be gauche, erotic, pornographic, subtle, understated, overstated, beautiful, crude, or something else—possible modifiers are endless. For my tastes, almost nothing is more beautiful than the understated, tight scroll found on a Purdey or other British-made shotgun. But of equal beauty to me is the Italian bulino or banknote engraving, which can have an almost photographic quality.

Many who are planning to shoot a high-grade shotgun rather than display it will probably buy it with the basic engraving that comes with the base price of the gun. However, just as many gun owners prefer to have their guns decorated, even though this may mean an additional, even long, waiting period. Some of the great shotgun manufacturers actually reserve time slots with top-notch engravers, as someone inevitably will order a

gun and ask for the services of that particular engraver.

Engraving should not be undertaken lightly. Rumor has it that there is presently an extremely high-grade shotgun in Britain or continental Europe that was allegedly ordered by an Arab sheik or prince. The engraving on the gun is so pornographic that the sheik, upon seeing the gun, backed out of the deal. Apparently no one else is willing to buy it, even at a greatly reduced price, simply because the engraving is so extreme.

Likewise, no aspect of a firearm so closely follows the adage that "You get what you pay for." Examples of engraving that should never have been done are readily found on shotguns that were worked on, inexpensively, in Asia. During the Vietnam War, servicemen and women stationed in Vietnam, on Okinawa, and elsewhere in the Far East found engravers willing to decorate their shotguns, typically

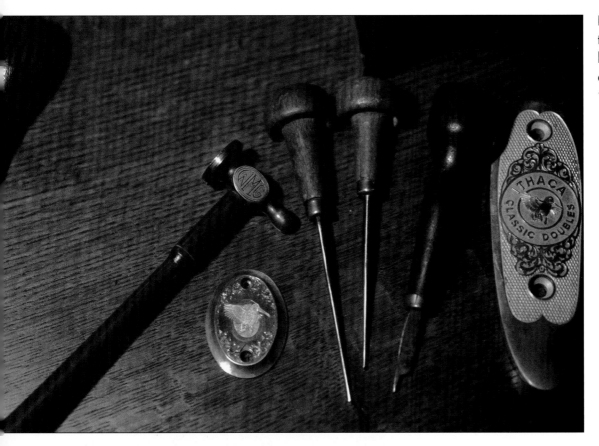

Engraving tools that were used by legendary Ithaca engraver William "Bill" McGraw.

The engraver's chisel begins an outline on a trigger guard, beginning a work of art on a fine shotgun.

Jack Jones engraves a trigger guard by cutting the metal using a very sharp chisel and a small hammer.

repeaters, for very little money. Some of these shotguns had silver and gold inlays; these are easy to spot, since most of the metal has fallen out.

Another problem with engraving occurs when someone applies a style that is foreign or completely out of place for the gun. In chapter 20 we'll look at the different styles of engraving, but in general, heavy, deep-relief engraving seems awkward on slim British or American doubles. Likewise, tight scrollwork common on fine British guns looks anemic on Germanic-style shotguns. Italian bulino seems at home on just about anything, and that's perhaps the exception. American engravers seem to have a good handle on blending deep relief with lighter engraving on the same gun.

Engraving can be absolutely exquisite, and when it is, it sets off a shotgun like nothing else, with the wood and engraving working together in harmony. If the wood and engraving don't complement each other—as on most of the Asian-engraved war guns—the firearm is simply an oddity with no special value. Also, engraving and wood are all a matter of personal taste, and what appeals to me may not to you. Perhaps that's why we have unusual mixes of engraving styles, and so long as the execution is good and it fits the gun to which it's applied, none can really be called wrong.

CHAPTER 20

Executing Engraving

There are three styles of engraving: English-style scroll, Germanic deep relief, and Italian bulino. The first two styles are sometimes blended, which makes their individual attributes blur. Bulino remains clearly itself. Each style is also executed in its own, special manner.

In the traditional method of applying scroll and deep-relief engraving, an artist taps a very sharp graver with a small hammer. Hundreds of light taps make the hardened graver cut into the metal. It takes great practice to be able to focus solely on the tip of the graver, while at the same time accurately tapping the hammer onto the back of the graver dozens of times a minute. A modern method of applying engraving uses a pneumatic hammer, which allows the engraver to hold the graver in his hand and control the "hammer" by means of a foot switch. There is no discernible difference between engraving done by the traditional hammer and graver, and by the pneumatic method. The results are solely due to the artist's abilities and style.

All engravers are talented artists, in the sense of being able to draw or paint. Years ago, as I stood in wonder and envy as a fellow college student sketched a bird on display in the biology wing of my alma mater, he said simply: "Drawing is easy. You just draw what you see." It was easy for him, but it sure wasn't for me. Engravers must be able to draw what they see, and often in a scale far reduced from the original. In the summer of 2004, I was treated to a tour of the Beretta factories in Gardone Val Trompia, Italy. Divided into two facilities, Beretta Uno is by far the smaller of the two, but in terms of interest to a fine-gun guy, it's larger than life. On the top floor on the south side of Beretta Uno, where sunlight floods the room, is the Beretta engraving salon. All their top-of-the-line guns are hand-engraved here (production guns are laser- or roll-engraved, or etched).

A Beretta sidelock over-and-under with magnificent engraving and gold inlays of different colored gold and ceramics that is stocked with the highest-grade wood; a glorious modern shotgun.

Here, too, is where Beretta's apprentice engraver program is run under the watchful eye of Mr. Giulio Timpini, Beretta's master engraver. One sees teenagers training for jobs in the gunmaking trade throughout the plants, but this is where the budding artists are trained.

"We are interested in training engravers, even if they don't remain with Beretta," Mr. Timpini told me. "We must ensure that the craft survives."

At benches along the walls, where big windows flood the room with light, apprentice, journeyman, and master engravers work shoulder to shoulder, some practicing on plain billets of gun steel while others apply engraving to finished firearms. Some are cutting stock

Giulio Timpini, Beretta's master engraver, who although officially retired, teaches apprentices enrolled in Beretta's training program.

Beretta's engraving salon in Gardone Val Trompia, Italy.

designs, while others are reproducing a beloved dog or other scene onto a shotgun, rifle, or pistol.

Beretta, like other firearms manufacturers, will engrave a firearm in any of several styles, but perhaps the most striking, and one that's solely Italian, is bulino.

With bulino, the artist uses only a handheld graver and cuts very small bits of metal with each stroke. The engraving is nearly photographic, and is sometimes called banknote engraving because of its likeness to that found on the plates used to print currency. In fact, if you were to ink a fine bulino engraving, you could produce a print that would look very much like a bill. This style of engraving lends itself to realism and, because of it, you'll find endless examples on fine guns, running the gamut from automobiles to game animals to the exotic and erotic. Fabbri shotguns are typically engraved in bulino.

Inlaying fine metals such as gold, silver, and platinum is also part of the engraver's art. To achieve this, the artist has to follow an outline and cut deeply into the gun's metal. Once the outline is achieved, the sides are carefully undercut to provide the means to hold the inlay securely. It is not uncommon for inlays

154

to pop out. Sometimes it's due to the quality of the work, but at other times it's attributable to heavy-recoil loads that jar and flex the action to the point that inlays will come loose.

Once the edges are undercut, fine gold, silver, or platinum wire is beaten into the prepared opening. The wire strands are laid side by side and hammered into a solid piece, and the inlay is either engraved to match the surrounding engraved steel or left as a stand-alone piece of art.

FAUX ENGRAVING AND INLAYS

New technology has vastly changed the appearance of lower-priced shotguns, as fine-appearing engraving can now be achieved with lasers or CNC machines that do the job in a matter of seconds. Recently, some firearms companies have begun providing higher-level engraving on some guns by special order. Some is done by hand, some is done by CNC or programmed machines. Some inlays or faux inlays are also done with a combination of mechanical and chemical reproduction.

Engraving adds the final touch to a fine shotgun. Engraving applied to fine shotguns is always commensurate with the overall quality of the gun. Poorly executed engraving stands out like a sore thumb, and is normally not done on a fine shotgun (but sometimes it is by a poorly guided owner). Remember the jumping, startled pheasant on the trigger plate

One of Beretta's engravers using the traditional hammer and chisel to cut away the metal.

of an otherwise nice British-made shotgun? In England, pheasants are walked up with dogs, just as we do here in America, but you can bet that engraving done on even a moderately priced British gun will depict a pheasant in flight, probably a driven bird in full glide, high over the guns. Just as fine-grained and finely finished wood are part of a fine gun, the engraving, even if done to an individual's tastes, should match and complement the overall gun. Too, just as wood and metal should flow together, so should engraving flow. Certainly, there are those who enjoy eccentric guns, wood, and engraving, but those guns should be all of one mind, and overall reflect the eccentricities of the owner. Owners of such guns need to realize that, in the resale market, barring an equally eccentric buyer, such guns bring less money, or in some cases are not even saleable, as evidenced by the sheik's pornographically engraved gun, which remains unsold to this day.

Engraving and wood are the frosting on the cake. Shotguns finished in deep blue, with no engraving, are called "funeral guns" in the gun trade. Although funeral guns can be beautiful, a shotgun that features understated, dark, oil-finished wood complemented with conservative and traditional tight scroll is perhaps the ultimate for the traditionalist. More flamboyant buyers will enjoy precious-metal inlays and deep, Germanic-style engraving, or beautiful bulino depicting a favorite scene. Regardless, engraving does nothing in terms of how a shotgun shoots. If one is buying a shotgun solely for its potential investment value, engraving and wood are of the highest priority. If you're planning to hunt and shoot with a particular shotgun, handling and other concerns take the driver's seat. You can have both, and never lose sight of the fact that beauty is in the eye of the beholder. It's your gun, and as the burger joint says, "Have it your way."

CHAPTER 21

The Bespoke Shotgun

I doubt there are many devoted shotgunners who do not dream about owning a bespoke shotgun, not one made for someone else and eventually sold secondhand, but an honest-to-God gun made just for them. Essentially, there are two avenues for getting a bespoke gun. One is to order it from a custom maker, and have the gun made specifically for you. Such a gun will come at a very high price and with a long waiting period. The other is to locate a manufacturer who offers catalogued guns, but with customizing options—including engraving patterns, upgraded wood, and a stock fitted and made to the customer's dimensions. Served up at a considerably lower price and with waiting periods measured in months instead of years, these guns can be excellent.

The true bespoke shotgun often takes years to finish. Once the buyer has selected the wood, engraving pattern, choking, and so on, the manufacturing begins. Current techniques make use of electric discharge erosion and computer numeric control (CNC) equipment to remove large quantities of metal, but, after that, everything else is hand-finished. Although the making of the gun is often accomplished in a year or two, in some cases true bespoke shotguns can take much longer, simply because top engravers have long waiting lists. In some cases, buyers have been known to die before their shotgun is delivered. In such cases, the gunmaking is often frozen until a new buyer is found; then the gun is finished for him, often in a year or so.

Let me tell you tales of two guns. One is about a new Ithaca from Ithaca Classic Doubles, which regrettably went bankrupt in 2003; the other is about a Perazzi sporting-clays gun.

In early 2003, I visited the Ithaca Classic Doubles factory in Victor, New York. While there, I was so impressed with the quality and affordability of their guns that I ordered a 20-gauge. Andrew McFarlane, their final or hard fitter, then checked the fit dimensions, although I told him not to cut the stock until I sent him firm dimensions from a shooting fitting. (Gun fitting by means other than actually shooting at a pattern plate borders on fraudulent.) Other aspects of the gun were settled on before I left Victor. I chose 30-inch barrels, simply because longer barrels swing better, and look fine even on a slim, proper 20-gauge action. I ordered double triggers and specified that the choking be .010 for the right barrel and .015 in the left—improved cylinder and light modified, just right for all-around use. I also ordered American black walnut for the stock and forend. Although Ithaca had a wood collection of beautiful Turkish walnut, Ithaca is an American gun, a modern version of the classic Ithaca NID, and an American shotgun ought to be stocked with American black walnut. I further ordered a slim beavertail forend. I planned to baptize this shotgun on an Argentina dove shoot, and felt the beavertail would afford some degree of additional protection from the hot barrels. I loathe extra-heavy beavertail forends that look like the hull of a battleship attached to the barrels. Shown an example, I was happy with this configura-

Cathy Williams being fitted by Silvio Zavaglio in the gun room of the Beretta Gallery in Milan, Italy. Many European gunmakers rely on in-store fitting, although British and many American stock fitters feel fitting can only be done by shooting at a pattern plate.

tion. The one item I left to Ithaca's owner Steve Lamboy's discretion was the engraving. I've never been a big engraving nut, so I asked that he provide something nice and unique. I had spent a morning with Ithaca's master engraver Jack Jones, and I knew that he would provide anything I liked, and he did. In terms of finish, I asked that the action be case-hardened, which was beautifully done by the incomparable Doug Turnbull, whose shop was about 20 minutes from the Ithaca facility. Turnbull specializes in restoration of classic firearms, and his case-hardening process is a carefully guarded secret. When I was there, I asked to take a photo of him quenching a basket of parts, and was politely but firmly rebuffed with the statement, "No one goes beyond that door." Only Turnbull and a couple of trusted workers know the formula, and they're not talking.

As seems my luck, following my ordering the shotgun, Ithaca Classic Doubles fell on hard times. Steve Lamboy told me that he simply miscalculated the amount of money it took to establish a gunmaking shop in this country. With my heart in my mouth, and wondering if I'd ever see my gun, or at least the hefty deposit I'd put down, I waited until Lamboy called. He told me that a few guns, including mine, were sufficiently completed. Mine was jointed and choke bored, and the stock finished to dimensions. It would be finished by Gunther Frommer, Lamboy's first hard fitter. Frommer indeed finished the metalwork, and sent the engraving to Jack Jones, the action to Doug Turnbull, and the stock and forend to master checkerer Ron Buck, also one of Lamboy's

workers. Once everything was done, I made my final payment, and took delivery of a shotgun made completely for me. It shoots exactly where I look and, with its case-hardened action and engraving just for me, is a thing of beauty that will be a joy forever.

Perazzi is about as well-known a name in clay-target circles as any. They continually make small changes to their line, but the basic Perazzi is a hard-shooting, durable shotgun that can be custom ordered. Perazzi makes bespoke shotguns on a regular basis, but I decided to take a shorter route, buying an existing model and specifying changes that they could accommodate, keeping time from initial order and deposit to delivery to about three months.

To buy a new Perazzi, I contacted Giacomo Arrighini, who runs Giacomo Sporting (6234 Stokes-Lee Rd., Lee Center, NY 13367; (315) 336-1356) in upstate New York. Although Perazzi's U.S. importer is in California, Arrighini is Italian by birth and is in constant contact with Daniel Perazzi, the firm's president. He speaks the language and knows the proper conversions from English to metric dimensions. When you can take advantage of that kind of liaison with the manufacturer, you're ahead of the game.

Once I told Arrighini of my stock dimensions, he told me he would order me a 12-gauge MX8 made to my specifications, and proceeded to outline what options I could have. He suggested some, and I had my own ideas. Arrighini knew what was possible and what was not, and between the two of us, we were able to order exactly the gun I wanted.

I chose a slightly different, slimmer forend than normal, a tapered rib, ventilated side ribs that end just inside the forend to allow better cooling, screw-in choking in both barrels, and a leather-covered pad. This is essentially the second type of bespoke shotgun: one that's in regular production yet made up to the buyer's specifications. I even specified that the patterns be 60 percent above the point of aim and 40 percent below.

Upon receiving the gun, I sent it to Briley Manufacturing company (1230 Lumpkin Road, Houston, TX 77043; phone: 800-331-5718), who installed a set of their lightest Ultra-Lite small-gauge tubes in 20- and 28-gauge and .410 bore. In addition, Briley provided a set of their new titanium choke tubes, which are far lighter than the steel tubes supplied by Perazzi. Because they are significantly lighter, the gun seems more alive in my hands. The completed gun is nothing short of a joy to shoot.

There are many things to consider, and ordering a bespoke shotgun should be undertaken with care, the process not rushed. When considering ordering a bespoke shotgun made in the United States by Tony Galazan or ordered through Orvis, Fieldsport, or others, or from Great Britain, language isn't a problem. If the gun of your dreams is coming from Italy or Spain, it is a good idea to use the services of

David Cruz (l.) discusses a Holland & Holland shotgun with Ramon Pascual in the New York gun room.

an American agent. Yes, the agent will receive a commission and up the price a bit, but a reputable agent or dealer will know the maker, and have someone, perhaps an intermediary, who speaks the language and can head off what could be a costly misunderstanding. If, however, you are planning a visit to the maker, let them know that you are coming and when you plan to arrive, and be sure that you and they are in agreement on dates and times. For the most part, gunmakers welcome visiting sportsmen and are happy to spend time with them planning a bespoke shotgun. Obtain a copy of the gunmaker's catalog in advance, read it carefully, and be prepared with a list of exactly what you want. Rare will be the gunmaker who will not ask what purpose the gun is intended for, and most will be prepared to verify your measurements, or, lacking them, do a fitting. However, many are content to do a gunroom fitting, without the benefit of actually shooting. Others may have access to a nearby range where they or one of the range's instructors will do the fitting. Beyond the specifics of the gun, the maker will want to know if you want it cased, and what kind of case to provide. Go to the factory if you wish; just be as well prepared as you can. If you can't travel there, order your gun through

The Italian National Proof House in Gardone Val Trompia, Italy. Unlike the United States, where manufacturers are responsible for the proofing of their firearms, in the remainder of the world proof houses are the responsibility of the government or gun trade associations that enforce the national proof laws.

one of their U.S. importers. It will save time and money.

When a gun is ordered, it is normal to pay a deposit of 25 to 50 percent of the *estimated* cost. While most makers and U.S. agents are up front and provide the best estimate of the price they can, currency fluctuations, cost of materials, choice of outside engravers, and other variables can change the final bottom line. In 2004, for example, the U.S. dollar slid against the euro, and that affected the price of shotguns made in Italy, Germany, and Spain. Prices quoted are on delivery, and as hard as gunmakers and reputable agents try to provide firm finished prices, be aware that they can vary.

Once the buyer is committed, a bespoke shotgun moves through several stages. The first is the rough machining of the metal, the selection of the barrel tubes (with special attention given to the finished weight), and selection of the bits and pieces, such as the trigger guard, that complete the parts list. These parts are initially rough finished, then fitted to nearly finished fit. Once the action is filed and the barrels joined, it is sent for provisional proof. Here the barrels and action are subjected to an approximately 50 percent overload. Provisional proofing allows the maker to be sure that, in its rough state, the gun is warranted safe, and that it will pass final proof. It's a simple matter of time and money. Why bring a gun to final finish, only to discover a flaw that renders the gun useless or in need of substantial rework before it can be sold? Once through prelimi-

nary proofing, the metal is polished and passed to the stocker.

Once the metalwork is nearly finished, the stocker takes over, carefully crafting the buttstock to near the final dimensions. In the top gun factories, the stockers also do the final filing of the action, and fit the individual parts into the action, file the forend iron, and finish

Stock blanks selected by customers with their specifications waiting heading up and finishing in the Beretta's Italian custom shop.

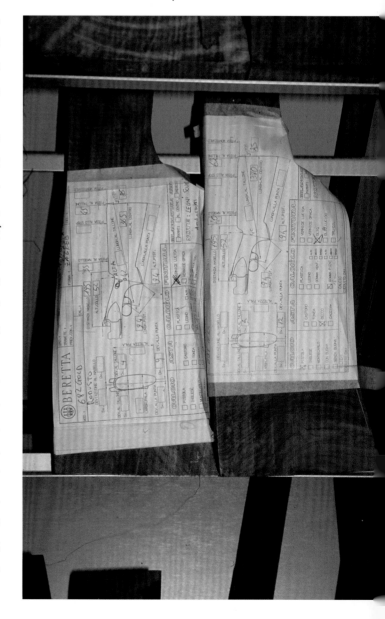

A common extra is an inletted oval engraved with the owner's initials on the buttstock of a fine shotgun.

the stock and forend while the metal is sent to the engraver. The stock of a London Best is traditionally oil-finished with a mixture of linseed oil, Japan dryers, and alkanet root, which gives the oil a reddish color. Each stockmaker has his own formula, although in recent years some have turned to Birchwood Casey's Tru-Oil, which is a combination of linseed oil and Japan dryers. Regardless of the formula, multiple coats of oil are rubbed on in very, very thin coats and each allowed to dry before the next coat is applied. Light sanding with very fine sandpaper is done to ensure that the grain is fully filled and sealed. Twenty or more coats of finish, applied over a period of weeks and even months, are required to complete the finishing of the wood. Finally, just prior

to final assembly, the grip and forend are checkered.

While the stock is being finished, the metal is at the engraver, who is executing the classic patterns used by the gunmaker or what is specified by the customer. Although the actual manufacturing takes a great deal of time, engraving often takes even longer. The great engravers are booked years in advance, and the gun must wait its turn.

Once engraved, the metal is case-hardened and/or blued, and then finally fitted, assembled, and submitted for final proof. At this point, no further work can be done to the barrels. There are very narrow parameters within which a pair of barrels can be altered from the original proof dimensions, so once they are chambered, choked, and polished, the gun is in final form. While this covers just the basics, it is not difficult to understand why a bespoke shotgun takes the months or even years to complete.

It's not uncommon for an order to be canceled while a shotgun is being worked on. This happens for any number of reasons—the customer or gunmaker passes away, someone runs into financial difficulty, or something else. The list of reasons is endless. This, of course, can be a windfall for someone seeking a bespoke shotgun. Often, guns will be block-stocked, with the stock headed up and attached to the action, but the rest remaining just as the blank came from the kiln. A great deal of variation can still be done in the final fitting of such a gun; it's semifinished, and can be delivered in a shorter period of time, and frequently at a better price.

There are several problems with bespoke guns. Once, while I was visiting the Holland & Holland gun room at 57th and Madison Avenue in New York City, a thirty-something Texan was looking hard at two shotguns that had belonged to an acquaintance of mine. He

Bending a stock by wrapping the stock's wrist in cotton saturated with hot oil. Once the heat softens the wood the bending jig is tightened to move the stock in its new direction. Others who bend stocks use heat lamps or other methods to make the wood pliable.

was tall and lanky, with long arms. The shotguns he was contemplating buying, a Purdey and a Holland & Holland, had once belonged to Colonel John (Jack) Pershing, the grandson of the famous general of the same name. Colonel Pershing was of short stature, with a powerful but very compact build. The chances of his shotguns—and he had a number of wonderful bespoke guns—fitting the man from Texas were slim. Furthermore, because of their basic dimensions, anything short of restocking them to fit our Texan friend was out of the question. Certainly, if a gun is close, the stock can be bent to fit, but drastic bending and modifications to fit individuals of drastically different builds just aren't in the cards. However, that being said, many bespoke shotguns have been and are made with fairly common dimensions. Certainly, shotguns made for the very tall, very short, very corpulent, and so on will have different dimensions, but those close to average can be adjusted.

As discussed in Chapter 19, the application of a favorite dog's portrait, the likeness of a lost love, or eccentric or pornographic engraving can greatly affect how a future buyer will consider the gun. Obviously, many who buy bespoke shotguns don't care a bit

about a future buyer, but if the shotgun is being bought as an investment, then eccentric specifications should be avoided. Often you can strike a good deal on a fine shotgun whose engraving or other aspects are far enough from the mainstream to detract from the resale value. Some oddities can occasionally be corrected with a new stock, screw-in choke job, or other radical surgery. Take any such after-purchase alterations into account when negotiating the price, and you may arrive at a better cost than the original price.

The ordering and buying of a bespoke shotgun is an anticipation-filled undertaking. Some buy bespoke guns simply for their investment value, and the waiting time is immaterial. Those ordering guns for shooting and hunting are often more impatient. Although waiting for the various phases of construction can be irritating, it is better to allow plenty of time during the ordering phase, and to sleep on all decisions, since they're hard to change once executed in steel and wood. Be sure of what you want, let it rest for a few days, then go back and make sure it's what you really want. Once that gun is finally in your hands, there is a thrill of ownership unlike any other.

CHAPTER 22

Shooting High-Grade Shotguns

New and in the box is the ideal image of a pristine shotgun. Yet many, many London Bests and top-of-the-line guns from around the globe have been shot—many have been shot a great deal. After all, shotguns are meant to be used. Certainly, there are investment-grade guns that repose in bank vaults and gun safes everywhere, sitting in their custom cases against that financial rainy day, or when retirement funds might dry up. Frankly, many of these end up being sold at estate sales and auctions by uncaring heirs. Don't get me wrong. If I had purchased a bunch of Winchester Model 21s during my youth, at, if memory serves me right, $296 each, I'd have a nice little nest egg. Of course the idea of having $296, even $29.60, all in the same place when 21s sold for that amount was about as remote as my sprouting wings and flying. Still, the thought continues to haunt and tantalize me. Yes, firearms, at least certain ones, have appreciated astronomically, and have done better than the stock market, but let's face it, many fine guns are used, and perhaps that's as it should be.

We have to decide if a shotgun owned by a famous person or made by a great gunmaking name is worth exposing to the elements and the dangers of modern travel. My thought is that, if the gun was regularly used and is apropos to the application, time afield is an extension of the original owner's and gunmaker's wishes and rewards the current owner with the joy of using a great shotgun where it belongs, in the field. After all, that was the initial purchaser's intention.

It's interesting that actor Larry Hagman, who played the villainous personality in the long-running television series *Dallas,* ordered a superbly made and engraved Holland & Holland. On it were reproduced, in gold inlays, various scenes and characters from the television series. He took delivery of the gun on a rainy day, and immediately proposed a duck hunt. In the pouring rain, Hagman delighted

A shooter swinging on a clay target with a fine hammer gun

in shooting ducks with his new, very expensive shotgun. Bravado, showing off? Apparently not. Hagman was a devoted hunter, and he bought his shotgun, exquisite as it was, to use. I have an A. H. Fox HE-grade Super Fox, the tight-shooting wildfowling gun made famous by the late Nash Buckingham. My Super Fox was ordered by his Memphis, Tennessee, sporting goods store, Buckingham, Ensley and Carrigan, during the time when Nash was an active member of the firm. I'm positive that he at least handled the gun, and there is recent evidence that it may have been owned by Buckingham for a short time. Do I shoot it? You bet, at every opportunity. Whether or not to

shoot a fine or legendary gun is a matter of personal choice, and must be tempered with some common sense, coupled with the condition of the gun.

Recent developments in technology, great gunsmithing, and the prevalence of specialty ammunition have made it possible for many shotguns to be taken afield and used on a regular basis. Even once-difficult-to-find 2- and 2½-inch cartridges are now readily available, although you may have to order them if you can't find them at your corner gun shop.

One of the biggest problems with using vintage shotguns is that many of them, and especially those made from 1870 through

An under-lever Holland & Holland from the early 1880s. One of several transitional locking devices for breech-loading shotguns, the Jones under-lever was immensely strong.

World War I, had Damascus, laminated, and twist-steel barrels. Damascus barrels were considered top-of-the-line, and indeed some of them exhibit exquisite patterns of tightly twisted steel and iron wires. Many of these high-quality Damascus barrels have immense strength, and some brave souls have attempted some destruction tests of these barrels, and found them to be nearly equal to modern steel barrels. But there's a problem.

Damascus barrels are made by welding together alternating strands of steel and iron—called "piling"—in a multilayered sandwich. The ultimate quality of the resulting Damascus barrels was governed by the number of layers initially used or piled. Normally, best-quality Damascus barrels were made of 60 percent steel and 40 percent iron. The highest-quality barrels consisted of 75 percent steel and 25 percent iron. Once these were welded and carefully inspected, one end of the rod was heated red hot and held in a vise, while the other end was put into a revolving chuck, which twisted the strands of steel and iron tightly together, forming what appeared to be a long screw. W. W. Greener's factory twisted the rod to about eight turns per inch. The cheapest Damascus barrels were then made of one of these strips, while higher-quality barrels were made of two or three. Four or five could be combined in

A nicely cased, older back-action Holland & Holland.

more decorative barrels, but they were not as strong as three-strand barrels. The tightly wound strips were then put together with the twist of one opposite the other, and hot-rolled and welded together into a flat ribbon, or riband. After that, one of these strips was wound into a spiral around a mandrel, with the rod being removed once the spiral was complete. Next, the spiral was heated and placed on another mandrel. Three craftsmen now got involved, with a foreman holding and turning the mandrel on a grooved anvil while the other two workers hammered away. The spiral was then forged into the front (muzzle) half of the barrel. Then a second thick spiral was heated and placed onto the rear of the mandrel and also heated and hammered until it was stretched to meet the forecoil; then the two were hammered together, welding the whole into a barrel tube. This was again heated

How a Damascus barrel is made. The individual strips of steel and iron are wound into ribbons that are welded and forged into a solid band that is wound around a mandrel and then welded and forged into a barrel tube.

and hammered until completely cool, thereby aligning the grain of the metal and increasing the tube's strength.

The key to making high-quality Damascus barrels is that the twist of the ribbons must be so perfect that welds could be made, and the fibers of the steel and iron intermingled so that they support each other. Once formed, this tube was then filed smooth or struck up, and bored, then milled for the breeching. The pattern produced by the alternating ribbons of steel and iron resulted in an exquisitely beau-

tiful barrel, a beauty enhanced by acid etching and finished by browning (a rusting process).

Laminated-steel barrels used a similar iron-and-steel arrangement, but the strips were laid differently. Twist barrels were often made of single ribbons of steel and iron in a 50-50 blend, which is not as strong as true Damascus.

Top-quality Damascus barrels were very labor- and skill-intensive, while steel barrels were only bored and profiled. This is why Damascus barrels commanded a premium, even as they

Prior to actual proofing, each firearm is carefully gauged to ensure it meets the established standard.

were being replaced by cheaper-to-make barrels that were stronger and capable of withstanding the forces of smokeless powder, which was rapidly overtaking blackpowder loads.

Despite the tests by some basement ballisticians, the fact is that regardless of the quality of the Damascus barrel, or the name of the maker, Damascus barrels must meet certain criteria before they can be used with modern smokeless-

powder loads. First, let's be clear that the height of the brass on any shotshell is no indicator of the pressure it generates. I answer numerous letters from individuals wanting to fire some relic with "low-brass shells." Low brass does not in any way imply that these shells generate low pressures. The opposite may be true. Current shotshell specifications that commercial ammunition companies adhere to provide only the service pressure, beyond which cartridges are considered unsafe. Therefore, no old shotgun can be fired unless it has been altered by an outfit such as Briley Manufacturing or has been submitted and passes proof at one of the proof houses in Britain, France, Spain, Germany, Austria, or Italy. Normally, Damascus-barreled guns are submitted to the London or Birmingham Proof Houses. London is the choice strictly for snob reasons, although London proof marks certainly can enhance the value.

In the United States, each manufacturer is responsible for ensuring that the firearms it produces meet the standards of the Sporting Arms and Ammunition Manufacturers Insti-

tute (SAAMI). Because of this, the United States does not have a national proof house. At any of the foreign proof houses, a firearm submitted for proof, new or old, is thoroughly inspected. The bores are checked for conformity to standards, the joining of the barrels to the action is examined, and so on. If accepted, the gun is then shot with at least two specially loaded proof rounds, which provide about 50 percent higher pressure than that exerted by the highest-pressure commercially made loads. For example, SAAMI standards dictate that a 2¾-inch, 12-gauge shell shall have a maximum service pressure of 11,500 pounds per square inch (psi), as measured by a piezoelectric trans-

The pressure gun used by Kent Cartridge America to check each run of ammunition, ensuring uniform pressures. Beyond the muzzle is a chronograph that verifies velocities.

ducer mounted in a pressure gun. Therefore, proof-test pressure for that load is in the neighborhood of 17,250 psi. It is normal for nitro-proofed Damascus barrels to be proofed to 850 bars, or 12,325 psi, quite a bit below SAAMI-standard proof loads and dangerously close to the 12-gauge service pressure. Those Damascus-barreled shotguns that pass proof—there is the distinct possibility that a shotgun submitted to proof may fail, making it instantly worthless—are therefore usable with low-pressure loads. Normally, these loads run in the 6,000- to 7,500-psi range, with the average pressures published right on the box.

Regardless of the original quality of Damascus and twist barrels, their propen-sity for corroding makes them useless unless submitted for proof, or actually reproof. During the period when Damascus and its less-expensive derivatives were in vogue, the priming mixtures contained potassium chlorate, a close relative to table salt. When fired, it combined with the moisture in the atmosphere, attacking the interior of the barrel, and unless this was completely removed—a difficult task—it soon caused the pitting so prevalent in shotgun barrels from this era. (This continued until 1945, when noncorrosive lead styphnate priming—now itself being replaced because of its lead content—came into use.) Once pitted, the soft iron component of Damascus barrels became a tunnel allowing

A small sampling of the ammunition kept on hand by the Italian National Proof House in Gardone Val Trompia, Italy.

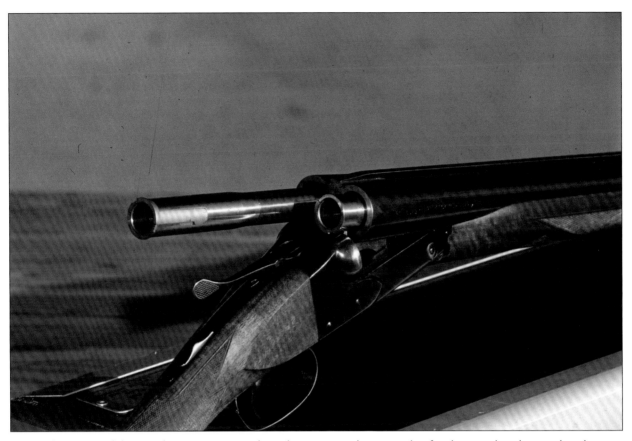

A Winchester Model 21 with a 20-gauge Briley tubes. It provides versatility for the traveling hunter, but these tubes also permit shooting of old shotguns with unsafe barrels.

corrosion to honeycomb the barrel. These barrels can often be rusted nearly through, yet the damage is undetectable without an optical bore scope. At this point they are unsafe with any ammunition.

Perhaps one of the easiest ways to make an old shotgun shootable is to have it equipped with a pair of full-length tubes of a smaller gauge. Briley Manufacturing in Houston, Texas, is a full-service shotgun-smithing company. They have breathed life back into many shotguns previously relegated to the back of the safe.

The alternative for suspect barrels, including deeply pitted steel barrels, is to have

them outfitted with chamber sleeves or full-length, small-gauge tubes. There are two styles of chamber sleeves or tubes: those that are permanently installed, and the relatively new ChamberMate and Side Kick tubes by Seminole Gun Works and Briley. These tubes slide into the chamber of a gun, and feature extractors that work with those in the gun. Seminole's ChamberMates use O rings, while Briley's Side Kicks employ small plastic buttons to keep the short tubes secured in the chamber. It should be emphasized that using these chamber tubes is contingent on the barrels being in good condition. They are not for heavily pitted bores or those that do not measure sufficiently thick to withstand the pressures associated with modern ammunition.

Chamber tubes reduce the gun by one gauge size, 10-gauge to 12-, 12-gauge to 20-, and so on. They use the existing barrel and choking. Because the pressure is halved as the volume doubles, pressures drop very quickly. This system is adaptable primarily to shotguns that have bores with no more than light pitting. Normally, heavy, 10-bore doubles can be permanently converted to a 3-inch 12-gauge with permanent chamber sleeving, and it works surprisingly well, even for firing nontoxic steel shot. Chamber tubes that are interchangeable between guns normally require a 2¾-inch chamber. This can be adjusted by taking the shoulder and forcing cone down a bit to accept the tube. Since the gun cannot be fired as is, any alteration to the chamber is moot. Full-length tubes are not intended for use with steel shot. They're made of aluminum, and not intended for this very hard shot.

Often there's a question about the safety of the action. It is imperative that any old shotgun being considered for use be inspected by a good gunsmith. It's worth the few dollars to have a really top-notch gunsmith evaluate any shotgun made prior to World War II before it's fired. Normally, the breeches of old doubles are solid. However, it is possible for them to crack, and in the event of firing a high-pressure load, they could break, with catastrophic results. Hence an inspection by a fine gunsmith is warranted. Normally, American-made doubles by A. H. Fox, L. C. Smith,

Ithaca, Lefever, and other top gunmakers fare very well.

The recent rise of cowboy action shooting has made old repeaters such as the Winchester Models 1893 and 1897 and Marlin 1898 much sought-after guns. In 1998, Marlin issued a service bulletin informing the public not to shoot the Model 1898, not only because of its age but also due to a lack of repair parts. The Winchester Model 1893 is probably unsafe to fire with smokeless powder loads, although the Model 1897 is probably safe for low-pressure loads. In any case, all these shotguns must be inspected before being fired to ensure the safety of the shooter and bystanders.

SAFETY AND ETIQUETTE

This book is about fine guns, not hunting and clays shooting. Still, one abhors going afield or to the clay range with an unsafe shooter. As controlled as ranges are, there is still the chance for an accident. Fortunately, fine shot is required on clay ranges, and unless someone is shot at very close range, the few incidents that occur are seldom fatal.

The one safety item that remains a problem, regardless of the range, is the inadvertent inserting of a 20-gauge shell into a 12-gauge gun or a 28-gauge load into a 16-gauge. In either case the smaller-gauge load will slip forward of the chamber and catch in the forcing cone. If the shooter does not check that his bore is clear, and then inserts a larger-gauge shell behind the small-gauge cartridge and fires the gun, grave personal injury can result. Not long ago, a member of our club was shooting at another, nearby range. He started the day by shooting a couple of rounds of 20-gauge skeet, then decided to shoot some trap. He didn't take the time to clear his pockets completely of 20-gauge shells, and he did the unthinkable. First, he loaded a 20-gauge shell into his 12-bore trap barrel. When it didn't fire, he loaded a 12-gauge shell and fired the gun. The barrel split, and our shooter's arm and hand were severely wounded. His hand was so badly mangled that it took months of reconstructive surgery before he had even limited use of it. Since then, he's stopped shooting altogether. Shooting is fun, and banter and conversation are important aspects of the whole scene, but when it comes to shooting, the focus must be on that and nothing else.

Shooting etiquette dictates that one does not shoot another's birds. Quail that flush in front of a hunter are his, not those of the guy on his far right. Little competitions and side bets to shoot the most birds can often lead to unsafe shooting. When shooting driven birds, an unsafe shooter will be asked to leave, or at least not invited back. Any move that endangers the beaters or other guns meets with immediate rebuke. Common sense dictates what is right and what is not, and when we become so wrapped up in trying to shoot the most or the fastest, danger lurks.

Shooting older shotguns is a lot of fun; to many, it doesn't get any better than that. Witness the growth of the Vintagers movement, whose participants shoot only side-by-sides, with most preferring hammer guns. Cowboy action shooting has an equally fast-growing following because shooting the guns of our ancestors or those that won the West is plain fun. Just remember that any arm brought to the clays course or field must be safe and always handled in a safe manner. There can be no deviation from this.

CHAPTER 23

Ammunition for High-Grade Shotguns

In general, high-grade shotguns are no different in their ammunition demands than the lowliest pump purchased at the local mart. Of course, many doubles are chambered for 2½-inch shells and older 16-gauge guns are often chambered for the now-obsolete 2⁹⁄₁₆-inch cartridges. Those issues can be dealt with by buying the correct ammunition, and a 16-gauge's chambers can be lengthened by a competent gunsmith. If there is a generalization to be made, it is to shoot light loads through high-grade guns.

That statement flies in the face of such top-of-the-line shotguns as the Fabbri, which is made for pigeon shooters and Olympic bunker and trap competitors. Pigeon loads are stiff, and trap and bunker shooters put thousands of rounds through their guns yearly, so to say that one should go light isn't necessarily correct!

Lighter is better when it comes to side-by-sides, however. By their design, quality over-and-unders withstand heavy recoil better than side-by-sides. Why? Because the over-and-under action takes the recoil in a vertical manner, with the side-to-side forces lessened by the stiffer barrels. Side-by-side design allows the forces of recoil not only to push the more flexible barrels downward, but also to torque them sideways. Over-and-unders will work loose when shot a great deal, but side-by-sides will do so even faster, and especially when they are subjected to loads that are heavier than what they are designed to shoot. Foreign-made shotguns will often be stamped with the maximum loads for which they were built. If you have a London Best or other best-quality shotgun in its original case, the load information may be on a card pasted in the lid of the case. If in doubt, lighter is better.

While repeated shooting of heavy loads can cause an action to loosen, nothing wears out double guns faster than slamming them shut. Shotguns should be shut firmly, but not

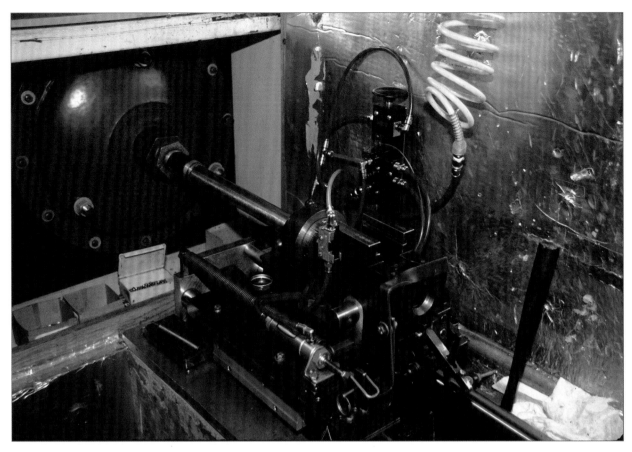

This pressure gun in the Hodgdon Powder Company's ballistics laboratory is fired using compressed air. The pressures are measure by a piezoelectric transducer and displayed on a computer screen.

slammed. I'm not sure that the old wives' tale of holding the top lever open, shutting the gun carefully, then allowing the top lever to be gently released is correct either. I believe that a shotgun should be shut with the lever allowed to snap, thereby allowing the locking bolt to engage with the locking lugs. Which is correct could be argued for eons, but the bottom line is that slamming shut a fine gun will wear it out much faster than any amount of shooting. It is traditional to hold the shotgun by the barrels at the forend, then close it while holding the butt. The barrels are pointed at the ground in front of the shooter, and so any accidental discharge will go harmlessly into the earth. More recent thinking recommends holding the buttstock firmly between the arm and ribs, then pivoting the barrels shut with the leading hand, keeping the muzzles pointing out into safe space.

CHAMBER LENGTHS

Whenever contemplating the purchase of a gun, the buyer must be sure to check all aspects of the gun, and that includes the length of the chamber. It wasn't until 1924 that 12-, 16-, and 20-gauge chambers were established as 2¾ inches long in the United States. Two-and-one-half-inch chambers were the standard in Great Britain long before that, and remain so to this day. Sixteen-gauge shotguns manufactured on the continent kept the 2⁹⁄₁₆-inch chamber well beyond the end of World War II. It is true that today's plastic-hull ammunition does not cause the kind of pressure spikes that paper hulls can. Still, firing long rounds in short chambers raises pressures and can ultimately lead to a catastrophic failure. At the very least, it can cause premature loosening of the action and barrels.

I recall a gun show where a late friend was planning to buy a 16-gauge side-by-side. He stopped at a booth and found a French-made gun that he really liked. Upon examination, however, he found that the gun had 2⁹⁄₁₆-inch chambers, marked 65mm on the barrel flats. I stopped the sale right there. I later told the dealer that I was sorry to take the sale from him, but didn't want my somewhat naive friend to buy a short-chambered gun. His answer was, "What difference does that make?" Here was a longtime gun man who dealt in shotguns, yet he didn't have the slightest idea of the problems associated with short chambers. Often the chamber length will be stamped with the proof marks, sometimes not. For those who want one, Tony Galazan sells a great chamber gauge for about $40. Called the Handy Model Chamber Length Gauge, it carries gauges for 10-, 12-, 16-, 20-, and 28-gauge and .410 bore, riveted together. The gauges are square on the end, so

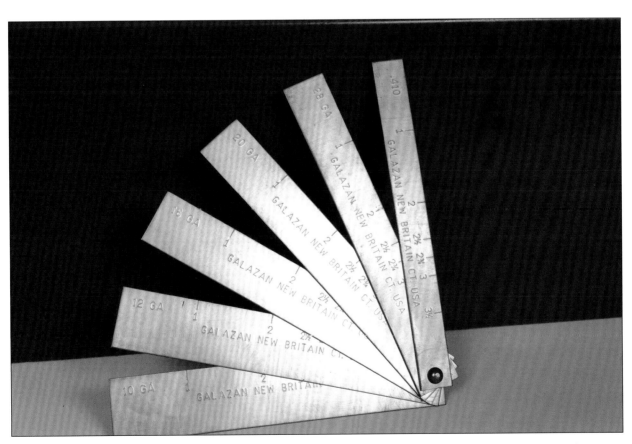

A set of Galazan chamber gauges that accurately measure chamber depth.

Two-inch, two-and-a-half-inch, two-and-three-quarter-inch, three-inch, and three-and-a-half-inch 12-gauge shells.

they bottom right at the head of the forcing cone. One caveat: In situations where chambers are cut to a more rapid taper, as they are in the Ansley H. Fox HE-Grade Super-Fox, which contributes to the gun's superior patterning performance, this gauge will not bottom at the forcing cone, and the chamber must be measured with a bore micrometer. However, rare is the gun that the Galazan gauge cannot measure. If you do a lot of buying, selling, and swapping, a good chamber gauge is a good investment. Buyers are often obsessed with the chokes in a particular gun, and it's important

that they be correct. But if the gun is going to be shot, it's even more important that the chamber lengths be verified.

At one time it was difficult to find short shells to fit 2- and 2½-inch-chambered shotguns. I once met a man who owned a lovely, 2-inch-chambered, 12-gauge Charles Lancaster. I had the opportunity to shoot it, and it handled like a magic wand. He traveled the Midwest wholesaling sporting goods to dealers and carried several tools and an MEC single-stage loader with him. He said that nights spent in motel rooms allowed him time to load

Joe Prather checking a pair of barrels with a barrel fork in the Griffin & Howe gun room. By moving the barrels over the fork, the precise thickness of the barrels can be determined; .030 inch thickness is deemed safe while those measuring .020 are unsafe.

his 2-inch shells. He had a cutter to trim the hulls, and his custom setup MEC single-stage loader allowed him to clamp it to any table and load the tiny shells.

Today, outfits such as Kent-Gamebore, B&P, RST (located in Pennsylvania and the only domestic U.S. company to load short shells), Fiocchi, and a few others provide a fairly wide selection of 2- and 2½-inch cartridges. Some of these manufacturers also provide short-length shells for 16-, 20-, and 28-gauge guns.

It seems I'm obsessed with short loads, but the truth is that many fine shotguns are chambered for these loads. It's a difficult deci-

sion, but sometimes it makes sense to have a really qualified gunsmith lengthen the chambers of one of these shotguns. Sometimes it will hurt the value, other times not much. If chambers are to be deepened, it is important that the work be done only by someone who can accurately determine the thickness of the barrels and make an intelligent decision about whether or not this particular gun has enough steel in the barrels to permit the work. If the chambers are lengthened, there must also be sufficient barrel thickness to provide for the lengthening of the forcing cones.

Some years ago, when the 3½-inch, 12-gauge magnum hit the market, an acquaintance took his Valmet over-and-under to a highly qualified gunsmith, seeking to have the chambers lengthened. The gunsmith refused, citing insufficient barrel thickness to make the alteration safely. Not only were the barrels too thin, but the 3½-inch, 12-gauge magnum generates extremely high chamber pressures (14,000 psi), and the project was deemed unsafe. Outfits such as Briley Manufacturing in Houston specialize in barrel work, and they and others who routinely perform such work are set up to properly gauge barrels, then do the work properly, or rule against it on safety grounds. If they or another good gunsmith refuse to lengthen the chambers of a shotgun, believe them, and either sell the gun or buy the proper, shorter-length shells.

While we've dwelt on the 12-gauge, it should be emphasized that 16-gauge shotguns often have 2$\frac{9}{16}$-inch chambers, and older 20-gauge guns often come with 2½-inch chambers. Again, it is important to verify the length of all chambers prior to purchasing or shooting any shotgun.

SHOT

Historically, shot was made of lead alloyed with antimony that acts as a surfactant that causes the pellets to form round spheres. Antimony also adds hardness to the lead. Typically, shot used in inexpensive hunting loads, often called promotional loads, has an antimony content of about 1 ½ percent. Target loads and premium hunting loads have as much

as 3 ½ percent antimony. Lead shot is formed by heating the lead-antimony mixture until molten, then pouring it through a sieve perforated with holes the size of the desired pellets. In the 1980s, there were numerous shot towers located throughout the Eastern United States. The Phoenix Shot Tower still exists in downtown Baltimore, Maryland. Today, Winchester, Remington, and independent shot makers still use 10-foot-high towers to make shot, while Federal and others use the German Bleimeister process that drops shot about three feet into hot water. Both processes produce excellent shot.

Prior to the 1991 hunting season, when nontoxic shot was mandated for all waterfowl hunting, lead shot was the standard, and had been for many years. Even as early as 1946, however, it was evident that waterfowl and other birds, including bald eagles, and a variety of animals were suffering from the effects of lead poisoning. The search for a type of shot that would be both ballistically lethal and nontoxic ultimately arrived at soft iron, best known as steel shot. Steel shot is made by cutting appropriately sized billets from wire of the diameter of the finished pellet. They are annealed by heating and cooling and then rolled, resulting in hard, round pellets. Measuring 90 to 120 on the diamond-pyramid hardness (DPH) scale, a system to measure the hardness of metal, shotgun barrel steel runs about 115 to 117 DPH, making it obvious that these hard steel pellets could easily score the bore or more likely peen a full choke, resulting in a circumferential bulge, commonly described as ring bulge. In the case of a double gun, on which the barrels

184

The historic Phoenix Shot Tower in downtown Baltimore, Maryland. Finished in 1828, at 234.25 feet tall, it was the tallest structure in the United States at that time. Lead was hoisted to the top where it was melted in a wood- or coal-fired furnace. The molten lead was poured through a sieve, and as the pellets dropped they cooled and solidified, finally plunging into a pool of water at the bottom.

Ron Petty with the author's 1924 Parker and a bouquet of mallards shot with Environ-Metal's Classic Doubles that is made specifically to be fired through older shotguns not up to the rigors of steel shot.

are very close, such a ring bulge can cause the barrels to separate, resulting in a very costly repair. The potential for ring bulge was easily corrected by opening chokes to .020 or larger, since mild constrictions seem unaffected by steel shot. Another initial problem was the lack of lethality. Over the years, ammunition manufacturers have developed different propellants, wads, and loading techniques that have resulted in today's steel shot being fired at very high velocities, most around 1,450 to 1,550 fps—Remington is introducing a steel-shot load for the 2010 waterfowl season that has a muzzle velocity of 1,700 fps—which greatly increases downrange lethality.

The problems of steel shot were easily corrected by more open chokes and choke tubes made from Vega or maraging steel, which has a zero coefficient of expansion. Briley Manufacturing pioneered this technique, and virtually all shotguns made within the past 20 years are capable of shooting steel shot without problems. Better wads and loading techniques have also helped.

Still, if you had a fine double, you had to leave it at home when you headed for the marsh. In the late 1980s a Canadian carpenter named John Brown began experimenting with bismuth pellets. More dense than steel—9.4 gr/cc versus 7.8 gr/cc for steel—but less dense than lead (10.9–11.1 gr/cc), bismuth is soft enough to prevent barrel damage, yet enough like lead to be more lethal than steel shot. Magazine magnate the late Robert Petersen saw the potential of bismuth shot, and provided the necessary

cash to test the pellets on live mallards. Petersen put up a heroic fight with the U. S. Fish and Wildlife Service (USFWS) to obtain approval of bismuth. While USFWS wasn't necessarily adversarial, there wasn't much in the way of protocols and guidelines for adopting alternative nontoxic pellets, so the USFWS required test after test to prove bismuth's nontoxic properties. Petersen persevered through several live-bird dosing tests, and ultimately won approval in 1992.

In the meantime, the British had been experimenting, using powdered tungsten with a plastic binder, calling it MolyShot. Never very successful, this technology awaited a group of Canadian investors led by Dem Rogers, who sought a nontoxic pellet that equaled lead in density. Taking the idea of powdered tungsten formed into a pellet using a binder, they sought the advice of a polymer chemist, who suggested very stiff "goo." The problem with MolyShot was that the tungsten was not uniformly distributed throughout the finished pellets. Weighted off center, the pellets did not pattern well. By blending the tungsten with a stiffer polymer, it was possible to form uniformly dense pellets. Kent Cartridge America and Canada offer the fine-gun hunter their wonderful Tungsten Matrix shot loaded in 12- and 20-gauge in a variety of hull lengths and shot charges and sizes, for any application from Canada geese and turkey to upland birds.

In 2009, Environ-Metal, who manufacture Hevi-Shot, released a new pellet named

Classic Doubles that is made of a blend of powdered tungsten, nickel, and iron that are then formed into pellets under extreme pressure. Soft enough to not damage old barrels but because of the very dense tungsten component is extremely lethal.

Although some fine guns can fire steel shot, I recommend using bismuth, Classic Doubles, or Tungsten Matrix. All are lethal, legal in any venue, and gentle on fine barrels, and respond well to choke, just like traditional lead shot.

In 2010, we have the greatest array of ammunition ever offered the hunting and shooting public. Finding ammunition is often but a few mouse clicks away on the Internet. The handloading industry has also taken note of fine guns and provides loading data and components for these shells. All in all, we're fortunate to have all these cartridges available. Just be sure of the chamber length you're working with, and remember, lighter is better. It's good for your shoulder, and even better for your shotgun.

CHAPTER 24

Caring for High-Grade Shotguns

Caring for high-grade shotguns is an ongoing process. If the guns are used, they must be regularly cleaned and properly lubricated. If they're not shot, you must still pay attention to them to avoid deterioration. Many things can damage a fine shotgun. In Chapter 23, we discussed how slamming a double shut will wear it loose faster than any amount of shooting. Equally harmful is too much lubrication—that's worse than none at all!

The human instinct is that if some is good, more is better. Not so when it comes to guns. Oil them sparingly! The biggest problem with the overzealous application of lubricants is that while oil never hurt metal, it sure damages wood. Go to any gun show and look at the older guns on any table. It doesn't matter if they're Model 12s, 21s, or Fox Sterlingworths—almost any shotgun from that era will do. Look at the color of the wood just behind the action and around the tang. I'll bet you that most all the

wood will be significantly darker in those areas. Why? Because of overlubrication and storing the gun butt down. As a youngster, I loved cleaning my dad's shotgun, and mine when I bought my Model 12 16-gauge when I was fourteen. (I no longer enjoy cleaning guns to the extent I did then.) My youthful enthusiasm told me that if some oil made it work well, then a lot more should make it work even better. Too, in the 1950s we were less than a decade from the introduction of noncorrosive priming, and most shotguns from the corrosive-priming era suffered from pitted bores. Oil and more oil seemed the answer. When aerosol cans of lubricant hit the market, we could really pour, or spray, it on. Squirting volumes of lube into every nook and cranny makes us feel good, and frankly, if it's a synthetically stocked Benelli Nova or Remington 1100/00-87 semiauto, so what? I'm not denigrating the Nova or 1100, but those guns are easily replaced, and synthetic replacement stocks are available from Cabela's and Bass Pro Shops. If you have a vintage Model 12, granddad's Browning Auto-5, or an L. C. Smith, however, apply oil sparingly.

As excess lubricant seeps back through the action, it is absorbed into the wood. The more poured in, the softer the wood becomes, until the stock rots and becomes worthless. It doesn't matter what brand of oil is used, from 3-in-1 Household Oil to the British favorite Rangoon Oil, oil-saturated stocks are among the major problems encountered with classic shotguns. A good gunsmith or stock man can often save an oil-soaked stock, but it's a long process. The head of the stock is covered with whiting, and this absorbs the old oil. Sometimes acetone can be used to dry out the head of the stock. Most of the time, however, older shotgun stocks cannot be sufficiently dried of old oil, and a new stock must be made if the gun is to be shot. I've done that with a couple of classic doubles, carefully keeping the original stock to preserve the original parts. I see no problem with restocking a high-grade shotgun if it's to be shot. If you're going to enjoy shooting a fine shotgun, it might as well fit, necessitating a restocking.

I have a big, old can of Rangoon Oil, at one time the universal British gun lubricant. It is somewhat like 3-in-1 Household Oil in this country. I used it for a while on a fine AyA, but stopped when it began to gum, and in fact a little bit of it petrified on the water table. I could scrub it off with acetone, but I keep it there as a memorial to when the sun never set on the British Empire, and Rangoon Oil had a better-sounding name than its practical value.

A can of Rangoon Oil. Once an integral part of British shotgun lubrication, this and whale oil have been replaced by a bevy of synthetic lubricants.

A complete set of turn screws or screwdrivers is an essential part of any shotgun enthusiast's tools. Having the screwdriver precisely fit the screw head often prevents burred screw heads. Burred screws greatly detract from the value of any firearm.

One important item that the gun cleaner needs is the correct set of tools. Screwdrivers *must* fit the screws *precisely*. Nothing detracts more from the aesthetics and value of a shotgun than burred or buggered screws from ill-fitting screwdrivers. Anytime a screw is to be removed, the shotgun should be held in a padded vise, and the screwdriver held in the screw head with plenty of downward pressure. Gunsmith Greg Wolf usually put his chin on the screwdriver and exerted pressure with his back muscles to ensure that the screwdriver didn't jump out of the head. Every screw head needs its own screwdriver. In addition, a long-shanked screwdriver is necessary for removing deeply set drawbolts. Sometimes English and metric

sockets are needed, as are drift punches, a soft-faced hammer, and other items. If there is any question in your mind about your ability to disassemble a gun, take it to a good gunsmith. Never experiment with a great shotgun.

The British take another avenue to gun care. The individual owner or one of his hired servants does the daily cleaning, but at the end of the shooting season, the shotgun is sent or taken back to the original maker for annual maintenance. In the Holland & Holland factory there is a separate area devoted exclusively to cleaning and repairs. There, the bores are thoroughly cleaned, and the action completely dismantled, cleaned, degreased, then relubricated. Often the gun is stored in the maker's vault until the following shooting season. It's impossible to take an A. H. Fox back to the maker, but a yearly cleaning by a competent gunsmith is a good idea for a heavily used fine gun. You pay for it, but a good gunsmith can also check for worn or potentially failing parts and replace them before they become problems. Guns never break down at home, only when you're close to the edge of the earth.

One of the great developments in shotshells has been the plastic hull and wad. By preventing gas leakage into the shot charge, cushioning the initial push of the propellant and protecting the shot as it goes down the barrel, plastic wads have done a great deal to improve patterning and downrange performance. The downside is that they deposit plastic throughout the length of the bore, and because plastic attracts moisture, it must be removed, lest the bore rust.

The plastic problem is also prevalent in shotgun chambers. Just as the all-plastic wad did great things for downrange performance, the all-plastic hull has provided a far better package than the old, moisture-sensitive paper hulls. Still, all-plastic ammunition can cause chambers to rust. So while our grandfathers needed to remove primer and powder residue and leading that covered the corrosive priming, we don't need to clean the bores of our shotguns as often. When we do, however, we have to remove the plastic, an effort as difficult as removing leading.

Fortunately, as solvents have evolved, several manufacturers have attacked the problem of plastic-wad residue, and developed concoctions that really cut plastic wad fouling. One of the best is Brownells Shotgun Wad Solvent. The only problem is that it has a strong odor, and is best used outdoors. Still, it cuts plastic residue about as well as anything I've tried. It is important that you have a good bronze or brass bore brush—some use stainless steel brushes, and while they work well, they are too hard for a high-grade barrel—and it takes some scrubbing to remove all the plastic. Brownells sells an excellent chamber brush, as do other cleaning equipment companies, and one is required to successfully remove plastic from chambers. Brushes are available in all gauges.

Plastic will frequently build up in the area of the choke. This accumulation of plastic can be quite thick, and can tighten the choke. When cleaning, it's imperative that you clean your gun with the screw-in choke tubes firmly in place. Without the tube, all the dirt, carbon, unburned powder, and dissolved plastic will be deposited into the choke cut and threads, creating a good old-fashioned mess. Never ever clean a shotgun without a choke tube in place.

To clean a heavily fouled choke tube, remove it and soak it in a glass jar filled with the solvent of choice (Brownell's EZ Soak and others supply choke-tube solvent in jars with lifters). Once the solvent has had the chance to work, remove the tube and brush vigorously to remove the plastic. It can take several cycles of soaking and brushing to remove all the plastic. It's sometimes even necessary to scrape the plastic out of the tube with a pocketknife, although great care is necessary to ensure that the choke tube is not cut. Some people chuck a short length of cleaning rod with a brass brush into an electric hand drill and use it to facilitate the removal of plastic from choke tubes. Brownells sells a brass, drill-chuckable cleaning rod that will cut through plastic quickly. Use care not to run the drill at high speed; a rather slow rotation seems to work best. I'd be cautious using one on a Purdey, but for workaday shotgun, it's perfect.

Once the plastic fouling has been removed, dry the bore with a few patches. I find that a paper towel works very well. Fold a sheet in two, then tear it into quarters, thirds, or halves—whatever size fits the gauge you're cleaning. That's all you need to do if the gun's going to be shot soon. If not, lubricate a patch lightly with a preservative-type oil, and push it through the bore several times, then follow it with a couple of dry patches. Don't leave lots of oil in the bore. If the gun is going to be stored, however, I'd put a thin film of preservative grease in the bore. Grease stays put, and doesn't migrate into the wood as readily as oil does.

The action should be exposed by removing the stock or the sidelocks, then cleaned with a cloth or one of the "crud blaster" cleaners, such as Birchwood Casey Gun Scrubber. Some good gunsmiths don't care for these, stating that they tend to break down the dirt, then blow it into every inac-

A complete, deluxe shotgun-cleaning kit with a joined rosewood rod, various brushes, jags, solvent, and oil.

193

cessible corner of the action. There's some validity to that, but I still like them for dirty or excessively lubricated actions. These solvents dissolve the lubrication, then evaporate, leaving bare metal. I then lubricate the actions with something like Rem Oil, from a spray bottle. Once I've coated everything, I let it sit for five minutes, then blot off all I can, and follow it up by using an air compressor and a blower nozzle to blow off every bit of oil I can. This blowing phase can take several minutes, since it is necessary to blow and blot with a paper towel several times. Try to blow away as much of the oil as possible from the corners of the action, and blot up all you can with pipe cleaners. I like pipe cleaners for lubricating, since you can put a slight amount of oil on the tip of one, and then apply it exactly where you want it. If you put down too much, you can reverse the cleaner and use the dry end to pick up the excess.

When lubing a sidelock shotgun, it's a good idea to moisten a patch with acetone and remove any excess oil from the inletting, being careful not to get any onto the finish. There is nothing better than acetone for removing excess oil and grease, but it must be used with care, and with adequate ventilation.

Once lightly lubricated, the gun can be reassembled.

In terms of storage, most people store their long guns butt down, but it's far better to store shotguns and rifles with their muzzles down. That way, any excess lubrication will drain down through the bore, not into the wood. This also prevents recoil pads from being constantly compressed, thereby misshaping them. If you need to store your long guns butt down, check them frequently for any sign of excess lubrication in and around the action and on the wood.

I store my firearms in a sturdy safe with a GoldenRod GunSaver Dehumidifier, which is simply a low-temperature heating element located at the back of the safe. The air is dried by being warmed, and the likelihood of rust is greatly diminished. Still, firearms stored in any safe or cabinet ought to be frequently checked for any rust or corrosion.

Lastly, and if at all possible, fine guns should not be stored in their cases. Cases are lined with fabric that attracts moisture, and in the closed environment where air cannot circulate, rust is a real threat. It's far better to store the guns in a safe and to keep the cases elsewhere. It's also a good idea to frequently check cases for any mold or mildew, which is frequently encountered in humid climates.

Owning fine guns, or ordinary guns for that matter, requires constant attention to their welfare. Out of sight, out of mind is a real enemy of fine guns. They need to be checked frequently for moisture and the effects of over-lubrication, so that they will remain in good shape for years to come. Just as a collector of fine art is only a custodian of a Renoir, Degas, or other great work of art, so is a fine-gun aficionado only a custodian, whose obligation is to pass on a Purdey, Fox, or other great gun to the next generation in the best possible condition.

CHAPTER 25

The Necessary Gunsmith

Into every life a little rain must fall, and when it does concerning a high-grade shotgun, there's only one place to turn, and that's to a fine, truly qualified gunsmith. I'm not talking about some guy down the block who took a correspondence course and coincidentally sharpens lawnmowers and chain saws, but an honest-to-God, real gunsmith.

I don't mean to be unnecessarily cruel to the Joe Jacklegs of gunsmithing, but in answering letter after letter from NRA members concerning shotguns, over and over I encounter individuals who have taken a gun to a "gunsmith" who not only did not properly repair the gun in question, but frequently made it worse. Good gunsmiths are expensive, but in return they provide the very best service for your shotgun. Some are individual proprietors, while others work for established firms such as Griffin & Howe or Doug Turnbull Restorations.

Fine guns need an equally fine gunsmith to care for them, and to advise the owner.

Often the only way to know whether a shotgun can be fired or not is to have it examined by a really good gunsmith. He will know how to measure the lengths of the chambers, and will have the necessary tools. In addition, he will check the barrels for thin spots, loose ribs, and other potential problem areas. If you frequently take work to him, the examination might be complimentary—if not, the charge will be small.

Barrel thickness is important when it comes to classic shotguns. Many British-made shotguns are made with very thin barrels to achieve balance, and any polishing out of the bores or re-striking to refinish or remove dents also removes metal, and can make them too thin for safe shooting. Most fine-gun dealers and gunsmiths who specialize in servicing fine guns will have a barrel fork, used to measure the thickness of individual barrels. Using a fork, the person doing the measuring can carefully work his way around and up and down

Now-retired gunsmith Greg Wolf removing a dent from a shotgun barrel.

the barrels, determining the thickness at each and every point.

When checking the thickness of shotgun barrels, the minimum should be 25 thousandths. Thirty thousandths would be better, which is still darned thin, but safe. Any thickness below 20 thousandths is unsafe, and guns with barrels that thin should be rejected. It is possible to verify barrel thickness using outside calipers and a bore micrometer, but that method is not nearly as accurate as using a barrel fork.

When contemplating any kind of refinishing job, keep in mind that the quality of polishing is extremely important. If the gunsmith is conscientious, he will avoid rolling over the sharp edges of the engraving and stamping. If possible, he'll even retouch the engraving after polishing so that everything stays as it was. Obviously, severe pitting and rust cannot be dealt with gently, and requires extra time and cost to rectify. The average gunsmith will probably get everything polished okay, but the stamping on the barrel will be smoothed over, and the sharp edge of the action will be rounded over. The truly fine gunsmith's polishing job will retain everything as if the gun had come from the factory. Yes, you can normally spot a refinish job, but the extra time and skill employed by a fine gunsmith will also be evident.

Beyond finish work, the really talented gunsmith will be able to make parts when none exist. As an aside, I answer many letters from people who are seeking parts for inexpensive

Following firing with proof loads, the overall gun is then inspected for any irregularity.

shotguns. The concept of making parts for such guns is sheer folly. However, a fine gun that's well cared for is eminently repairable, and a fine gunsmith will be able to do everything necessary.

It should be noted that many gunsmiths are specialists. Some do wood, some do metal, and a few do both. Those who specialize in one or the other normally work with a colleague who specializes in the other discipline.

It must be kept in mind that the services of truly good gunsmiths are constantly in demand, and therefore it normally takes longer for them to complete a job. Sometimes a restocking job will take a year. Provided you're a good customer, simple repairs might be done while you wait. The rule, however, is that any repair takes some time, and extensive work takes even longer. Don't show up on your gunsmith's door the night before opening day, expecting some kind of sleight-of-hand miracle. Anytime work is needed, plan, plan, plan. Allow plenty of time, and if you expect to take your shotgun on a trip, be sure you inform your gunsmith up front when you need it. If he's honest, he'll tell you whether or not he can accomplish the work in time, and will strive to do so.

There are many gunsmiths who can replace parts in a Remington 870 or 11-87, but, when presented with a fine gun, will do more harm than good. Fine gun work is not inexpensive and often not performed quickly, but the price and wait are worth it.

CHAPTER 26

Storing High-Grade Shotguns

I know a man who collected shotguns and kept them in a rental storage unit. I have one of those, and dust gets in, and the temperature inside is what it is outside. Only the rain and snow are kept out. I'd like to have a collection that is so large that I need a storage locker, but fine guns need more shelter than that provided by a rental cubicle.

Because fine guns often come in oak-and-leather, trunk-style cases, owners are tempted to just leave them in the cases. The problem is that most are baize- or felt-lined, and felt attracts moisture. Certainly, if a temperature- and humidity-controlled room is available, storage in cases is possible, but still risky. Many guns stored in their cases end up having the imprint of the case's lining embossed on them by rust. It's much better to store fine guns separately. There still are problems, however.

Some shotguns have never left the original box. Last assembled at the factory for final testing, the gun has never been assembled since

purchase. Shotguns such as these are absolutely pristine, and should never be assembled unless the owner intends to shoot them. Most don't. Therefore it is best to devote a secure room with controlled temperature and humidity to their storage. Such a room isn't that hard to find—you just need a room that remains cool with low humidity that can be provided by a dehumidifier that costs a few dollars at a home center.

Fine guns that are used, or have been used, are best kept assembled and stored in a quality gun safe. Safes are secure, most are fireproof, and they can be kept dry with the installation of a GoldenRod GunSaver Dehumidifier, which is placed at the back of the safe, and keeps the air warmed while driving out humidity. Obviously, if you live in an arid climate, humidity isn't a problem.

When buying a safe, be sure it has sufficient space for your collection, and allow some spare room for additional acquisitions. More

A secure
gun safe
is the best
way to
store a gun
collection.

than one safe may be required to hold an extensive collection, or permit the addition of new shotguns.

One concern is getting the safe into your home or office. A good friend recently purchased a safe, and suggested that the deliverymen bring it around the house and carry it in through the basement sliding door. The deliverymen thought it would be quicker to go down a long, narrow flight of stairs. Following hours of hard work and frustration, they had made no progress, and were not even close to the basement. Finally the safe company owner arrived with a number of sheets of plywood and a forklift, and the safe was brought around the outside.

In my case, the safe I wanted could not be navigated down our stairs and make the sharp turn at the bottom. I finally bought two smaller safes which, combined, had more overall capacity. Plus, the two men who delivered them were able to get them into the basement without difficulty. Actually, two safes turned out to

Storing shotguns muzzle down prevents excess lubrication from migrating into the buttstock.

be a better idea than one in another aspect as well: I've been able to separate my guns into my favorites—those I shoot frequently—and those I seldom use, or use only for photos.

As mentioned in Chapter 24, because of the damage that excess lubrication can do to wood, I prefer to store my shotguns muzzle down. Any excess oil drains out the muzzle, not into the wrist of the stock. Those shotguns with recoil pads will also benefit, since muzzle-down storage will not compress the pad. If guns are stored muzzle down, they all fit into the safe just fine, and maybe even a bit better than muzzle up. In a glass-fronted cabinet, displayed guns should be stored butt down, lest they appear strange. So stored, they should be checked monthly for excess oil in the stock.

Truly, any kind of safe is a good idea, be it a locked closet, an old, locking trunk, or a secured locker. Lacking that, store guns outside soft cases, as these attract and hold moisture that will cause rust—and once that sets in, even the finest gun is disfigured for life.

CHAPTER 27

Accessories

Some people are accessory junkies, while others ignore even the most basic, and often necessary, accessories. Those who own fine guns should have some basic accessories, simply because fine guns deserve them.

Snap caps: No fine gun ought to be snapped, i.e., the trigger pulled, without snap caps in the chambers. A snap cap is a dummy cartridge. Normally made of nickel-plated brass, it is shorter than a cartridge, and has some kind of resilient material where the primer would be located on a real shell. When the hammer drops and the striker or firing pin snaps forward, the snap cap will stop it. Fox, Ithaca, and Winchester 21 doubles have strikers that are integral with the hammers, and these shotguns do not suffer from snapping without caps, although snap caps are still a good idea. Shotguns with separate strikers or firing pins that are repeatedly snapped without snap caps can actually end up with broken firing pins. If the pin is driven forward without

a snap cap, it travels its full length before being stopped by the larger base of the pin. Over time, the firing-pin holes or the breech can be deformed. More frequently, the pin breaks from fatigue.

Cleaning: I suspect that every gun owner has a collection of cleaning rods, jags, brushes, and solvents. Although some of the all-steel rods are attractive, coated or wooden rods are better. I have an old Herter's one-piece wooden cleaning rod that is slotted at the tip for a large patch. I use paper towels folded in half and torn to fit whatever gauge I'm cleaning. Over the years, all shooters seem to collect their own favorite cleaning equipment, but that old Herter's rod from the 1950s is my favorite.

Mat: It's a good idea to have a cleaning or bench mat. Remington and Brownells offer them, as do others. These make a nice, soft work area for your fine guns. They come in a couple of sizes, about 12 to 16 inches wide and 24 to 54 inches long. I have two, one for the

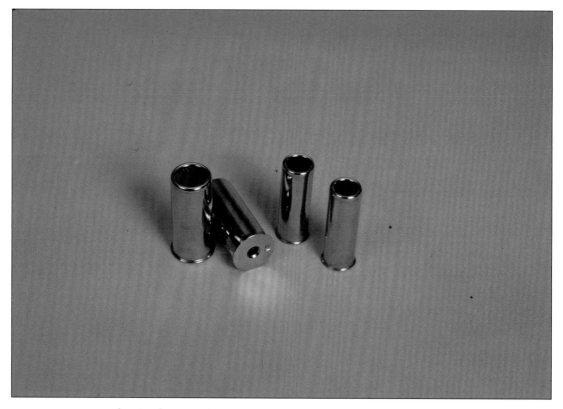

Snap caps are necessary for dry firing and releasing the mainsprings on a fine gun.

bench and a second for the other parts of the gun that I'm not currently working with. They absorb liquids, and provide a nice nonslip work surface. In addition, small parts, springs, and screws are easy to see, and because of the short nap, do not roll off the bench.

Gloves: It's best to handle a fine shotgun with gloves to prevent skin oils from transferring to the metal or wood, and in the field gloves provide a good, solid grip. A few pairs of white cotton museum gloves are a good idea for handling especially valuable guns. Another benefit of a good glove is that it will keep your leading hand from getting burned while you're shooting in a hot dove corner, or if you're simply doing a lot of shooting at the trap, skeet, or clays course.

Cartridge bag: Every gentleman shooter should have a good-quality shell bag. That may sound snobbish, but why not? I like a good British-style shell bag for dove hunting. I'm using only one type of ammunition, and depending on my level of shooting on that day, I may need lots of shells. The open-top design allows quick access, plus, if I put seventy-five 12-gauge shells into a hundred-cartridge bag, there is sufficient room for my shooting glasses, gloves, and hearing protection.

Handguard: The purpose of a traditional splinter forend is to hold the barrels to the action, aid in cocking the hammers, and provide space for the ejectors. Even beavertail forends often do not adequately insulate the fingers, since shooters with long arms often grip the

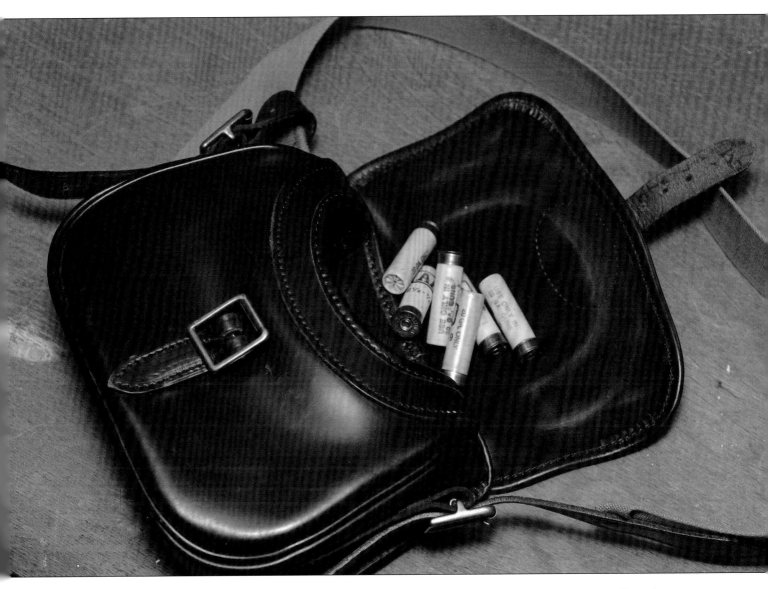

Although expensive a fine leather cartridge bag will last for decades and is an easy way to carry shells in the field.

barrels beyond the beavertail. Many companies manufacture leather-covered, metal handguards that slip onto the barrels from the muzzle. The handguard is stopped by the forward end of the forend, and helps somewhat in protecting your fingers from hot barrels. Take care not to pick up the gun by these handguards, since they can easily slip, causing the gun to fall.

Barrel micrometer and wall-thickness gauge: This is not necessary unless you frequently trade or collect shotguns. The barrel micrometer will provide information regarding the actual inside bore diameter. If the gun is of British manufacture, it is easy to compare the current bore diameter to the diameter at time of proof, and determine if the barrels have been

Atop a cleaning kit are a leather hand guard, barrel tampions that are intended to keep shotgun bores dust free, but can also rust into the barrels, and a shell extractor made nearly redundant by plastic-cased ammunition.

polished to remove pitting. It also measures actual choke constriction.

A wall-thickness gauge—Anthony Galazan of Connecticut Shotgun Manufacturing Company makes one—is necessary only for someone dealing in older used shotguns. It will register the thickness of the barrels at virtually any point, except where the barrels are connected by the top and bottom ribs. To be safe, barrels ought to measure at least .025 inches thick, though .030 inches is better. A wall-thickness gauge can quickly help you determine barrel thickness, and the inherent safety of those barrels.

Chamber-length gauge: If you frequently trade guns or shop for guns at gun shows, a little pocket chamber-length gauge is invaluable. Costing about $40 from Connecticut Shotgun Manufacturing Company, the gauge will quickly and accurately measure chambers from 10-gauge through .410 bore. Be aware that a few shotguns, including the A. H. Fox HE-Grade Super Fox, have tightly tapered chambers that cannot be measured with a conventional chamber-length gauge. However, the chamber length is stamped on the barrel flats, and that dimension can be relied on. When dealing with older, American-

A workman at the Holland & Holland factory measuring the bore of a shotgun barrel he is lapping.

made firearms and shotguns from overseas, remember that chamber lengths can vary, with most being short, so a chamber-length gauge can be valuable.

Tampions and bore ropes: Tampions are muzzle plugs. Normally mounted on springs that are compressed to insert them into the muzzles of a shotgun, tampions were initially thought to be necessary to properly store shotguns so that nothing could enter the muzzles. We now know that good air circulation is necessary to prevent rust. In extremely dusty conditions, a set of tampions would perhaps prevent dust from entering the muzzles, but great care must be exercised to ensure they are removed prior to shooting.

Now anachronisms, bore ropes were soaked in oil, and then pulled into the barrel. Supposed to prevent off-season rust, most dried out, picked up moisture, and rusted firmly in place. They're fun to collect—just leave them in the original boxes as conversation pieces.

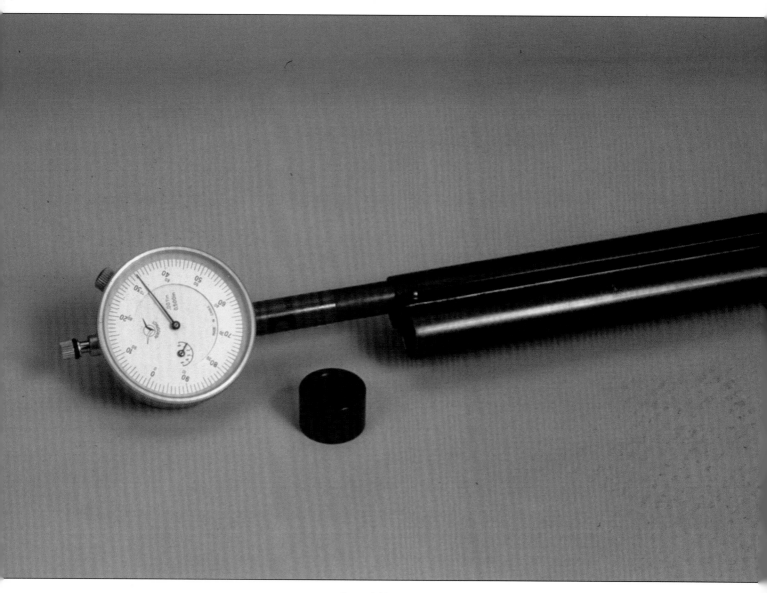

Barrel Micrometer.

CHAPTER 28

Cases for High-Grade Shotguns

Nothing protects a fine shotgun better than an equally fine case. Cases come in two types: hard and soft. In almost all situations, a hard case will provide the maximum protection, soft cases less so.

OAK-AND-LEATHER CASES

The classic hard case for a fine shotgun is a fitted case made of leather-covered oak. The inside is carefully fitted to the individual gun, and the deluxe ones also come complete with a set of fitted turnscrews or screwdrivers, cleaning equipment, oil bottles, containers for extra strikers or firing pins and springs, snap caps, and other accessories, all carefully fitted into their own compartments. Many top-quality fine guns, regardless of their age, often come in an oak-and-leather case. If in good repair, these cases provide great protection at the expense of weight, as oak-and-leather cases weigh a ton. Too, trunk cases were designed in an era of land travel. Gentlemen and ladies trav-

eled by rail, horse-drawn carriages, then automobiles, and trips abroad were by steamer. It was in this era of genteel travel, and servants who carried the bags, that the oak-and-leather case was the premier case. Even in those years, lighter but still hard cases, called "motor cases," were also in vogue. Lighter in weight, they provided adequate protection for fine guns when traveling by car. Don't forget that the oak-and-leather case was born in an era of servants, and it didn't matter how much it weighed since one's "man" handled it.

There is little in addition to a first-quality shotgun in excellent condition that sets it off more than a fine oak-and-leather case. Even one in shabby condition adds to the prestige, especially if it is the original case that came with the gun from the maker. In that instance, inside the lid will be the maker's label and cards listing the load for which the gun was made and with which it was expected the gun would be used. There are several indi-

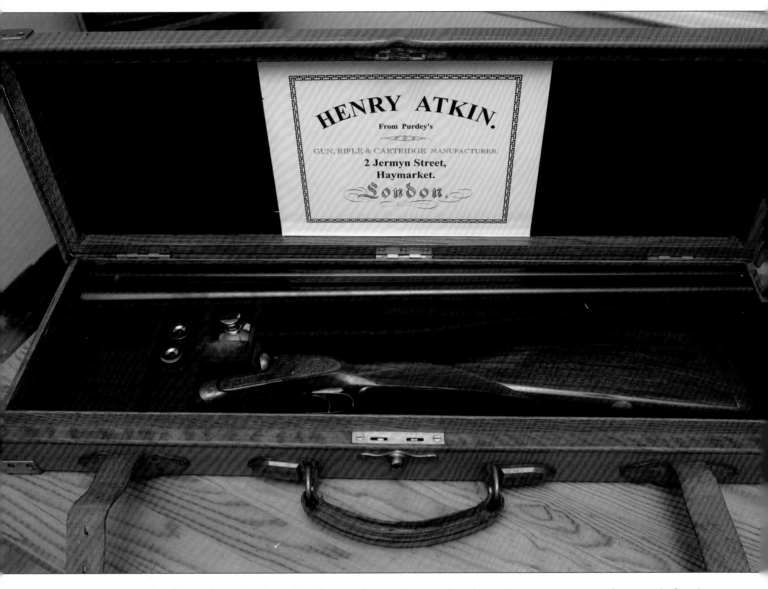

An example of a traditional oak-and-leather trunk case that weighs about the same as an anvil. Precisely fitted to the individual shotgun, these cases add to the value of any shotgun.

viduals who specialize in rehabilitating dilapidated cases. Their services include repair of the leather and cleaning or completely relining the case and rebuilding broken partitions. A case in poor condition can be brought back to nice condition and that will increase it and the gun's value.

I have a wonderful old Henry Atkin that came in an oak-and-leather case. Regrettably, it wasn't the original, but the gun was made about 1900—quality lasts—and it would be a miracle if the original case could have lasted that long. It came in a nice, moderately good, oak-and-leather case, but not a precisely fitted case, and while it adds some value, it's not much. A case restorer could reblock the interior to better fit the gun and accommodate the accessories. Someday, maybe.

Melvin Huey and a few others currently make oak-and-leather cases. They are beautiful, functional works of art at commensurately high prices. That's not a condemnation, because these cases are very labor-intensive to produce, and they must be built one at a time because each is unique. Worth the money, perhaps. If you own a vintage Purdey or other great shotgun, then investing in a top-of-the-line, oak-and-leather case is worth every penny.

FLIGHT CASES

As wonderful as oak-and-leather cases are, they are not designed nor intended for air travel. The exterior leather covering is susceptible to all manner of gouging and scuffing by mechanical and human baggage handling. True, canvas case covers are available to protect the exterior, but due to their great weight, and the savage attitude of baggage handlers to anything heavier than a box of Kleenex, an oak-and-leather case would be punished far more than necessary.

A whole industry has sprung up to serve the flying sportsman. The Federal Aviation Administration (FAA) requires that all firearms be declared at the moment of check-in for a flight. They must be unloaded and contained in a locked, hard case. That's all. Some airlines have other restrictions, but from experience, if I arrive at the ticket counter with my shotguns in a good-quality, hard, locked case, there is no problem. I prefer cases in which the shotguns are broken down. Most airline ticket agents are not shooters, and they receive virtually no training in checking firearms. However, if guns

are broken down it is obvious that they are not capable of being fired in that state, and consequently they meet all the criteria, and normally present few problems to ticket agents. After you sign a form that is put inside the case with the firearm, the case is locked, and you're on your way.

I have talked with Transportation Security Administration (TSA) officers, and they advise that once the firearm is declared and the declaration form is placed inside the case, I should lock the case and send it through inspection. However, I always hang around until my guns are cleared, just in case they want to look. Always lock your case before handing it over. If TSA inspectors want to look inside, they will page you. Always provide plenty of extra time at the check-in end of a flight. It might not be necessary, but mark my words, the one time you check in late, you'll encounter an obstinate agent. I use Americase cases, but a plethora of cases are available, most of which more or less copy each other. I have a double double-gun case that takes two 30-inch-barreled side-by-sides or over-and-unders and also provides plenty of space for choke tubes, oil, grease, knife, and other accessories. For the most part, I can put my knife and other small accessories in with my shotguns, saving space and weight elsewhere. Be aware that choke tubes must be in your checked baggage, since they are parts of a firearm. Don't argue the point—just pack them. If you want to pack ammunition, it too must be in your checked baggage. Normally, ammo can go in your main bag, but be certain to declare it. There are severe penalties for

This Americase is the best bet for traveling with a high-value shotgun. These cases provide excellent protection and can be purchased configured for one shotgun, two shotguns, shotguns with several barrels, etc.

failing to declare firearms and ammunition. At the very least, the hassles can be trying. Just play the game by the rules, and the problems diminish greatly.

The choice of hard cases is wide, and while a very cheap case complies with FAA rules, it may not protect your fine shotgun. On a trip to Uruguay, a fellow writer's guns were in a full-length aluminum case, but when we arrived at Montevideo, the entire end of one side of the case had been peeled back, revealing the barrel of one and stock of the other. The bird boys bent it back and repaired it fairly well for his return trip, and he also mummified it with duct tape. Those with better cases had no problems. Quality pays, and the more compact the case, the less chance you run of having it—and your fine guns—damaged.

This slip is the best way to transport shotguns around a shooting facility, between pegs on a driven shoot, in a duck boat or car, or any time the protection of a hard case is unnecessary.

SOFT CASES

For travel by car, a good-quality soft case is hard to beat. The gun is assembled and ready to go, with no need to put the gun together in the blowing dust, driving rain, or snow. Soft cases will guard against most damage, but not all. Rolling around in the back of a pickup truck with a bunch of metal fence posts, chain saws, tools, etc., is not a good environment for a gun, cased or not. Dented barrels are the primary problem. You can shoot a shotgun with a dent in the stock, but a dented barrel should never be fired. Repair is not cheap, as it often requires rebluing, so a soft case must be used with care.

Another problem with soft cases is how they open. Some use zippers, some spring clips, some hook-and-loop material, and some ties. The problem is that all of these can fail. Always carry a shotgun in a soft case with the muzzle end down, since this is the end that is completely closed. Don't rely on the fasteners to keep it closed.

I use soft cases all the time. I feel a gun is best protected in a soft case when traveling by car to the gun club or to hunt. There is no need to assemble the gun in adverse weather, and if you're rushing to get started, proper lubrication is often neglected. With a soft case, the knuckle and hinge are lubed at home, and ready to go. However, if I'm taking a long trip by car to hunt or shoot clays, I always opt for hard cases. They pack well, the guns are fully protected, and they handle well moving in and out of motel rooms, etc. I carry a couple of soft cases for field use, but on long trips hard cases are best.

SLIPS

When shooting driven game, it is almost mandatory to carry shotguns from point to point in a slip. A gun slip is no more than a light, soft case with a shoulder strap for easy carrying. More for safety and ease of handling than anything else, the gun must be in a slip whenever the shooter is not in his butt. In proper slip use, the gun is withdrawn until the action is barely free, and then the action is opened and the gun withdrawn fully. When you're moving to another butt, the broken gun is pushed into the slip up to the action, which is then closed and the gun fully encased.

I use a Cordura gun slip from Avery Outdoors anytime I hunt waterfowl. The company offers a floating model for boats, but anytime I'm going to walk to a pit, slog through a marsh to a blind, or walk to a dove corner, my gun is in its Avery slip. This slip has a good nonslip shoulder strap, and a pocket for a couple of choke tubes or a small bottle of lubricant, and the latest model has a pocket for a goose flag. It keeps my hands free for other gear or just keeping my balance in the mud. Don't leave home without a slip with a shoulder strap.

The types and numbers of case styles are vast. Choosing the correct case is important, either to the value of the gun, or for keeping a fine gun in good shape despite the violence of modern-day baggage handling, or as a convenient way to transport a shotgun a few miles to the range or field. Choose well—as a good case will last for many years.

CHAPTER 29

Shopping for High-Grade Shotguns

In the Internet age, the prospective gun buyer can go to endless sources to find what he is looking for. If he wants to go online and buy a gun without having personally inspected the firearm, then buying a gun is just a click of the cursor away. Another option is to go to traditional gun shops, which can vary from a guy's converted garage to the lavish gun rooms of Holland & Holland in New York, Anthony Galazan's Connecticut Shotgun Manufacturing Company in Connecticut, or Briley in Texas. Yet another option is to go to a gun show or to an annual event such as the Vintagers Shoot, which attracts dozens of fine-gun makers and dealers to Pintail Point near Queenstown, Maryland; about a twenty-minute drive from the eastern end of the Chesapeake Bay Bridge. The Safari Club International (SCI) Annual Hunters' Convention in Reno, Nevada, is still another possibility.

Shows such as the one at Pintail Point showcase mostly side-by-side shotguns. The SCI Convention features all kinds of firearms, mostly large-caliber rifles, but all the fine makers are there, and many display their shotguns. Events such as the annual Grand American trap shoot also have numerous vendors, although the arms at that event are mainly trap guns. All these event-driven shows offer a broad variety of shotguns for sale, albeit within the niche of the specific event.

Local gun shows often have a few high-grade shotguns spread among the various tables. Some of these are good buys, but in the main, gun show prices are quite high, and are often set that way to provide bargaining space. If you go to such a show, be wide awake and prepared to look at every detail, since often the guy sitting at the table doesn't know much about fine shotguns, save the price.

When attending a gun show where I might want to buy something, I carry a bore micrometer, a chamber-length gauge, snap caps in 12-, 20- and 28-gauge, a small tape measure

The entrance to the gun room at Holland & Holland's London store.

to check barrel length, and the latest edition of the *Blue Book of Gun Values*. If I find a shotgun I'm interested in, I'll ask the owner to disassemble it, or do it myself with his permission. I can then check the barrel flats and water table or action flats for whatever markings might be there. There may be little to see on American guns, but a great deal to see on British, Italian, French, Belgian, German, or Austrian shotguns. A Parker shotgun will tell me the grade, barrel steel, action size (stamped on the bottom of the barrel lug), and year of manufacture (with the serial number), but often not the length of the chamber. In the lowest grade, the Parker VH or VHE—the E stands for automatic ejectors—came standard with

Vulcan steel barrels. An action stamped with a W indicates Whitworth steel barrels, although these are rare because this was Parker's lowest-priced graded gun, and few customers opted for add-ons, except for automatic ejectors, which themselves are not particularly common. If you're contemplating purchasing a Parker, do lots of homework and understand all the various markings that Parker used, so you can decipher the specifications of the original shotgun. Understanding the proof marks of a British shotgun should also be an integral part of shopping for a British-made shotgun. The markings are your guide to the origins of the gun, and from them you can often tell how much of the original gun is still there.

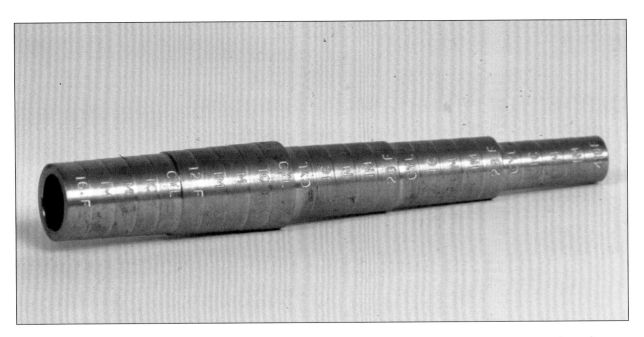

This brass gauge will provide a rough estimate of the amount of choke in a shotgun barrel. Only a barrel micrometer can accurately measure bores and chokes. Gauges like this are handy when shopping at gun shows.

When examining a used shotgun, first check out the wood. Wood that's been refinished more than once, or that a ham-handed refinisher has worked on, will no longer stand proud of the metal. Heavily refinished wood can often be pared down too much, detracting from the value. If you look at a gun that reveals marked divergence from the original—such as heavily refinished wood, refinished metal that's polished over the stampings and engraving, barrels that appear to have been cut, checkering that varies from stock to forend—walk away from it. Tell the seller you're simply not interested. If the seller realizes that you know that the gun has problems, he may be willing to reduce the price, but it had better be so low that you can afford to have the firearm properly repaired. If you're looking for a particular shotgun that's fairly rare, it might be worth bargaining for, but only if it's something you really want, and only if the defects don't render it dangerous or useless. An HE-Grade Super Fox whose barrels have been cut from 32 to 30 inches, or that shows heavy wear but is still solid, might be worth pursuing, for example.

Shopping for a new high-grade shotgun is a lot easier. All well-known gun rooms and gun dealers will offer quality guns at appropriate prices. Certainly, there may be room for bargaining, but often the price is set, and it's up to you to decide if you want to pay it. Handmade shotguns are not cheap to produce, and the price tag will reflect not only the components used, but the intensive labor involved in making the gun. On the other hand, nothing beats sitting with a patient and knowledgeable salesperson and discussing every aspect of a new shotgun so that nothing is neglected or forgotten. I've seen individuals like Chris Batha take orders for $60,000 shotguns. It's his job to guide each client through the ordering process, never rushing but keeping to the task at hand, ensuring that the customer gets exactly the gun he wants.

Experienced shooters are far easier to deal with. They will have been to several shooting schools, have solid, repeatable gun mounts, and will have had at least one if not several gun fittings. With their stock dimensions set— they change as we age and our body contours settle—much of the work is already done. An experienced shooter will have a pretty good idea about what he wants in terms of choking, stock style, barrel length, and so on. No beginning shooter should ever consider ordering a bespoke shotgun until he has attended a good shooting school and had several sessions with a recognized shooting instructor. From this instruction should come the beginnings of a good gun mount, as well as preliminary stock dimensions. Once the proper gun mount is stabilized, a bespoke shotgun can be considered.

Shopping for a high-grade shotgun via the Internet or advertisements in one of the several periodicals that cater to high-grade gun aficionados can be risky. The majority of those who advertise are highly reputable individuals or firms, but there are always bottom feeders lurking out there. Any reputable dealer will allow a three-day inspection period from the date the gun is received. Normally, the buyer calls the seller when the gun arrives, and the clock begins running. If for any reason the gun isn't what you thought it would be, or if you just

don't like it, you have every right to return it. However, it must be returned in the condition received, and expect to pay the return shipping. Don't expect to take a Parker duck hunting and roll it around in the bottom of your boat for the weekend, then send it back Monday. If you wish to shoot the gun, ask if that is permitted, then take it to the clay range or game farm—but remember that it must be returned in the same condition as received. It also goes without saying that if the seller sent it via overnight or second-day express service, you must return it by the same means. In short, the seller, who wants for you to like the shotgun and keep it, is entitled to the same treatment the buyer expects. If a problem occurs because of heavy-handed shippers, it's remedied through the carrier, but don't blame UPS for a scratched stock—bent barrels maybe, but not scratches from briers.

On the other hand, if the seller says, "I'll send it and you've bought it," hang up. Do not buy a shotgun of any kind from anyone who is not willing to hold your check until you've had a fair time to inspect and ruminate about the purchase. Anything other than a firm commitment to this arrangement should send up a multitude of red flags.

Are there any bargain high-grade shotguns? Probably not, at least as far as new guns are concerned. Perhaps a gun room will take several new guns into stock, and for whatever reason decide to move them along. One of those could be a bargain. Often the seller will offer to bend the stock for a reduced fee to better fit the buyer, or some other enticement. These deals are few and far between, but they do occur from time to time. Occasionally one of the major gun rooms will reduce the prices on used guns to clear out accumulated stock, and that's when real bargains can be found.

If you know what you want, good bargains can be had on the used market. I found a vintage Henry Atkin at the Vintagers Shoot a couple of years ago. It had several problems. The stock was oil-soaked at the head, it came in a nice oak-and-leather case that was not the original, and it had thin-walled Briley screw-in choke tubes. Some people would have rejected this gun immediately, but I was attracted to it. I feel that screw-in chokes are perhaps the greatest development in shotgun technology since the breechloader was defined. They provide the user flexibility, and the fact that some of the world's finest bespoke shotguns can be so choked speaks volumes. I traded a composed pair and an American shotgun that I never could shoot well for the Atkin. I saw my trades listed by the dealer at high prices, but that's how the game is played. I then spent some money to have my new Atkin shotgun's buttstock replaced with a piece of Bastogne walnut and fitted to my measurements, and put the old stock aside to go with the gun should I ever decide sell it. The seller's price, against which I was trading, was about a third to half that of a similar Atkin on another table. Mine's not a collector's gun, but a shooter's gun, and that's just fine with me.

When seeking a trade, remember that you're trading your gun at wholesale against the seller's gun that's at retail. Seldom if ever is anyone willing to trade wholesale against wholesale. Keep in mind, too, that prices in the *Blue Book of Gun Values* and similar publications are guidelines only. They represent a good yardstick against which to measure a gun in hand in regard to condition, and then to arrive at a mutually agreeable price. Seldom do sellers receive the prices listed in these books. Yes, you can be swindled, and if your heirs are not wise in the ways of guns, be sure that they know they should take your collection to a reputable dealer who will give them a fair price. Selling guns on consignment normally requires a 10- to 20-percent commission for the seller. Often selling a gun or an entire collection outright is easier, even though this normally brings the seller only about 35 or 40 percent of the gun's retail price. Selling unique guns this way puts the onus on the buying dealer to sell it, and relieves the seller the hassles of weighing offers.

I've got about all the shotguns I need, but probably not all I want. The quest for a particular shotgun is fun, and often takes many twists and turns. Often you'll meet some wonderful people, though you may also run across some whose photos and fingerprints belong on a wanted poster in a post office. For my part, the majority have been great people who were frequently fonts of knowledge, and who added greatly to my personal education about guns. I've tried to not spend much time with the others.

Appendix A
HIGH-GRADE SHOTGUN MANUFACTURERS AND IMPORTERS

Aguirre y Aranzabal AYA (USA)
P.O. Box 647
Old Saybrook, CT 06475
(860) 388-3989

Arietta Manufacturas, S.L.
Morkaiko, 5
Elgoibar
Spain 20870

Pedro Arrizabalaga, S.A.
Errekatux, 5
Eibar, Guipuscoa
Spain 20600
43-11743

Asprey & Garrard
The Gun Room
167 New Bond St.
London
W1S 4AR, UK
011-44-20-7493-6767, Ext. 2865

Atkin, Grant & Lang
Broomhill Leys, Windmill Rd.
Markyate, St. Albans
Hertfordshire
AL3 8LP, UK
011-44-1582-842280

Beretta USA
17601 Beretta Dr.
Accokeek, MD 20607
(800) 636-3420

Armi Fratelli Bertuzzi
Via Alessandro Volta 65
25063 Gardone Val Trompia
Italy
39-03-08912188

Thomas Bland & Sons
Woodcock Hill
192 Spencers Rd.
Benton, PA 17814
(570) 864-3242

Blaser USA
403 East Ramsey, Ste. 301
San Antonio, TX 78216
(210) 377-2527

Fabbrica Armi Luciano Bosis
Via G. Marconi 30
25039 Travagliato
Brescia
Italy
011-39-030-660413

Boss & Co., Ltd
110 Kew Green
Richmond, London
TW9 3AP, UK
44-020-8948-2781

Briley Manufacturing
1230 Lumpkin Road,
Houston, TX 77043
(800) 331-5718

Browning
One Browning Place
Morgan, UT 84050
(800) 333-3288

Caesar Guerini USA
700 Lake St.
Cambridge, MD 21613
(410) 901-1131

Charles Boswell Gunmakers
43 Pinckney Coloney Rd.
Okatie, SC 29909
(866) 254-2405

Connecticut Shotgun Manufacturing Co.
100 Burritt St.

New Britain, CT 06506-4004
(860) 225-6581

Dakota Arms
1310 Industry Rd.
Sturgis, SD 57785
(605) 347-4686

Darne, S.A.
4T, Rue de la Convention
42100 St.-Étienne
France
04.77.37.00.96

Dickson & MacNaughton
21 Frederick St.
Edinburgh, Scotland
EH2 2NE, UK
44-131-225-4218

William Evans, Ltd.
67A St. James St.
London
SW1A 1PH, UK

Fabbri snc
Via Don Filippo Bassi 6 – 25075
Nave (BS) Italy
39-030-2715300

Famars di Abbiatico & Savinelli
Via Valtrompia, 16/18
25063 Gardone Val Trompia
Brescia, Italy
39-030-891-2894

Johann Fanzoj
Fanzoj Jagdwaffen GmbH
Griesgasse 3
9170 Ferlach, Austria
43-4227-2867

Fausti Steffano SRL
Via Martiri dell'Indipendenza, 70
25060 Marcheno V.T.
Brescia, Italy
39-030-861-0155

Auguste Francotte & Cie
See: Connecticut Shotgun Manufacturing Co.

Galazan
See: Connecticut Shotgun Manufacturing Co.

Renato Gamba
Via Artigioni, 93
25063 Gardone V.T
Brescia, Italy
03-030-891-0265

Armas Garbi
Uki, 12-14
Eibar, Guipuzcoa
Spain 20600
43-113873

Giacomo Sporting
6234 Stokes-Lee Rd.,
Lee Center, NY 13367
(315) 336-1356

Griffin & Howe
33 Claremont Rd.
Bernardsville, NJ 07924
(908) 766-2287

Grulla Armas
P.O. Box 453
Eibar, Guipuzcoa
Spain 20600
43-118756

GSI (Merkel and Hyem)
P.O. Box 129
7661 Commerce Ln.
Trussville, AL 35173
(205) 655-8399

Hartman & Weiss GmbH
Rahlstedter Bahnhofstr. 47
22143 Hamburg
Germany
49-40-677-5585

Peter Hofer Jagdwaffen
Kirshgasse 24
9170 Ferlach
Austria
43-42-273683

Holland & Holland Ltd. (USA)
10 E. 40th St., Suite 1910
New York, NY 10016
(212) 752-7755

Holloway & Naughton
Turners Barn Farm, Kibworth Rd.
Three Gates, Illston-on-the-Hill
Leicestershire
LE7 9EQ, UK
44-116-259-6592

Armas Kemen
Ermuraranb ide, 14 – apartado n. 60
20870 Elgoibar, Guipuzcoa
Spain
43-43-74-4401

Krieghoff International
P.O. Box 549
7528 Easton Rd.
Ottsville, PA 18942
(610) 847-5173

Lebeau-Courally
386, Rue Saint-Gilles
4000 Liège
Belgium
32-41-52-2008

S. Lucchini Shotguns
25060 Ponte Zanano, V.T.
Sarezzo, Italy
39-30-89-11573

David McKay Brown
32 Hamilton Rd.
Bothwell
G71 8N, UK
44-1698-853727

Merkel
See: GSI

**William Larkin Moore & Co.
(Importer)**
8340 E. Raintree Dr., Suite B-7
Scottsdale, AZ 85260
(480) 951-8913

The Orvis Company
P.O. Box 798
Manchester, VT 05254
(802) 362-2580

Perazzi USA
1010 W. Tenth St.
Azusa, CA 91702
(626) 334-1234

Piotti Fratelli snc
Via Cinelli, 10-12
25063 Gardone Val Trompia

Brescia
Italy
39-030-891-6522

William Powell & Son, Ltd
35-36 Carrs Lane
Birmingham
B4 7SX, UK
44-121-643-2689

James Purdey & Sons
57-58 South Audley St.
London
W1K 2ED, UK
44-20-7499-1801

Remington Arms Co.
P.O. Box 700
870 Remington Dr.
Madison, NC 27025
(800) 243-9700

John Rigby & Co.
500 Linne Rd., Suite D
Paso Robles, CA 93446
(805) 227-4236

Fabbrica D'Arma Fratelli Rizzini snc
Via X Giornate, N. 9
25063 Magno V.T.
Brescia
Italy
39-030-891-1400

Ignacio Ugartechea, S.A.
P.O. Box 21
Eibar, Guipuzcoa
Spain 20600
3443-121669

Appendix B
Helpful References

L. C. Smith Collectors Association
Frank Finch, Executive Director
1322 Bay Avenue
Mantoloking, NJ 08738
(732) 899-1498
www.lcsmith.org

The Parker Gun Collectors Association
P.O. Box 115
Mayodan, NC 27027
www.parkergun.org

Information about Ansley H. Fox, Savage, and Stevens firearms
J. T. Callahan
53 Old Quarry Rd.
Westfield, ME 01085

German Gun Collectors Association
P.O. Box 429
Mayfield, UT 84643
(435) 979-9723
info@germanguns.com
www.germanguns.com

A. H. Fox Collectors Association
www.foxcollectors.com

The Blue Book of Gun Values
Blue Book Publications
8009 34th Avenue South, Suite 175
Minneapolis, MN 55425
(800) 877-4867, Ext. 3 (Orders only)
www.bluebookinc.com

Appendix C
Manufacture Dates

1900	9100

Lefever Arms Co.
Lefever Sidelock Model Guns

YEAR	GUN #
1880	5000
1881	5500
1882	6500
1883	7500
1884	8049
1885	8500
1886	9500
1887	10000
1888	10500
1889	11500
1890	12500
1891	14552
1892	17240
1893	20264
1894	22112
1895	23288
1896	24856
1897	25556
1898	27180
1899	28916
1900	31632
1901	36364
1902	40480
1903	45408
1904	49496
1905	51064
1906	54592
1907	57924
1908	60164
1909	61704
1910	62824
1911	65092
1912	65512
1913	69544
1914	71336
1915-1919	73000 plus

Lefever Nitro Special
(Made by Ithaca Gun Co.)

YEAR	GUN #
1921	100,000 - 101599
1922	119899
1923	158699
1924	185399
1925	214399
1926	233007
1927	252699
1928	272999
1929	297199
1930	298699
1933	298749
1934	299249
1935	299999
1935	325000-327299
1936	336399
1937	345099
1938	345899
1939	347099
1940	353099
1941	354999
1942	356299
1946	357299
1947	361199

Lefever A Grade
(Made by Ithaca Gun Co.)

YEAR	GUN #
1934	300000-300654
1935	301007
1936	301023
1937	301037
1938	301045
1935	301050-301699
1936	302099
1937	302399
1938	302456
1939	302496

Lefever Single Barrel Guns - (Made by Ithaca Gun Co.)

YEAR	GUN #
1927	8505
1928	15729
1929	20280
1930	20799
1931	21799
left open	21899
1935	22299
1936	23099
1937	23499
1938	23799
1939	24579
1940	24604
1941	24607

PARKER

YEAR	GUN #
1867-1878	1-10000
1878	13000
1879	16000
1880	18000
1881	23000
1882	28000
1883	35000
1884	38000
1885	47000
1886	50000
1887	57000
1889	60000
1890	40000
1891	70000
1892	75000
1893	79000
1894	80000
1895	83000
1896	86000
1897	87000
1898	90000
1899	94000
1900	99000
1901	106000
1902	114000
1903	122000
1904	128000
1905	131000
1906	139000
1907	145000
1908	148000
1909	151000
1910	154000
1911	157000
1911	158000
1913	165000
1914	169000
1915	172000
1916	175000
1917	178000
1918	181000
1919	185000
1920	191000
1921	196000
1922	201000
1923	206000
1924	209000
1925	215000
1926	220000
1927	223000
1928	227000
1929	231000
1930	235000
1931	235500
1932-33	236000
1934	237000
1935	238000
1936	240000
1937	241000
1938-47	242385

PIOTTI

YEAR	GUN #
1962	1
1962	515
1963	1285
1964	1913
1965	2594
1966	2988
1967	3351
1968	3954
1969	4787
1970	5018
1971	5499
1972	5815
1973	6180
1974	6437
1975	6650
1976	6839
1977	7025
1978	7236
1979	7388
1980	7524
1981	7663
1982	7797
1983	7918
1984	8038
1985	8179
1986	8318
1987	8465
1988	8605
1989	8753
1990	8878
1991	8978
1992	9063

JAMES PURDEY

YEAR	GUN #
1814	974
1826	1149
1827	1324
1828	1549
1829	1874
1830	1999
1831	2247
1832	2421
1833	2497
1834	2697
1835	2773
1836	2848
1837	3098
1838	3223
1839	3298
1840	3473
1841	3623
1842	3698
1843	3848
1844	3998
1845	4048
1846	4098
1847	4223
1848	4348
1849	4473
1850	4599
1851	4720
1852	4844
1853	4944
1854	5093
1855	5167
1856	5267
1857	5443
1858	5542
1859	5747
1860	5997
1861	6271
1862	6422
1863	6671
1864	6871
1865	7121
1866	7420
1867	7646
1868	7896
1869	8246
1870	8322
1871	8646
1872	8821
1873	9096
1874	9288
1875	9505
1876	9648
1877	10153
1878	10440
1879	10800
1880	10900
1881	11082
1882	11342
1883	11669
1884	12036
1885	12171
1886	12530
1887	12875
1888	13150
1889	13468
1890	13662
1891	14000
1892	14520
1893	14851
1894	15134
1895	15362
1896	15726
1897	16095
1898	16420
1899	16736
1900	17078
1901	17227
1902	17547
1903	17849
1904	18148
1905	18400
1906	18686
1907	18987
1908	19272
1909	19546
1910	19813
1911	20147
1912	20400
1913	20770
1914	21086
1915	21332
1916	21465
1917	21541
1919	21574
1920	21892
1921	22111
1922	22312
1923	22491
1924	22896
1925	22937
1926	23283
1927	23284
1928	23551
1929	23854
1930	24139
1931	24387
1932	24567
1933	24647
1934	24743
1935	24920
1936	25130
1937	25325
1938	25526
1939	25711
1940	25783
1941	25793
1942	25813
1943	25844
1945	25851
1946	25901
1947	25990
1948	26051
1949	26128
1950	26206
1951	26275
1952	26349
1953	26423
1955	26531
1975	28003
1979	28546
1981	28569

WESTLEY RICHARDS

YEAR	GUN #
1869	12000
1877	13000
1884	14000
1893	15000
1901	16000
1908	17000
1924	18000
1935	18500
1957	19000

JOHN RIGBY

YEAR	GUN #
1822	5341
1825	5745
1830	6667
1835	7640
1840	8531
1845	9487
1850	10171
1855	10634
1860	10986
1865	12418
1870	13416
1875	14227
1880	15076
1885	15660
1890	16106
1895	16410
1900	16700
1905	17250
1910	17550
1930	18162

RIZZINI
Sidelock Gun

YEAR	GUN #
1980	1
1981	21
1982	41
1983	61
1984	81
1985	101
1986	121
1987	141
1988	161
1989	181
1992	200

W.&C. Scott & Son
(Guns in Bold Typeface Webly & Scott)

YEAR	GUN #
1865	1
1868	1000
1871	2000
1872	3000
1873	4000
1874	5000
1875	6000
1876	7000
1877	8000
1878	10000
1866	11000
1867	12000
1869	13000
1870	14000
1871	15000
1872	16000
1873	17000
1874	19000
1875	20000
1876	21000
1877	22000
1878	23000
1879	25000
1880	27000
1881	29000
1882	31000
1883	33000
1884	35000
1885	37000
1886	39000
1887	42000
1888	43000
1889	44000
1890	45000
1891	47000
1892	49000
1893	51000
1894	53000
1895	55000
1896	57000
1897	**53000**
1898	**54000**
1899	**56000**
1900	57000
1897	58000
1898	60000
1899	61000
1900	62000
1901	63000
1902	65000
1903	66000
1904	68000
1905	69000
1900	**70000**
1902	**71000**
1904	**73000**
1905	**74000**
1906	**75000**
1907	**76000**
1908	**77000**
1909	**78000**
1911	**79000**
1906	80000-81000
1907	82000
1908	84000
1909	85000
1910	87000
1911	88000
1912	90000
1914	91000
1916	92000
1920	94000
1921	95000
1922	96000
1924	99000
1913	**100000**
1915	**101000**
1920	**102000**
1924	**103000**
	104000
	105000
not	**106000**
assigned	**107000**
	108000
	109000
1925	110000
1926	111000
1927	112000
1929	113000
1932	114000
1936	115000
1939	116000
1947	117000
1948	118000
1949	119000
1950	120000
1951	122000
1952	123000
1953	125000
1955	126000
1956	127000
1957	128000
1958	129000
1960	130000
1961	131000
1962	132000
1963	133000
1964	135000
1965	136000
1966	137000
1967	138000
1968	139000
1969	140000
1970	141000
1971	142000
1973	143000
1975	144000
1976	145000
1978	146000
1966	200000
1978	**701000**
1978	**702000**
1976	**712000**
1971	**720000**
1971	**728000**

L.C. SMITH
(Manufactured by Hunter Arms Co. 1890-1918)

Hammerless (Non-ejector) - 20 Gauge

YEAR	GUN #
1907	1000-1204
1908	1329
1909	1788
1910	2587
1911	3615
1912	4630
1913	4999
1913	10000-10786
1914	11451
1915	11873
1916	12361
1917	12666
1918	12753

Hammerless (Non-ejector) - 10 and 12 Gauge

1890	30000-32527
1891	34381
1892	36615
1893	37324
1894	38892
1895	40334

Hammerless (Non-ejector) - 8, 10, 12 and 16 Gauge

1896	40335-42219
1897	44104
1898	45999

Hammerless (Non-ejector) - 16 Gauge

1895	60000-60144
1896	60289
1897	60434
1898	60579
1899	60724
1900	60869
1901	61014
1902	61159
1903	61402
1904	61685
1905	62156
1906	62653
1907	63698
1908	64226
1909	65021
1910	65861
1911	66821
1912	67683
1913	68704
1914	69681
1915	69999
1915	400000-401758

Hammerless (Non-ejector) - 10 and 12 Gauge

1899	105210
1900	105917
1901	111681
1902	119035
1903	120767
1904	124419
1905	124999
1904	300000-300301
1905	305787
1906	311528
1907	318079
1908	322129
1909	329476
1910	333081
1911	336572
1912	341717
1913	345493
1914	350857
1915	352431
1916	355068
1917	359624
1918	361071

Hammerless (Non-ejector) - 10, 12 and 16 Gauge

1891	500-559
1898	3173
1901	6959
1902	9000
1902	200000-200025
1903	201758
1904	203272
1905	205098
1906	207093
1907	209368
1908	210579
1909	211885
1910	213084
1911	214246
1912	215615
1913	216939
1914	218260
1915	218829
1916	219603
1917	219750

Hammer Guns - 20 Gauge

1907	5000-5131
1908	5379
1909	5677
1910	6238
1911	6593
1912	7076
1913	7521
1914	7828
1915	7935
1916	8149
1917	8250

Hammer Guns - 10, 12 and 16 Gauge

1894	50000-50867
1895	51735
1896	52602
1897	55301
1898	58000
1900	79000-84943
1901	89999
1902	125000-129700
1903	133039
1904	137445
1905	144409
1906	150221
1907	156901
1908	159519
1909	163160
1910	166705
1911	168761
1912	171415
1913	173371
1914	175483
1915	176091
1916	176576
1917	178522
1918	179841

All Gauges 1918-1950 **(These serial numbers include all types of L.C. Smith, Fulton and Hunter Shotguns)**

YEAR	GUN #
1918	101-3850
1919	18252
1920	35228
1921	44566
1922	51985
1923	64187
1924	75897
1925	86695
1926	93841
1927	103900
1928	114817
1929	125347
1930	132827
1931	134242
1930-1938	136741
1932	137779
1933	138371
1934	140146
1935	144296
1936	151123
1937	162670
1938	171179
1939	181701
1940	190280
1941	197124
1942	201794
1943	202959
1944	204084
1945	205423
1946	1-8595
1947	25661
1948	41825
1949	55608
1950	56800

Western Long-Range -

YEAR	GUN #
1929	16-Jan
1930	24499
1931	29999
1932	30399
1934	30849
1935	34599
1936	41699
1937	47299
1938	49299
1939	52899
1940	59199
1941	64199
1946	65779

JAMES WOODWARD

YEAR	GUN #
1874-1879	3268-3717
1885	4102
1891	4608
1897	5230
1903	5712
1909	6044
1915	6433
1921	6637
1927	6832
1933	7014
1939	7153
1948	718

FREDERICK BEESLEY

YEAR	GUN #
1891	1100
1895	1300
1900	1650
1929	2733

BOSS & COMPANY

YEAR	GUN #
1830	680
1850	1400
1857	1600
1900	4700
1920	6618
1930	7730
1945	8711
1951	8912
1953	8920
1963	9219
1970	9559

CHURCHILL LTD

YEAR	GUN #
1891	156
1892	339
1893	384
1894	480
1895	569
1896	655
1897	761
1898	923
1899	1047
1900	1156
1924	2834
1957	6901

JOHN DICKSON

YEAR	GUN #
1812 - 1854	1 - 1500
1860	2000
1864	2500
1870	3000
1878	3500
1885	3933
1886	4000
1889	4889
1892	4500
1898	5000
1903	5500

A.H. FOX

12 Gauge Grade A-F

YEAR	GUN #
1907	7500
1908	7600
1909	9900
1910	15000
1911	18700
1912	20000
1913	20700
1914	21500
1915	22000
1916	23200
1917	24300
1918	24700
1919	25000
1920	25900
1921	27000
1922	27900
1923	29000
1924	30000
1925	30900
1926	31600
1927	32000
1928	32900
1929	33850
1930	33900
1931	33999
1932	34100
1933	34200
1934	34300
1935	34400
1936	34500
1937	34750
1938	34900
1939	35150
1940	35280

16 Gauge Grade A-F

YEAR	GUN #
1912	300075
1913	300200
1914	300400
1915	300600
1916	300700
1917	300750
1918	300800
1919	300900
1920	301100
1921	301300
1922	301500
1923	301800
1924	302000
1925	302300
1926	302500
1927	302650
1928	302800
1929	303000
1930	303050
1931	303100
1932	303200
1933	303300
1934	303350
1935	303400
1936	303500
1937	303650
1938	303800
1939	303850
1940	303870
Last Gun Made	303875

20 Gauge Grade A-F

YEAR	GUN #
1912	200100
1913	200250
1914	200500
1915	200700
1916	200800
1917	200900
1918	201000
1919	201300
1920	201500
1921	201600
1922	201800
1923	202000
1924	202200
1925	202400
1926	202500
1927	202800
1928	202950
1929	203100
1930	203150
1931	203200
1932	203300
1933	203350
1934	203500
1935	203700
1936	203750
1937	203800
1938	203830
1939	203900
1940	203970
Last number in series	203974

12 Gauge Sterlingworth

YEAR	GUN #
1910	53800
1911	59000
1912	63500
1913	66500
1914	74200
1915	75600
1916	77500
1917	79000
1918	82000
1919	84500
1920	89500
1921	92300
1922	94500
1923	97500
1924	99000
1925	100600
1926	105500
1927	113500
1928	119000
1929	122600
1930	128500
1931	130000
1932	132000
1933	134000
1934	136000
1935	138000
1936	139000
1937	145000
1938	150000
1939	155000
1940	161500
Highest number	161556

16 Gauge Sterlingworth

YEAR	GUN #
1913	351000
1914	351600
1915	352300
1916	353000
1917	353700
1918	354200
1919	355000
1920	356500
1921	357000
1922	357800
1923	358500
1924	359500
1925	359900
1926	360300
1927	362000
1928	364500
1929	366400
1930	367500
1931	368000
1932	368600
1933	369200
1934	369900
1935	372000
1936	373500
1937	374200
1938	374800
Highest Number	378481

20 Gauge Sterlingworth

YEAR	GUN #
1912	250100
1913	252000
1914	253000
1915	254500
1916	254600
1917	254700
1918	255000
1919	255300
1920	255800
1921	256100
1922	256400
1923	256800
1924	257200
1925	257700
1926	258200
1927	259300
1928	260500
1929	262000
1930	263600
1931	263800
1932	264000
1933	264300
1934	264600
1935	266500
1936	268500
1937	270500
1938	270800
1939	271200
1940	271225
Highest number	271304

Single Barrel Trap Guns - Grade J-K-L-M

YEAR	GUN #
1919	400090
1920	400250
1921	400275
1922	400300
1923	400325
1924	400350
1925	400375
1926	400385
1927	400395
1928	400400
1929	400410
1930	400415
1931	400425
1932	400500
1933	400525
1934	400540
1935	400568

AUGUSTE FRANCOTTE

Best Grade

YEAR	GUN #
1887	14211
1888	14229
1889	14706
1890	15034
1891	15199
1892	15443
1893	15544
1894	15735
1895	15881
1896	16040
1897	16163
1898	16192
1899	16310
1900	16410
1955	20456
1956	20556
1957	20719
1958	20800
1959	21000
1960	21136
1961	21187
1962	21244
1963	21278
1964	21326
1972	21443
1981	21617
1982	21654
1983	21731
1984	21746
1985	21758
1986	21777
1987	21790
1988	21810
1989	21833

Medium Grade

YEAR	GUN #
1890	18888
1891	19475
1892	20437
1893	21465
1894	22411
1895	23195
1896	27898
1897	29614
1900	33891
1901	35010
1902	36477
1903	37400
1904	39218
1905	60353
1907	64469
1908	66800
1910	70907
1911	72277
1912	74087
1914	77950
1915	78669
1919	78670
1920	79409
1921	81060
1926	84464
1927	84689
1928	85578
1929	86417
1930	86851
1931	87232
1932	87537
1933	87559
1934	87792
1935	87920
1936	88080
1937	88263
1938	88460
1939	88590
1940	88709
1941	88784
1942	88820
1943	88980
1944	89050
1945	89200
1946	89500
1947	89700
1948	89750
1949	89800
1950	89960
1956	90155
1957	90215
1958	90280
1959	90300
1960	90350
1961	90389
1962	90520
1963	90578
1964	90700
1965	90740
1966	90800
1967	90911
1968	90970
1969	91000
1970	91031
1971	91071
1972	91111
1973	91173
1974	91214
1975	91257
1976	91337
1977	91374
1978	91403
1979	91446
1980	91490
1981	91538
1982	91600
1983	91631
1984	91680
1985	91739
1986	91771
1987	91800
1988	91817
1989	91844

Bottom Grade*

YEAR	GUN #
1894	303318
1895	304261
1896	305025
1897	305265
1898	305561
1899	305769
1900	305923
1901	306060
1902	306180
1903	306249
1904	306417
1905	306505
1906	306638
1907	306760
1908	306882
1909	306957
1910	306992
1911	307039
1912	307072
1913	307198
1914	307327
1920	307358
1921	307600
1922	94879
1926	99753
1927	1390
1928	2222
1929	3590
1930	4130
1931	4456
1932	4632
1933	5712
1934	6384
1935	7304
1936	9922
1937	12637
1938	16359
1939	18530
1940	19743
1941	19370
1942	19492
1943	20191
1944	20865
1945	21075
1946	21547
1947	21656
1948	22260
1949	22390
1950	22616
1951	22839
1952	22989
1953	23140
1954	23261
1955	23360
1956	23424
1957	23523
1958	23622
1959	23709
1961	23946
1962	24017
1963	24068
1964	24100
1965	24117
1986	25099
1987	25161
1988	25170
1989	25176

*Serial number range changes in 1922 & 1927

STEPHEN GRANT

YEAR	GUN #
1867	2480
1870	3000
1875	3900
1880	4750
1885	5450
1890	6100
1895	6700
1896	6857
1900	7300

W W GREENER

YEAR	GUN #
1878	19304
1880	22860
1895	38917
1902	50911
1915	58536
1920	62621
1930	68635
1967	79259

HOLLAND & HOLLAND

Best Guns

YEAR	GUN #
1899	22000
1900	22500
1902	23000
1903	23500
1906	25000
1907	25500
1910	27000
1911	27250
1912	27500
1913	27750
1914	29000
1915	29100
1919	29200
1920	29400
1921	30500
1922	30700
1924	30800
1925	30900
1926	31500
1928	31800
1929	32500
1930	32700
1931	32800
1932	32900
1934	33000
1935	33100
1936	33200
1937	33400
1939	33500
1946	33600
1948	33700
1950	33800
1952	33900
1954	36251
1956	36300
1958	36400
1959	36500
1962	36600
1964	36700
1965	36800
1967	36900
1970	40006
1972	40100
1974	40200
1978	40400
1980	40500

Paradox Guns

YEAR	GUN #
1894	15035
1895	15347
1900	15558
1903	15655
1905	15750
1906	15825
1907	15860
1911	15900
1914	15950
1919	15960
1922	15970
1930	15980

Over & Under Guns

YEAR	GUN #
1950	3600
1952	3010
1954	3020
1967	3036

Plain Guns

YEAR	GUN #
1907	26200
1908	26300
1909	26500

Ithaca Gun Co.

Baker Model Ithaca Double Guns

YEAR	GUN #
1880-1885	2447
1886	4104
1887	7003
1888	8787
1889 (Jan-Aug)	10534

Crass Model Ithaca Double Guns

YEAR	GUN #
1892	17235-21999
1893	25421
1894	25759
1895	27762
1896	28713
1897	30222
1898	33026
1899	38399
1900	46627
1901	61609
1902	76599
1903	94108

Lewis Model Ithaca Double Guns

YEAR	GUN #
1904	94109-105999
1905	119320
1906	123677

Flues Model Ithaca Double & Single Guns

YEAR	GUN #
1908	175000-182031
1909	192499
1910	205399
1911	216499
1912	230099
1913	242599
1914	256699
1915	268199
1916	276899
1917	289299
1918	299799
1919	315399
1920	343335
1921	356513
1922	361849
1923	372099
1924	390499
1925	398352
1926	398365

Ithaca N.I.D. Model Double Guns

YEAR	GUN #
1925	425000-425299
1926	439199
1927	451099
1928	454530
1929	457299
1930	458399
1931	459139
1932	459162
1933	459195
1935	459637
1936	459649
1935	460799
1936	462399
1937	464699
1938	464827
1939	464850
1940	464899
1938	465199
1939	465999
1940	466999
1941	467146
1946	467199
1941	468099
1946	468699
1947	468794
1948	468799
1947	469949
1948	469979
1948	470099

Ithaca - Magnum Doubles

YEAR	GUN #
1932-1942	500000-501000

Ithaca Knick Model Single-Barrel Trap Guns

YEAR	GUN #
1922-1944	400000-402789

CHARLES LANCASTER

YEAR	GUN #
1826	100
1830	600
1840	1200
1850	2100
1860	3200
1861	3400
1862	3540
1863	3693
1864	3805
1865	3914
1866	3999
1867	4087
1868	4183
1869	4271
1870	4328
1871	4401
1872	4477
1873	4562
1874	4644
1875	4714
1876	4769
1877	4833
1878	4892
1879	4924
1880	4949
1881	4982
1882	5079
1883	5186
1884	5359
1885	5497
1886	5627
1887	5764
1888	5926
1889	6136
1890	6406
1891	6671
1892	6988
1893	7189
1894	7360
1895	7548
1896	7709
1897	7940
1898	8132
1899	8353
1900	8529
1901	8700

JOSEPH LANG

YEAR	GUN #
1858	2085
1860	2332
1865	2970
1870	3916
1875	5180
1880	6000
1885	7031
1890	7546
1895	8150

Appendix D
PROOF MARKS

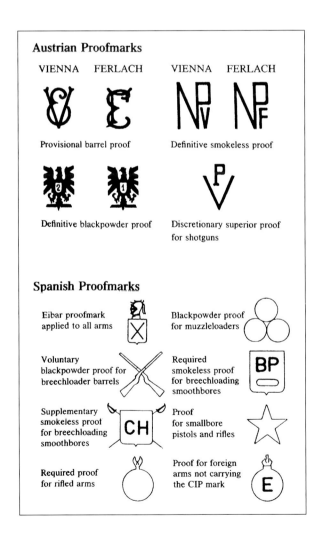

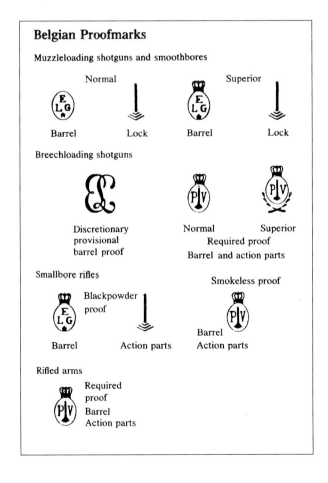

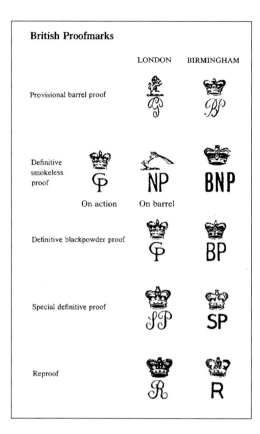

British Proofmarks

	LONDON	BIRMINGHAM
Provisional barrel proof		
Definitive smokeless proof	On action	NP On barrel	BNP
Definitive blackpowder proof		BP
Special definitive proof		SP
Reproof		R

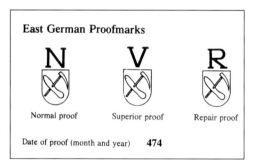

East German Proofmarks

N — Normal proof V — Superior proof R — Repair proof

Date of proof (month and year) **474**

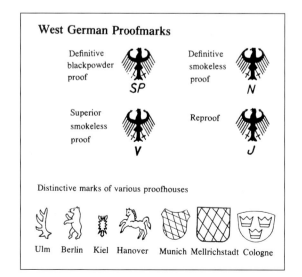

West German Proofmarks

Definitive blackpowder proof — SP
Definitive smokeless proof — N
Superior smokeless proof — V
Reproof — J

Distinctive marks of various proofhouses

Ulm Berlin Kiel Hanover Munich Mellrichstadt Cologne

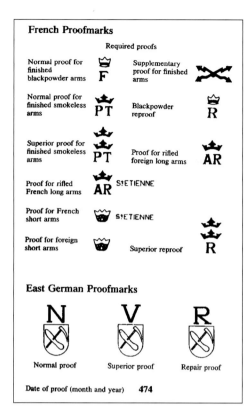

French Proofmarks

Required proofs

Normal proof for finished blackpowder arms — F
Supplementary proof for finished arms
Normal proof for finished smokeless arms — PT
Blackpowder reproof — R
Superior proof for finished smokeless arms — PT
Proof for rifled foreign long arms — AR
Proof for rifled French long arms — AR StETIENNE
Proof for French short arms — StETIENNE
Proof for foreign short arms
Superior reproof — R

East German Proofmarks

N — Normal proof V — Superior proof R — Repair proof

Date of proof (month and year) **474**

Italian Proofmarks

Distinctive mark of the Gardone proofhouse applies to all arms
Definitive blackpowder proof — PN
Definitive smokeless proof — PSF
Discretionary superior smokeless proof — PSF
Additional mark for arms proved in a finished state — FINITO

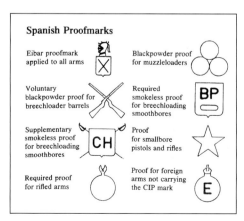

Spanish Proofmarks

Eibar proofmark applied to all arms
Blackpowder proof for muzzleloaders
Voluntary blackpowder proof for breechloader barrels
Required smokeless proof for breechloading smoothbores — BP
Supplementary smokeless proof for breechloading smoothbores — CH
Proof for smallbore pistols and rifles
Required proof for rifled arms
Proof for foreign arms not carrying the CIP mark — E

Bibliography

Adams, Cyril S., and Robert S. Braden. *Lock, Stock, and Barrel.* Long Beach, CA: Safari Press, 1996.

Amor, Damián Ferman Vaquero. *Perdices.* Barcelona: Editorial Hispano Europea, S. A., 1983.

Andrews, John. *The Best Shooting in Scotland.* Moffat, Scotland: Lochar Publishing, 1991.

Arnold, Richard, *Automatic and Repeating Shotguns.* New York: A.S. Barnes Company, 1958.

Baer, Larry L. *The Parker Gun.* North Hollywood, CA: Bienfield Publishing, 1980.

Batha, Chris, *Breaking Clays.* Shropshire, England: Swan Hill Press, 2005.

Bauer, Erwin A. *The Duck Hunter's Bible.* Garden City, NY: Doubleday & Company, 1965.

Beaumont, Richard. *Purdey's: The Guns and the Family.* London: David & Charles, 1984.

Begbie, Eric, and John Humphreys. *The Beacon Shooting Buyer's Guide.* Wellingboro, England: Beacon Publishing, 1986.

Bellrose, Frank C. *Ducks, Geese and Swans of North America.* Harrisburg, PA: Stackpole Books, 1976.

Black, James E. *Black's Wing and Clay: The Complete Shotgunner's Guide to Equipment, Instruction and Destinations.* Red Bank: Black's Sporting Directories, 1998.

Bodio, Stephen. *Good Guns.* New York: Nick Lyons Books, 1986.

Boothroyd, Geoffrey. *The Shotgun.* London: A & C Black; Long Beach, CA: Safari Press, 1985.

Boothroyd, Geoffrey. *Shotguns and Gunsmiths.* London: A & C Black; Long Beach, CA: Safari Press, 1986.

Bowlen, Bruce. *The Orvis Wing-Shooting Handbook.* New York: Nick Lyons Books, 1985.

Bowman, Steve, and Steve Wright. *Arkansas Duck Hunter's Almanac.* Fayetteville, AR: Ozark Dekti Press, 1998.

Brister, Bob. *Moss, Mallards & Mules.* New York: Winchester Press, 1969.

Brister, Bob. *Shotgunning: The Art and Science.* New York: Winchester Press, 1976.

British Proof Authorities. *Notes on the Proof of Shotguns & Other Small Arms.* The Worshipful Company of Gunmakers of the City of London and the Guardians of the Birmingham Proof House (The Proof House, 48 Commercial Road, London El1LP; The Gun Barrel Proof House, Banbury Street, Birmingham B5 5RH).

Brophy, Lt. William S. *L. C. Smith Shotguns.* North Hollywood, CA: Bienfield Publishing, 1979.

Browning, John, and Curt Gentry. *John M. Browning: American Gunmaker.* Garden City, NY: Doubleday & Company, 1964.

Buckingham, Nash. *"Mr. Buck": The Autobiography of Nash Buckingham.* Edited by Dyrk Haistead and Steve Smith. Traverse City, MI: Countrysport Press, 1990.

Burrard, Maj. Sir Gerald. *In the Gunroom.* London: Herbert Jenkins, 1930.

Butler, David F. *The American Shotgun.* New York: Winchester Press, 1973.

Buxton, Aubrey. *The King in His Country.* Woodstock, VT: The Countryman Press, n.d.

Carder, Charles E. *Recognizing Side-by-Side Shotguns.* Delphos, OH: Avil Orize Publishing, 1996.

Carder, Charles E. *Side-by-Sides of the World.* Delphos, OH: Avil Orize Publishing, 1997.

Churchill, Robert. *Game Shooting.* Revised by MacDonald Hastings. Harrisburg, PA: Stackpole Books, 1971.

Churchill, Robert and MacDonald Hastings. *Robert Churchill's Game Shooting.* Traverse City, MI: Countrysport Press, 1990.

Connett, Eugene V., ed. *Wildfowling in the Atlantic Flyway.* New York: Bonanza Books, 1949.

Connett, Eugene V., ed. *Wildfowling in the Mississippi Flyway.* New York: D. Van Nostrand Co., 1949.

Cradock, Chris. *A Manual of Clayshooting.* London: B. T. Bratsford, 1986.

Davies, Ken. *The Better Shot.* London: Quiller Press, 1992.

Evans, George Bird. *The Best of Nash Buckingham.* New York: Winchester Press, 1973.

Evans, George Bird. *Dear John—: Nash Buckingham's Letters to John Bailey.* Old Hemlock, NY: George and Kay Evans, 1984.

Evans, George Bird. *Opus 10: Men Who Shot and Wrote About It.* Old Hemlock, NY: George and Kay Evans, 1983.

Evans, George Bird. *Upland Gunner's Book.* Clinton: Amwell Press, 1979.

Evans, George Bird. *The Upland Shooting Life.* New York: Alfred A. Knopf, 1971.

Fackler, Kurt D., and M. L. McPherson *Reloading for Shotgunners*. Iola, WI: Krause Publications, 1997.

Fjestad, S. P. *Blue Book of Gun Values, 31st Ed.* Minneapolis: Blue Book Publications, 1998.

Garwood, Gough Thomas. *Gough Thomas's Gun Book*. Auburn Hills, MI: Gunnerman Press, 1994.

Garwood, Gough Thomas. *Shotgun Shooting Facts*. New York: Winchester Press, 1978.

Grassi, Rodolfo. *El Gran Libro del Cazador*. Barcelona: Editorial De Vecchi, S. A., 1984.

Greener, W. W. *The Gun and Its Development, 9th Ed.* New York: Bonanza Books, 1910.

Gresham, Grits. *The Complete Wildfowler*. New York: Winchester Press, 1973.

Weatherby: The Man, The Gun, The Legend. Natchitoches, LA: Cane River Publishing, 1992.

Grozik, Richard S. *Game Gun*. Oshkosh, WI: Willow Creek Press, 1986.

Harbour, Dave. *Hunting the American Wild Turkey*. Harrisburg, PA: Stackpole Books, 1975.

Harlan, Howard, and W. Crew Anderson. *Duck Calls: An Enduring American Folk Art*. Nashville, TN: Harlan Anderson Press, 1988.

Hartman, B. C. (Barney). *Hartman on Skeet*. Toronto: McClelland and Stewart, 1967.

Hastings, MacDonald. *How to Shoot Straight*. New Jersey: A. S. Barnes and Company, 1970.

Hastings, MacDonald. *The Other Mr. Churchill*. New York: Dodd, Mead & Company, 1965.

Hastings, MacDonald *The Shotgun*. London: David & Charles, 1983.

Hatch, Alden. *Remington Arms: An American History*. Ilion, NY: Remington Arms Company, 1972.

Hearn, Arthur. *Shooting and Gun Fitting*. London: Herbert Jenkins, n.d. (ca. 1930).

Heilner, Van Campen. *A Book on Duck Shooting*. Philadelphia: Penn Publishing Company, 1939.

Herter's Inc. *Herter's Wholesale Catalog No. 81*. Waseca: Herter's, 1970.

Hightower, John. *Pheasant Hunting*. New York: Alfred A. Knopf, 1946.

Hill, Gene. *A Hunter's Fireside Book*. New York: Winchester Press, 1972.

Hill, Gene. *Mostly Tailfeathers: Stories about Guns and Dogs and Other Odds and Ends*. Piscataway, NJ: New Century Publishers, 1974.

Hinman, Bob. *The Duck Hunter's Handbook*. Prescott: Wolf, 1993.

Hinman, Bob. *The Golden Age of Shotgunning*. New York: Winchester Press, 1975.

Holmgren, Christer. *Praktiskt Jaktsyttc*. Rabén and Sjögren, Sweden: ICA Bokforlag, 1991.

Holmgren, Christer. *Vapnet Och Jakten*. Västerás, Sweden: ICA Bokforlag, 1988.

Humphreys, John, ed. *The Shooting Handbook*. Northampton, MA: Beacon Publishing, 1985.

Hughes, Steven Dodd. *Fine Gunmaking: Double Shotguns.* Iola, WI : Krause Publications, 1998.

Jackson, Anthony. *So You Want to Go Shooting.* London: Arlington Books, 1974.

Jeffrey, W. J., & Co. *Jeffrey & Co. Guns, Rifles & General Shooting Accessories.* London: W. J. Jeffrey, 1912-13.

Johnson, Peter H. *Parker: America's Finest Shotgun.* New York: Bonanza Books, 1961.

King, Peter. *The Shooting Field: One Hundred and Fifty Years with Holland & Holland.* London: Quiller Press, 1985.

Knap, Jerome. *All About Wildfowling in America.* New York: Winchester Press, 1976.

Knight, Richard Alden. *Mastering the Shotgun.* New York: E. P. Dutton Co., 1975.

Lancaster, Charles. *The Art of Shooting.* London: McCorquodale & Co., 1954.

Lind, Ernie. *The Complete Book of Trick and Fancy Shooting.* Secaucus: Citadel Press, 1972.

Madis, George. *The Winchester Model Twelve.* Brownsboro: Art and Reference House, 1982.

Marchington, James. *Book of Shotguns.* London: Pelham Books, 1984.

Marcot, Roy. Remington: *The Official Authorized History of Remington Arms Company.* Madison: Remington Arms, 1998.

Marshall-Ball, Robin. *The Sporting Shotgun: A User's Handbook.* Surrey, UK: Saiga Publishing Co., 1982.

Martin, Brian P. *British Game Shooting, Rough Shooting and Wildfowling.* North Pomfret, VT: Trafalgar Square Publishing, 1988.

Martin, Brian P. *The Great Shoots.* London: David & Charles, 1987.

Matunas, Edward A. *American Ammo.* Danbury: Outdoor Life Books, 1989.

McCawley, E. S., Jr. *Shotguns & Shooting.* New York: Van Nostrand Reinhold Company, 1965.

McGrath, Brian. *Duck Calls and Other Game Calls.* Plano: Thomas B. Reel Co., 1988.

McIntosh, Michael. *Best Guns.* Traverse City, MI: Countrysport Press, 1989.

McIntosh, Michael. *The Best Shotguns Ever Made in America.* New York: Charles Scribner's Sons, 1981.

McIntosh, Michael. *More Shotguns and Shooting.* Selma, AL: Countrysport Press, 1998.

McIntosh, Michael. *Shotguns and Shooting.* Traverse City, MI: Countrysport Press, 1995.

Missildine, Fred, and Nicky Karas. *Score Better at Skeet.* New York: Winchester Press, 1972.

Muderlak, Ed. *Parker Guns: The Old Reliable.* Long Beach: Safari Press, 1997.

National Rifle Association of America. *NRA Firearms Fact Book.* Washington, D. C.: National Rifle Association of America, 1989.

National Rifle Association of America. *Waterfowl Hunting.* Washington, D.C.:

National Rifle Association of America. 1988.

National Rifle Association of America. *Wild Turkey Hunting.* Washington, D.C.: National Rifle Association of America, 1988.

Nichols, Bob. *Skeet and How to Shoot It.* New York: G. P. Putnam's Sons, 1947.

Nonte, George C., Jr. *Firearms Encyclopedia.* New York: Harper and Row, 1973.

Norman, Geoffrey. *The Orvis Book of Upland Bird Shooting.* New York: Nick Lyons Books, 1985.

Norris, Dr. Charles C. *Eastern Upland Shooting.* Traverse City: Countrysport Press, 1989.

O'Connor, Jack. *The Shotgun Book.* New York: Alfred A. Knopf, 1974.

Popowski, Bert. *Oft's Hunting Handbook.* Pekin, IL: P. S. Olt Company, 1948.

Purdey, T. D. S. and J. A. *The Shotgun.* London: Adam & Charles Black, 1965.

Rose, Michael. *The Eley Book of Shooting Technique.* London: Chancerel Publishers, 1979.

Ruffer, J. E. M. *The Art of Good Shooting.* New York: Drake Publishers, 1972.

Ruffner, Jonathan Garnier. *The Big Shots: Edwardian Shooting Parties.* New York: ARCO Publishing Co., 1977.

Scharff, Robert. *Complete Duck Shooter's Handbook.* New York: G.P. Putnam's Sons, 1957.

Schwing, Ned. *Winchester's Finest: The Model 21.* New York: Krause Publications, 1990.

Smith, A. J. *Sporting Clays.* Wautoma, WI: Willow Creek Press, 1989.

Stadt, Ronald W. *Winchester Shotguns and Shotshells.* Tacoma, WA: Armory Publications, 1984.

Stanbury, Percy, and G. L. Carlisle. *Shotgun and Shooter.* London: Barrie & Jenkins, 1970.

Shotgun Marksmanship. Cranbury, NJ: A. S. Barnes & Co., 1969.

Stanford, J. K. *The Complex Gun.* London: Pelham Books, 1968.

Tate, Douglas. *Birmingham Gunmakers.* Long Beach, CA: Safari Press, 1997.

Taylor, John M. *The Shotgun Encyclopedia,* Long Beach, CA: Safari Press 2004.

Taylor, John M. *Shotshells & Ballistics,* Long Beach, CA: Safari Press 2007.

Taylor, Zack. *Successful Waterfowling.* New York: Crown Publishers, 1974.

Walker, Ralph T., and Jack Lewis. *Shotgun Gunsmithing.* Northfield, MN: DBI Books, 1983.

Wallack, L. R. *American Shotguns: Design and Performance.* New York: Winchester Press, 1977.

Wieland, Terry. *Spanish Best: The Fine Shotguns of Spain.* Traverse City, MI: Countrysport Press, 1994.

Willow Creek Press's Editors. *Back Then: A Pictorial History of Americans Afield.* Wautoma, WI: Willow Creek Press, 1989.

Wood, J. B. *The Gun Digest Book of Firearms. Assembly/Disassembly: Part V Shotguns.* Northfield, MN: DBI Books, 1980.

Woods, Shirley E. *Gunning for Birds and Wildfowl.* New York: Winchester Press, 1976.

Yardley, Michael. *Gunfitting.* Long Beach, CA: Safari Press, 1993.

Zutz, Don. *The Double Shotgun.* Piscataway, NJ: New Century Publishers, 1985.

Zutz, Don. *Modern Waterfowl Guns & Gunning.* South Hackensack, NJ: Stoeger Publishing Co., 1985.

Zutz, Don, and Ron L. Reiber. *Hodgdon Powder Company Shotshell Data Manual.* Shawnee Mission, KS: Hodgdon Powder Company, 1996.

Periodicals:

The Double Gun Journal (Double Gun Journal, Inc., East Jordan, Mich.)

Index

Gun manufacturers named after people are sorted by the appropriate last name (e.g., A.H. Fox Gun Company can be found under *F*.) Significant discussion of individual gun models are included as subheadings under the entry for the appropriate manufacturer. Page numbers followed by *ph* indicate a photograph or its caption.